Android™ Application Development

FOR DUMMIES®

A Wiley Brand

3rd Edition

by Michael Burton

FOR DUMMIES®
A Wiley Brand

Android™ Application Development For Dummies®, 3rd Edition

Published by: **John Wiley & Sons, Inc.,** 111 River Street, Hoboken, NJ 07030-5774, www.wiley.com

Copyright © 2015 by John Wiley & Sons, Inc., Hoboken, New Jersey

Published simultaneously in Canada

For general information on our other products and services, please contact our Customer Care Department within the U.S. at 877-762-2974, outside the U.S. at 317-572-3993, or fax 317-572-4002. For technical support, please visit www.wiley.com/techsupport.

Wiley publishes in a variety of print and electronic formats and by print-on-demand. Some material included with standard print versions of this book may not be included in e-books or in print-on-demand. If this book refers to media such as a CD or DVD that is not included in the version you purchased, you may download this material at http://booksupport.wiley.com. For more information about Wiley products, visit www.wiley.com.

Library of Congress Control Number:

ISBN: 978-1-119-01792-9
ISBN 978-1-119-01793-6 (ePDF); ISBN 978-1-119-01794-3 (ePUB)

Manufactured in the United States of America

10 9 8 7 6 5 4 3 2 1

Table of Contents

Part III: Creating a Feature-Rich Application 155

Chapter 9: Designing the Tasks Application.....................157

Chapter 10: Creating the Task Detail Page 181

Chapter 11: Going a la Carte with Your Menu....................199

Chapter 12: Handling User Input 211

Introduction

●●●

Welcome to *Android Application Development For Dummies*!

When Android was acquired by Google in 2005 (yes, Android was a start-up company at one point), a lot of people didn't have much interest in it because Google hadn't yet entered the mobile space. Fast-forward to a few years later, when Google announced its first Android phone: the G1. It was the start of something huge.

The G1 was the first publicly released Android device. It didn't match the rich feature set of the iPhone at the time, but a lot of people believed in the platform. As soon as Donut (Android 1.6) was released, it was evident that Google was putting some effort into the product. Immediately after version 1.6 was released, talk of 2.0 was already on the horizon.

Today, we're on version 5.0 of the Android platform, with no signs that things are slowing down. Without doubt, this is an exciting time in Android development.

About This Book

Android Application Development For Dummies is a beginner's guide to developing Android applications. You don't need any Android application development experience under your belt to get started.

The Android platform is a *device-independent* platform, which means that you can develop applications for various devices. These devices include, but aren't limited to phones, watches, tablets, cars, e-book readers, netbooks, televisions, and GPS devices.

Finding out how to develop for the Android platform opens a large variety of development options for you. This book distills hundreds, if not thousands, of pages of Android documentation, tips, tricks, and tutorials into a short, digestible format that allows you to springboard into your future as an Android developer. This book isn't a recipe book, but it gives you the basic knowledge to assemble various pieces of the Android framework to create interactive and compelling applications.

Conventions Used in This Book

Throughout the book, you use the Android framework classes, and you'll create Java classes and XML files.

Code examples in this book appear in a monospace font so that they stand out from other text in the book. This means that the code you'll see looks like this:

```
public class MainActivity
```

Java is a high-level programming language that is case-sensitive, so be sure to enter the text into the editor *exactly* as you see it in the book. The examples follow standard Java conventions so you can transition easily between the book examples and the example code provided by the Android Software Development Kit (SDK). All class names, for example, appear in `PascalCase` format.

All the URLs in the book appear in monospace font as well:

```
http://d.android.com
```

Foolish Assumptions

To begin programming with Android, you need a computer that runs one of the following operating systems:

- Windows 2003, Vista, 7 or 8
- Mac OS X 10.8.5 or later
- Linux GNOME or KDE

You also need to download Android Studio (which is free) and the Java Development Kit (or JDK, which is also free), if you don't already have them on your computer. Chapter 2 outlines the entire installation process for all the tools and frameworks.

Because Android applications are developed in the Java programming language, you need to understand the Java language. Android also uses XML quite heavily to define various resources inside the application, so you should understand XML too. You don't have to be an expert in these languages, however.

You don't need a physical Android device, because all the applications you build in this book will work on an emulator.

How This Book Is Organized

Android Application Development For Dummies has five parts, described in the following sections.

Part I: Getting Started with Your First Android Application

Part I introduces the tools and frameworks that you use to develop Android applications. It also introduces the various SDK components and shows you how they're used in the Android ecosystem.

Part II: Building and Publishing Your First Android Application

Part II introduces you to building your first Android application: the Silent Mode Toggle application. After you build the initial application, you create an app widget for the application that you can place on the Home screen of an Android device. Then you publish your application to the Google Play Store.

Part III: Creating a Feature-Rich Application

Part III takes your development skills up a notch by walking you through the construction of the Tasks application, which allows users to create various tasks with reminders. You implement an SQLite backed content provider in this multiscreen application. You also see how to use the Android status bar to create notifications that can help increase the usability of your application.

Part IV: Android Is More than Phones

Part IV takes the phone app you built in Part III and tweaks it to work on lots of other devices, including tablets, wearables, televisions, and the Amazon Fire.

Part V: The Part of Tens

Part V gives you a tour of sample applications that prove to be stellar launching pads for your Android apps, and useful Android libraries that can make your Android development career a lot easier.

Icons Used in This Book

 This icon indicates a useful pointer that you shouldn't skip.

 This icon represents a friendly reminder about a vital point you should keep in mind while proceeding through a particular section of the chapter.

 This icon signifies that the accompanying explanation may be informative but isn't essential to understanding Android application development. Feel free to skip these snippets, if you like.

 This icon alerts you to potential problems that you may encounter along the way. Read and remember these tidbits to avoid possible trouble.

 This icon signifies that you'll find additional relevant content at www. dummies.com/extras/androidappdevelopment.

Beyond the Book

In addition to the content in this book, you'll find some extra content available at the www.dummies.com website:

- ✔ The Cheat Sheet for this book at www.dummies.com/cheatsheet/ androidappdevelopment
- ✔ Online articles covering additional topics at www.dummies.com/ extras/androidappdevelopment

Here you'll find the articles referred to on the page that introduces each part of the book. So, feel free to visit `www.dummies.com/extras/ androidappdevelopment`. You'll feel at home there . . . find coffee and donuts . . . okay, maybe not the coffee and donuts, but you can find cool supplementary information about things we couldn't fit into the book, such as testing, GPS location tracking, voice control, and other fun topics.

✔ Updates to this book, if any, at `www.dummies.com/extras/ androidappdevelopment`

✔ Don't want to type all the code in the book? You can download it from the book's website at `www.dummies.com/go/androidappdevfd`.

✔ If there are ever updates to this book, you can find them at `www. dummies.com/go/androidappdevfdupdates`.

Part I

Getting Started with Your First Android Application

In this part . . .

Part I introduces you to the Android platform and describes what makes a spectacular Android application. You explore various parts of the Android software development kit (SDK) and see how to use them in your applications. You install the tools and frameworks necessary to develop Android applications.

Chapter 1

Developing Spectacular Android Applications

Google rocks! Google acquired the Android platform in 2005 (see the sidebar "The roots of Android," later in this chapter) to ensure that a mobile operating system (OS) can be created and maintained in an open platform. Google continues to pump time and resources into the Android project. Though devices have been available only since October 2008, over a billion Android devices have now been activated, and more than a million more are being added daily. In only a few years, Android has already made a *huge* impact.

It has never been easier for Android developers to make money by developing apps. Android users trust Google, and because your app resides in the Google Play Store, many users will be willing to trust your app, too.

Why Develop for Android?

The real question is, "Why *not* develop for Android?" If you want your app to be available to millions of users worldwide or if you want to publish apps as soon as you finish writing and testing them or if you like developing on an open platform, you have your answer. But in case you're still undecided, continue reading.

Market share

As a developer, you have an opportunity to develop apps for a booming market. The number of Android devices in use is greater than the number of devices on all other mobile operating systems combined. The Google Play Store puts your app directly and easily into a user's hands. Users don't have to search the Internet to find an app to install — they can simply go to the preinstalled Google Play Store on their devices and have access to all your apps. Because the Google Play Store comes preinstalled on most Android devices (see Chapter 19 for some exceptions), users typically search the Google Play Store for all their application needs. It isn't unusual to see an app's number of downloads soar in only a few days.

Time to market

Because of all the application programming interfaces (APIs) packed into Android, you can easily develop full-featured applications in a relatively short time frame. After you register as a developer at the Google Play Store, simply upload your apps and publish them. Unlike other mobile marketplaces, the Google Play Store has no app approval process. All you have to do is write apps and publish them.

Though anyone can publish almost any type of app, maintain your good karma — and your compliance with the Google terms of service — by producing family-friendly apps. Android has a diverse set of users from all over the world and of all ages.

Open platform

The Android operating system is an *open platform:* Any hardware manufacturer or provider can make or sell Android devices. As you can imagine, the openness of Android has allowed it to gain market share quickly. Feel free to dig into the Android source code to see how it works, by visiting `https://source.android.com`. By using open source code, manufacturers can create custom user interfaces (UIs) and even add new features to certain devices.

Device compatibility

Android can run on devices of many different screen sizes and resolutions, including watches, phones, tablets, televisions, and more. Android comes

The roots of Android

Though most people aren't aware of it, Google didn't start the Android project. The first version of the Android operating system was created by Android, Inc., a small start-up company in Silicon Valley that was purchased by Google in August 2005. The founders (who worked for various Internet technology companies, such as Danger, Wildfire Communications, T-Mobile, and WebTV) became part of the Google team that helped create what is now the full-fledged Android mobile operating system.

supplied with tools to help you develop applications that support multiple types of devices. If your app requires a front-facing camera, for example, only devices with front-facing cameras can "see" your app in the Google Play Store — an arrangement known as *feature detection*. (For more information on publishing your apps to the Google Play Store, see Chapter 8.)

Mashup capability

A *mashup* combines two or more services to create an application. You can create a mashup by using the camera and the Android location services, for example, to take a photo with the exact location displayed on the image. Or you can use the Map API with the Contacts list to show all contacts on a map. You can easily make apps by combining services or libraries in countless new and exciting ways. A few other types of mashups that can help your brain juices start pumping out ideas include the following:

- **Geolocation and social networking:** Suppose that you want to write an app that tweets a user's current location every ten minutes throughout the day. Using the Android location services and a third-party Twitter API (such as iTwitter), you can do it easily.

- **Geolocation and gaming:** Location-based gaming, which is increasingly popular, is a helpful way to inject players into the thick of a game. A game might run a background service to check a player's current location and compare it with other players' locations in the same area. If a second player is within a specified distance, the first one could be notified to challenge her to a battle. All this is possible because of GPS technology on a strong platform such as Android. If you're interested in developing games for Android, check out `https://developers.google.com/games/services/` for more information about Google Play Games services.

✔ **Contacts and Internet:** With all the useful APIs at your disposal, you can easily make full-featured apps by combining the functionality of two or more APIs. You can combine the Internet and names from the Contacts list to create a greeting-card app, for example. Or you may simply want to add an easy way for users to contact you from an app or enable them to send your app to their friends. (See "Google APIs," later in this chapter, for more information on the APIs.)

Developers can make Android do almost anything they want, so use your best judgment when creating and publishing apps for mass consumption. Just because you want live wallpaper to highlight your version of the hula in your birthday suit doesn't mean that anyone else wants to see it.

Android Development Basics

Thank goodness you don't have to be a member of Mensa to develop Android applications! Developing in Android is simple because its default language is Java. Though writing Android applications is fairly easy, writing code in general is no easy feat.

If you've never developed applications before, this book may not be the best place to start. Pick up a copy of *Beginning Programming with Java For Dummies,* by Barry Burd (John Wiley & Sons, Inc.) to learn the ropes. After you have a basic understanding of Java under your belt, you should be ready to tackle this book.

Although the Android operating system consists primarily of Java code, some of the framework isn't written in Java. Android apps use small amounts of XML in addition to Java. You need to cement your basic understanding of XML before delving into this book.

If you need an introduction to XML, check out *XML For Dummies,* by Lucinda Dykes and Ed Tittel (John Wiley & Sons, Inc.).

If you already know how to use Java and XML, then congratulations — you're ahead of the curve.

Java: Your Android programming language

Android applications are written in Java — not the full-blown version of Java that's familiar to developers using Java Platform, Enterprise Edition (JEE), but a subset of the Java libraries that are most useful on Android.

This smaller subset of Java excludes classes that aren't suitable for mobile devices. If you have experience in Java, you should feel right at home developing apps in Android.

Even with a Java reference book on hand, you can always search at www.google.com or www.stackoverflow.com to find information about topics you don't understand. Because Java isn't a new language, you can find plenty of examples on the web that demonstrate how to do virtually anything.

Not every class that's available to Java programmers is also available on Android. Verify that it's available to you before you start trying to use it. If it's not, an alternative is probably bundled with Android that can work for your needs.

Activities

An Android application can consist of one or more activities. An *activity* serves as a container for both the user interface and the code that runs it. You can think of activities as *pages* of your app — one page in your app corresponds to one activity. Activities are discussed in more detail in Chapters 3 and 5.

Fragments

Every "page" in an Android application is a separate activity. In older versions of Android, you would place any element that you wanted to display onscreen directly into the Activity class. This arrangement works well when viewed on a phone's small screen, on which you typically can't see a lot of information at once. You may be able to see a list of tasks, or a task that you're editing, but cramming both elements onto the screen at the same time is impossible.

On a tablet, however, you're swimming in real estate. Not only does it make sense to let users see a list of tasks and edit them on the same page, but it also looks silly not to let them do so. The screen size on a tablet is simply too big to fill with a single long list of items or lots of empty space.

Android doesn't allow you to easily put two activities on the screen at the same time. What to do? The answer is *fragments*.

Using fragments, a single list fragment can occupy half the screen, and an edit fragment can occupy the other half. Now each page of your app can contain multiple fragments. You can find out how to use fragments in your phone application in Chapter 9 and how to scale your app to tablets in Chapter 17.

You can think of fragments as miniature activities: Because every fragment has its own lifecycle, you know when it's being created and destroyed, among other information. Fragments go inside activities.

Intents

Intents make up the core message system that runs Android. An intent is composed of two elements:

- ✔ **An action:** The general action to be performed (such as view, edit, or dial) when the intent is received
- ✔ **Data:** The information that the action operates on, such as the name of a contact

Intents are used to start activities and to communicate among various parts of the Android operating system. An application can send and receive intents.

Sending messages with intents

When you send an intent, you send a message telling Android to make something happen. The intent can tell Android to start a new activity from within your application or to start another application.

Registering intent filters

Sending an intent doesn't make something happen automatically. You have to register an *intent filter* that listens for the intent and then tells Android what to do — whether the task is starting a new activity or another app. If more than one receiver can accept a given intent, a chooser can be created to allow the user to decide which app to use to complete the activity — such as how the YouTube app allows the user to choose whether to watch videos in the YouTube app or in a browser.

Various registered receivers, such as the Gmail and the Hangouts apps, handle image-sharing intents by default. When you find more than one possible intent filter, a chooser opens with a list of options to choose from and asks what to do: Use email, messaging, or another application, as shown in Figure 1-1.

Follow best practice and create choosers for intents that don't target other activities within your application. If the Android system cannot find a match for an intent that was sent, and if a chooser wasn't created manually, the application crashes after experiencing a runtime exception — an unhandled error in the application. (Android expects developers to know what they're doing.) See `http://d.android.com/training/basics/intents/sending.html` for more information about using intent choosers.

Figure 1-1:
A chooser.

Cursorless controls

Unlike the PC, where you manipulate the mouse to move the cursor, an Android device lets you use your fingers to do nearly anything you can do with a mouse. Rather than right-click in Android, however, you long-press an element until its context menu appears.

As a developer, you can create and manipulate context menus. You can allow users to use two fingers on an Android device, rather than a single mouse cursor, for example. Fingers come in all sizes, so design the user interface in your apps accordingly. Buttons should be large enough (and have sufficient spacing) so that even users with larger fingers can interact with your apps easily, whether they're using your app on a phone or tablet.

Views

A *view,* which is a basic element of the Android user interface, is a rectangular area of the screen that's responsible for drawing and event handling. Views are a basic building block of Android user interfaces, much like paragraph `<p>` or anchor `<a>` tags are building blocks of an HTML page. Some common views you might use in an Android application might be a `TextView`, `ImageView`, `Layout`, and `Button`, but there are dozens more out there for you to explore. You can also implement your own custom views.

Many more views are ready for you to use. For complete details about views, check out the `android.widget` and `android.view` packages in the Android documentation at `http://d.android.com/reference/android/widget/package-summary.html`.

Background operations

There are various ways to run multiple operations at the same time on Android without having to manage a thread yourself (which is generally not recommended). When loading data from a database to show on the screen, you'll generally find yourself using loaders. *Loaders* take care of managing background threads for you, and they also watch your database for changes so that your UI updates when the data changes. You can find out more about loaders in Chapter 13.

For other kinds of background operations, you may find yourself using the `AsyncTask` class to run an operation on a background thread. `AsyncTask(s)` let you start a task to run in the background, and then they return the result to your foreground thread so that you can update your UI. This creates a clean programming model for asynchronous processing.

Threads let you run multiple sets of instructions at the same time on the same device. They all share the same memory and CPU, but when one thread is blocked waiting for something, other threads can be resumed to keep the CPU busy.

You use asynchronous processing for tasks that might take more than a small fraction of a second, such as network (Internet) communication; reading or writing to storage; or media processing. When users have to wait for your task to complete, use an asynchronous call and an element in the user interface to notify them that something is happening.

Failing to use an asynchronous programming model can cause users of your application to (correctly) believe that it's buggy. Downloading the latest Twitter messages via the Internet takes time, for example. If the network slows and you aren't using an asynchronous model, the application will lock up and the user will likely assume that something is wrong because the application isn't responding to her interaction. If the application fails to respond within a reasonable length of time, the user sees the Application Not Responding (ANR) dialog box, as shown in Figure 1-2. The user can then choose whether to close the application or wait for it to recover. Most of the time, users press OK and close your app.

To follow the best practice, run CPU-intensive or long-running code inside another thread, as described in "Keeping Your App Responsive" on the Android developer site (`http://d.android.com/guide/practices/design/responsiveness.html`).

Background services

You may already know what a *service* is: It's an application that runs in the background and doesn't necessarily have a user interface. A classic example

Figure 1-2:
The ANR
dialog box.

is an antivirus application that usually runs in the background as a service. Even though you don't see it, you know that it's running.

Android apps can also have background services. Most music players that can be downloaded from the Google Play Store, for example, run as background services. Users can then listen to music while checking email or performing other tasks that require the use of the screen.

Android support library

It's always so much fun to write apps for the latest and greatest devices! However, you may find yourself wanting to support older devices from time to time. After all, not all of your users may be running the very latest versions of Android.

Luckily, Android provides a solution. You can use the Android support library to make your apps compatible with devices all the way back to the Android Stone Age (circa 2010 A.D. or even earlier).

In addition to supplying fragments and loaders, the support library adds several other newer APIs to old devices, such as:

- ✔ RecyclerView: Creates an endless scrollable list of views
- ✔ CardView: A "card" you can use with a RecyclerView to create a scrollable list of cards in your apps
- ✔ ViewPager: Swipes pages left and right
- ✔ ShareCompat: For sharing things with your friends

Visit `https://developer.android.com/tools/support-library/features.html` to see the complete list of features in the Android support library. Visit `https://developer.android.com/about/dashboards` to see how many Android users are using which versions of Android.

Action bar

The *action bar* is where you'll put many of the buttons and menus that will enable users to interact with your application. The action bar is almost always present across the top of the screen — and it's therefore extremely difficult *not* to notice. See Figure 1-3 for an example of the action bar from the YouTube application.

Figure 1-3:
The YouTube action bar for a funny cat video.

| You Tube | Supercats: Episode 1 — The Funniest Cat Video!   ⊞ < Q |

Check out these elements on the action bar:

- ✔ **Up Button, app logo:** Tap the Up button or the app logo on the action bar to move up one level.

  Note the subtle distinction between the Up button and the Back button: Pressing the Back button returns the user to the previous activity, regardless of which app is being used; pressing the Up button returns the user to the previous activity *in the current application,* even if that activity wasn't an activity the user was just performing.

  Suppose that you're viewing a web page in the Chrome browser and you tap a link to open the YouTube app. Pressing the Back button returns you to Chrome; pressing the Up button takes you to the YouTube app's home page.

- ✔ **Page:** Next to the application icon on the action bar is the title of the current page. If your application lets you filter data on the current page, you can add a drop-down menu there to allow users to change the filter.

- ✔ **Action:** You can see, on the right end of the action bar, various actions that the user can perform. In the YouTube app shown in Figure 1-3, the user can add the video to a list, share the video, or search for more videos. Actions can take the form of text or icons (as shown in the figure) or both. You can add as many actions as you want. Actions that don't fit onscreen are placed on an overflow submenu on the right end.

- ✔ **Context action bar (not shown):** The action bar can change to show what the user is doing. For example, if a user chooses several items from a list, you can replace the standard action bar with a contextual action bar to let users choose actions based on those items. For example, if you want to allow bulk deletions, you can provide a Delete Items button on the contextual action bar.

Visit `http://d.android.com/guide/topics/ui/actionbar.html` for more information about the versatility that this element of the user interface can add to your app.

The action bar doesn't exist at all on Android 2.x and earlier! Any action bars you add to your application will not show up in these versions of Android. But don't despair, you can use the action bar on 2.1 or later by using the support library.

Widgets and notifications

Users might want to access information from your app without explicitly starting it up first. For example, think about how the Gmail app allows users to preview emails in a notification before they open the Gmail app, or how you can see the current time on your launcher without having to open the clock app. These are examples of using notifications and launcher widgets.

- ✔ **Launcher Widgets:** Widgets are like "mini apps" that provide access to functionality in your app directly from the phone's launcher (also known as Home screen). Widgets are easy to find in the Applications list. They can display information, contain buttons, and even contain *list views* to handle limited swiping and scrolling.

- ✔ **Notifications:** Android notifications are expandable and collapsible to allow users to see more information about them. For example, if your mother sends you a photo of her new puppy in a text message, you can see it directly in the notification without having to open the app. A notification about a new email message can show a preview of the message text so that it can be read directly.

   In addition, a notification also lets the user take action on it directly from whichever app is being used. To reply to a birthday email from Grandma, for example, simply tap the Reply button on the notification to launch Gmail with an editor so that you can thank her.

Hardware Tools

Google gives developers the tools necessary to create top-notch, full-featured mobile apps. Google makes it simple to tap into, and make use of, all available hardware on a device.

To create a spectacular Android app, you should take advantage of all that the hardware has to offer. Don't get us wrong — if you have an idea for an app that needs no hardware assistance, that's okay, too.

Android devices come supplied with several hardware features that you can use to build apps. Table 1-1 describes the hardware features available on most Android devices.

Table 1-1	Android Device Hardware
Android Hardware Feature	*What It Does*
Accelerometer	Indicates whether the phone is moving
Bluetooth radio	Indicates whether a headset is connected
Compass	Indicates in which direction the user is heading
Camera	Take pictures and record video
GPS receiver	Indicates the user's location

Most Android devices are released with the hardware discussed in the following four sections, but not all devices are created equal. Android is free for hardware manufacturers to distribute, so it's used in a wide range of devices, including some made by small manufacturers overseas (and it isn't uncommon for some of these devices to be missing a feature or two).

Android devices come in all shapes and sizes: phones, tablets, ebook readers, watches, televisions, and cars. The engineers behind Android provide tools that let you easily deploy apps on multiple screen sizes and resolutions. Don't worry — the Android team has done all the hard work for you. Chapter 4 covers the basics of screen sizes and densities.

Touchscreen

The Android touchscreen opens a ton of possibilities to enhance users' interaction with your apps. Users can swipe, flip, drag, or pinch to zoom, for example, by moving a finger on the touchscreen. You can even supply custom gestures in your app, which opens even more possibilities.

Android also supports *multitouch* capability, which lets a user touch the entire screen with more than one finger at a time.

Hardware buttons are old news. You can place buttons of any shape anywhere on the screen to create the user interface best suited for your app.

GPS

Combining the Android operating system with the GPS receiver on a device lets the developer access, and track, a user's location at any time. The Foursquare social networking app is a good example — it uses the GPS feature to determine the user's location and then accesses the web to determine the closest venues to the user.

Another helpful example is the Maps application's ability to pinpoint a user's location on a map and provide directions to that person's destination. Combining Android with GPS hardware gives you access to the user's exact GPS location. Many apps use this combination to show users where the nearest gas station, coffeehouse, or even restroom is located.

Accelerometer

An *accelerometer* is a device that measures acceleration, and Android comes packed with accelerometer support. The accelerometer tells you whether a user's device is being moved or shaken, and even in which direction it's being turned. You can then use this information as a way to control your application.

You can use the accelerometer to perform simple tasks, such as determining when the device has been turned upside down and then completing an action. For example, you can immerse users in game play by having them shake their device to roll the dice. This level of usefulness is setting mobile devices apart from typical desktop personal computers.

 Android has *activity recognition* built in, which uses various sensors such as the accelerometer and the GPS to determine whether your user is likely walking, running, driving, or bicycling right now. Check out `http://d.android.com/training/location/activity-recognition.html` for more information about using activity recognition.

SD card

Android gives you the tools you need to access (save and load) files on the device's *SD card* — a portable storage medium that you can insert into compatible phones, tablets, and computers. To avoid bloating your app with extra required resources and hogging limited built-in memory, you can download some or all of your application's resources from your web host and save them to the device's SD card (which makes users less likely to uninstall your app when they need to clear space on their devices).

 Not every device has an SD card preinstalled, though most do. Always ensure that a device has an SD card installed and that adequate space is available before trying to save files to it. Also, be aware that any file you place on an SD card is not secure, and can be read by other apps on the user's phone.

Software Tools

Various Android tools are at your disposal while you're writing Android applications. The following sections outline some of the most popular tools to use in your day-to-day Android development process.

Internet

Thanks to the Internet capabilities of Android devices, users can find real-time information on the Internet, such as the next showing of a new movie or the next arrival of a commuter train. As a developer, you can have your apps use the Internet to access real-time, up-to-date data, such as weather, news, and sports scores, or (like Pandora and YouTube) to store your application's icons and graphics.

 You can even offload your application's more intense processes to a web server when appropriate, to save processing time or to streamline the app. In this well-established software architecture, known as *client–server computing,* the client uses the Internet to make a request to a server that's ready to perform some work for your app. The built-in Maps app is an example of a client that accesses map and location data from a web server.

Audio and video support

Including audio and video in your apps is a breeze in the Android operating system. Many standard audio and video formats are supported, and adding multimedia content to your apps — such as sound effects, instructional videos, background music, and streaming video and audio from the Internet — couldn't be easier. Be as creative as you want to be. The sky's the limit.

Contacts

Your app can access a user's Contacts list, which is stored on the device, to display the contact information in a new or different way, or you can create your own Contacts list. You might even write an app that couples the contact information with the GPS system to alert the user whenever she's near a contact's address.

Don't use information from the Contacts list in a malicious way. Use your imagination, but be responsible about it. (See the next section, "Security.")

Security

Suppose that someone releases an app that sends a user's entire Contacts list to a server for malicious purposes. For this reason, most functions that modify a user's Android device or access its protected content need specific *permissions*. For example, if you want to download an image from the web, you need permission to use the Internet so that you can download the file to your device, and you need a separate permission to save the image file to an SD card. When your app is being installed, the user is notified of the permissions your app is requesting and can decide whether to proceed. Though asking for permission isn't optional, it's as easy as implementing a single line of code in your application's manifest file. (Manifest files are described in Chapter 3.)

Google APIs

Users of the Android operating system aren't limited to making calls, organizing contacts, or installing apps. As a developer, you have great power at your fingertips — you can even integrate maps into your application, for example, by using the Google Maps API.

Pinpointing locations on a map

Perhaps you want to write an app that displays a user's current location to friends. You can spend hundreds of hours developing a mapping system, or you can use the Google Maps API. You can embed the API in your application without investing hundreds of development hours or even a single cent. Using the Maps API, you can find almost anything that has an address. The possibilities are endless — a friend's location, the nearest grocery store, or your favorite gas station, for example.

Showing your current location to friends is cool, but the Google Maps API can also access the Google Navigation API, to pinpoint your location and show your users how to reach it.

Messaging in the cloud

Suppose that your application's data is stored in the cloud (the Internet) and you download all of its assets the first time it runs. And then you realize that an image is outdated. To update the image, the app needs to know that the image has changed. You can use the Google Cloud Messaging framework to send a cloud-to-device notification (a message from the web server to the device) to direct the app to update the image. This process works even if your app isn't running. When the device receives the message, it dispatches a message to start your app so that it can take the appropriate action.

The KISS principle

The most difficult task in developing applications is remembering the KISS principle: Keep It Simple, Stupid. One way to unnecessarily complicate the code you create is to dive into development before understanding the role of the built-in APIs. Choosing this route may take more of your time than simply glossing over the Android documentation; you don't have to memorize the documentation, but do yourself a favor and at least skim it. Then you can see how easily you can use the built-in functionality — and how much time it can save you. You can easily write multiple lines of code to complete a one-line task. Changing the volume of the media player or creating a menu, for example, is a simple process, but if you don't know how to use the APIs, you may cause more problems by having to rewrite them.

Another way to muck things up is to add unnecessary functionality. Just give users the simplest way to operate their devices. For example, avoid designing a fancy, custom-tab layout when a couple of menu items will suffice. Also, Android comes supplied with enough widgets (built-in controls) to help you accomplish virtually any task. Using these controls makes your app even easier for users to work with because they already know and love them.

Chapter 2

Prepping Your Development Headquarters

All the software that you need to develop Android applications is *free*. That's where the beauty of developing Android applications lies. The basic building blocks you need to develop rich Android applications — the tools, the frameworks, and even the source code — are free. No one gives you a free computer, but you get to set up your development environment and start developing applications for free, and you can't beat free. Well, maybe you can — if someone pays you to write an Android application, but you'll reach that. This chapter walks you through the necessary steps to install the tools and frameworks so that you can start building kick-butt Android applications.

Developing the Android Developer Inside You

Becoming an Android developer isn't a complicated task. And it's likely simpler than you believe. To see what's involved, ask yourself these questions:

✔ Do I want to develop Android applications?

✔ Do I like free software development tools?

    ✓ Do I like to pay no developer fees?

    ✓ Do I have a computer to develop on?

If you answered yes to every question, today is your lucky day — you're ready to become an Android developer.

There's always a catch, right? You can develop for free to your heart's content, but as soon as you want to publish your application to the Google Play Store, where you upload and publish your apps, you need to pay a small, nominal registration fee. At this writing, the fee is $25.

If you're developing an application for a client, you can publish your application as a redistributable package to give to him. Then your client can publish the application to the Google Play Store, using his Google account, to ensure that you don't have to pay a fee for client work. You can then be a bona fide Android developer and never have to pay a fee. That's *cool.*

Assembling Your Toolkit

After you know that you're ready to be an Android developer, grab your computer and get cracking on installing the tools and frameworks necessary to build your first blockbuster application.

Linux kernel

Android was created on top of the open source Linux kernel. The Android team chose to use this kernel because it provided proven core features on which to develop the Android operating system. The features of the Linux kernel include (but aren't limited to)

    ✓ **Security model:** The Linux kernel handles security between the application and the system.

    ✓ **Memory management:** The kernel handles memory management, leaving you free to develop your app.

    ✓ **Process management:** The Linux kernel manages processes well, allocating resources to processes as they need them.

    ✓ **Network stack:** The Linux kernel also handles network communication.

    ✓ **Driver model:** The goal of Linux is to ensure that the application works. Hardware manufacturers can build their drivers into the Linux build.

Android source code

You should be aware that the full Android source code is open source, which means that it's not only free to use but also free to modify. If you want to download the Android source code and create a new version of Android, you're free to do so. Check out the Android Open Source Project at `https://source.android.com`.

Android framework

Atop the Linux kernel, the Android framework was developed with various features. These features were pulled from numerous open source projects. The output of these projects resulted in these elements:

- ✔ **The Android runtime:** The Android runtime is composed of Java core libraries and ART (the Android RunTime). Older versions of Android (4.x and earlier) use the Dalvik runtime.

- ✔ **Open GL (graphics library):** This cross-language, cross-platform application program interface (API) is used to produce 2D and 3D computer graphics.

- ✔ **WebKit:** This open source web browser engine provides the functionality to display web content and to simplify page loading.

- ✔ **SQLite:** This open source relational database engine is designed to be embedded in devices.

- ✔ **Media frameworks:** These libraries allow you to play and record audio and video.

- ✔ **Secure Sockets Layer (SSL):** These libraries are responsible for Internet security.

See Figure 2-1 for a list of common Android libraries.

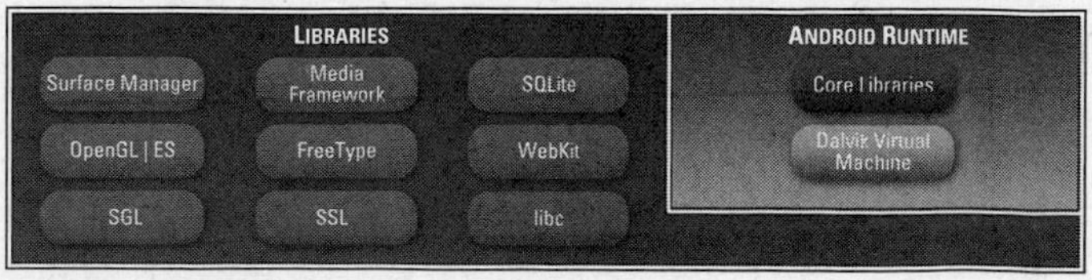

Figure 2-1:
Android and other third-party libraries that sit atop the Linux 3.4 kernel.

Application framework

If you've read the preceding section, you may say, "Well, that's all nice and well, but how do these libraries affect me as a developer?" It's simple: All these open source frameworks are available to you via Android. You don't have to worry about how Android interacts with SQLite and the surface manager; you use them as tools in your Android tool belt.

The Android team has built on a known set of proven libraries, built in the background, and has given them to you, all exposed through Android interfaces. These interfaces wrap up the various libraries and make them useful to the Android platform and to you as a developer. You benefit from these features because you don't have to build any of the functionality they provide. Some of these interfaces include

- **Activity manager:** Manages the activity lifecycle.
- **Telephony manager:** Provides access to telephony services as well as to certain subscriber information, such as phone numbers.
- **View system:** Handles the views and layouts that make up your user interface (UI).
- **Location manager:** Finds the device's geographic location.

Take a look at Figure 2-2 to see the libraries that make up the application framework.

From kernel to application, the Android operating system has been developed with proven open source technologies. You, as a developer, can therefore build rich applications that have been fostered in the open source community. See Figure 2-3 for a full picture of how the Android application framework stacks up. The Applications section is where your application sits.

Figure 2-2:
A glimpse at part of the Android application framework.

APPLICATION FRAMEWORK

Activity Manager   Window Manager   Content Providers   View System

Package Manager   Telephony Manager   Resource Manager   Location Manager   Notification Manager

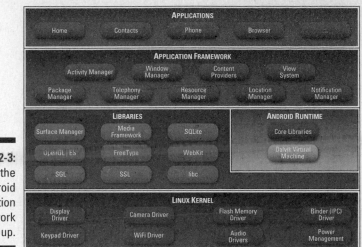

Figure 2-3:
How the
Android
application
framework
stacks up.

Sometimes when you're developing an Android application, you want to use
the same resource as in the core Android system. A good example is an icon for
a Settings menu option. By accessing the Android source code, you can browse
the various resources and download the resources you need for your project.
Having access to the source code also allows you to dig in and see exactly how
Android does what it does. Be aware though that you need to follow the
requirements of the license, as well as follow Google's branding guidelines
when borrowing these resources. Find out more at `http://d.android.com/`
`distribute/googleplay/promote/brand.html`.

Java knowledge

The Java programming language is one of the glorious tools that make programming Android a breeze compared with programming for other mobile
platforms. Whereas other languages insist that you manage memory, allocate
and de-allocate bytes, and then shift bits around like a game of dominoes, the
Java runtime helps take care of that for you. The Java runtime allows you to
focus on writing code to solve a business problem by using a clean, under-
standable programming language (or to build that next cool first-person
shooter game you've been dreaming of) instead of focusing on the "plumbing" just to get the screens to show up.

You're expected to understand the basics of the Java programming language
before you write your first Android application. If you're feeling rusty and
need a refresher course on Java, you can visit the Java tutorials site at
`http://docs.oracle.com/javase/tutorial`.

Though you find a little Java information in this book, you may want to spend some time with a good book like *Java All-in-One For Dummies,* by Doug Lowe (John Wiley & Sons, Inc.), if you have no Java experience.

Tuning Up Your Hardware

You can develop Android applications on various operating systems, including Windows, Linux, and Mac OS X. In this book, you find a combination of the Windows 8 operating system and Mac OS X, but you can use Linux as well.

Operating system

Android supports these platforms:

- ✔ Windows XP or later
- ✔ Mac OS X 10.5 or later
- ✔ Linux with GNOME or KDE

Throughout this book, some examples use Windows 7 64-bit Edition. Windows paths look similar to this:

```
c:\path\to\file.txt
```

Some examples use Mac OS X; a Mac or Linux path looks similar to this:

```
/path/to/file.txt
```

Computer hardware

Before you start installing the required software, make sure that your computer can run it adequately. Just about any desktop or laptop computer manufactured in the past four years will suffice. A computer with 4 or 8 gigabytes (GB) of RAM should work just fine.

To ensure that you can install all the tools and frameworks you'll need, make sure that you have enough hard drive space to accommodate them. The Android developer site has a list of hardware requirements, outlining how much hard drive space each component requires, at `https://developer.android.com/sdk/installing/studio.html`.

To save you time, you need at least 3GB of free hard drive space to install all the tools and frameworks necessary to develop Android applications.

Installing and Configuring Your Support Tools

It's time to put these exciting Android concepts into action, but before you can do so, you need to install and configure a few tools, including the SDKs:

- ✔ **Android Studio:** An easy to use Integrated Development Environment (IDE) that brings together Java and the Android SDK to make it simple to write Android apps.
- ✔ **Java JDK:** The Java Development Kit. Lays the foundation for the Android SDK.
- ✔ **Android SDK:** Included in Android Studio. Provides access to Android libraries and allows you to develop for Android.

The following sections show you how to acquire and install all these tools.

A benefit of working with open source software is that, most of the time, you can get the tools to develop the software for free. Android is no exception to that rule. All the tools that you need to develop rich Android applications are free.

Installing Android Studio

To download Android Studio, first go to `https://developer.android.com/sdk/installing/studio.html` and download Android Studio. Then go through the following steps to get to the Android Studio boot screen, as in Figure 2-4:

Mac users

If you're a Mac user, follow these steps to download Android Studio:

1. **Open the downloaded** `DMG` **file,** `android-studio-ide-*.dmg`.

2. **From the resulting Android Studio DMG volume, drag and drop Android Studio into the** `Applications` **folder.**

3. **Eject the Android Studio DMG volume so that you don't accidentally run the wrong Android Studio.**

4. **Open the `Applications` folder and double-click Android Studio.**

   Depending on your security settings, when you attempt to open Android Studio, you might see a warning that says the package is damaged and should be moved to the trash. If this happens, choose System Preferences⇨Security & Privacy and, under Allow applications downloaded from, select Anywhere. Then open Android Studio again.

5. **Depending on your Mac, you may be asked to install Java at this point.**

   Click OK and Java will be automatically installed for you.

Figure 2-4:
The Android Studio boot screen.

Windows users

If you're a Windows user, follow these steps to download Android Studio:

1. **Launch the downloaded `EXE` file, `android-studio-bundle-*.exe`.**

2. **Follow the setup wizard to install Android Studio.**

3. **Open the Start screen and launch Android Studio.**

   On some Windows systems, the launcher script does not find where Java is installed. If you encounter this problem, you need to set an environment variable indicating the correct location.

Choose Start menu⇨Computer⇨System Properties⇨Advanced System Properties. Then choose Advanced tab⇨Environment Variables and add a new system variable, `JAVA_HOME`, that points to your `JDK` folder — for example, `C:\ProgramFiles\Java\jdk1.8.0_20`.

If you do not have the Java JDK installed, see the next section.

Installing Java 7

On some systems, you may see an error that the system cannot find the Java 7 JDK.

If this happens, visit `www.oracle.com/technetwork/java/javase/downloads/jdk7-downloads-1880260.html` to download the Java 7 JDK appropriate for your machine. Install it, then run Android Studio again.

If you're on a Mac and you continue to see the same error after installing Java 7, you may also need to install Java 6. Visit `http://support.apple.com/kb/DL1572` to install Java 6 on your Mac, then try again.

Adding SDK Packages

Now that you have Android Studio installed, you need to make sure that you download all the latest SDK components. The first time you launch Android Studio, it may install part of the SDK for you, but you need to install the full SDK using the following steps:

1. **Choose Tools⇨Android⇨SDK Manager to launch the SDK manager tool.**

2. **Click New to select all new packages that are not currently on your machine, then click the Install button.**

3. **Click each group in the list and click Accept License for each, then click Install.**

Now hum the theme from *Jeopardy*.

Once this is done, do it again. No seriously. Click New to select all the new packages, accept the license agreements again, and click Install again. You shouldn't have to do it more than twice, but heck, check it a third time while you're at it.

Navigating the Android SDK

Now that you've installed the Android SDK, take a look inside the `SDK` folder:

On a Mac, open the Terminal app in Applications⇨Utilities (or by search-ing for "Terminal" in Spotlight), then type `cd "/Applications/Android Studio.app/sdk"`. On Windows, open the Start menu and search for "cmd" to launch a command prompt, then type `cd "\Users\<user>\AppData\ Local\Android\android-studio\sdk\"` where `<user>` is your username.

Whoa — you'll find a lot of folders in the SDK! Don't worry: The folder struc-ture of the Android SDK is easy to understand when you get the hang of it. You need to understand the structure of the SDK to master it. Table 2-1 out-lines the contents of each folder.

Table 2-1	Folders in the Android SDK
SDK Folder	*What It Contains*
`tools`, `build-tools`, and `platform-tools`	Various tools that are available for use during development — such as for debugging, view management, and building.
`platforms`	The platforms you target when you build Android applica-tions, such as folders named `android-16` (which is Android 4.1) and `android-8` (which is Android 2.2).
`extras` and/or `add-ons`	Additional APIs that provide extra functionality. The Google APIs in this folder include mapping functional-ity. This folder remains empty until you install any of the Google Maps APIs.

Specifying Android Platforms

Android platform is a fancy way of saying *Android version*. At this writing, many versions of Android are available, ranging up through version 5.0. When we say "specifying an Android platform," that means that we are developing our app so that it will work on devices running that specific Android version or later.

Several versions of Android are still widely used on phones. If you want to reach the largest number of users, target an earlier version. If you want to keep your development quick and simple, or if your app requires functionality that older platforms can't support, then by all means specify the newer platform. It would make no sense to write a Bluetooth toggle widget targeting any platform earlier than 2.0 because earlier platforms can't use Bluetooth.

To view current platform statistics, visit `http://d.android.com/`
`resources/dashboard/platform-versions.html`.

Using SDK Tools for Everyday Development

The SDK tools are the building blocks you use in developing Android apps.
New features packed into every release enable you to develop for the latest
version of Android.

Saying hello to the emulator

Google provides not only the tools you need to develop apps but also an
awesome little emulator to test your app. The emulator has some limitations
(for example, it cannot emulate certain hardware components, such as the
accelerometer) but not to worry — plenty of apps can be developed and
tested using only an emulator.

When you're developing an app that uses Bluetooth, for example, you should
use a physical device that has Bluetooth on it. If you develop on a speedy
computer, testing on an emulator is fast; on slower machines, however, the
emulator can take a long time to complete a seemingly simple task. If you're
developing on an older machine, use a physical device. When you're developing on a newer, faster machine, use the emulator.

The emulator is handy for testing apps at different screen sizes and resolutions. It isn't always practical or possible to have several devices connected
to your computer at the same time, but you can run multiple emulators with
varying screen sizes and resolutions.

Getting physical with a real Android device [Windows]

If you develop on a Windows machine and you want to test your app on
a real-life device, you need to install a driver. If you're on a Mac or Linux
machine, you can skip this section because you don't need to install the
USB driver.

When you downloaded the SDK, you also downloaded the USB driver that you need. To install it, do the following:

1. **Plug in your device.**

2. **Choose Control Panel⇨Device Manager.**

3. **Expand Other Devices (Figure 2-5), right-click your device, and select Update Driver Software.**

   Select Browse my computer for driver software.

4. **Type** `\C:\Users\<user>\AppData\Local\Android\android-studio\sdk\extras\google\usb_driver` **(replacing** `<user>` **with your username), and click Next.**

   If you can't find the `AppData` directory on your computer, it's because it's hidden by default. What you can do is type **%appdata%** in the location field and then click Browse. That unhides the directory and allows you to navigate the rest of the way there.

5. **When asked if you would like to install this device, click Install.**

Figure 2-5:
Finding your device in the Windows Device Manager.

```
Device Manager                                             _  □  ×
File  Action  View  Help
← →  |  ⊡ | 🔲 | 🛈 🔲 | 🗗 | 🖳 🖳 🖳
▲ 🖥 WIN-I02UBCEFNIQ
  ▷ 🔊 Audio inputs and outputs
  ▷ 🔋 Batteries
  ▷ 🟦 Bluetooth
  ▷ 💻 Computer
  ▷ 👝 Disk drives
  ▷ 🖳 Display adapters
  ▷ 💿 DVD/CD-ROM drives
  ▷ 🖫 Floppy disk drives
  ▷ 🖫 Floppy drive controllers
  ▷ 🕹 Human Interface Devices
  ▷ ⟺ IDE ATA/ATAPI controllers
  ▷ ⌨ Keyboards
  ▷ 🖫 Memory devices
  ▷ 🖱 Mice and other pointing devices
  ▷ 🖥 Monitors
  ▷ 🖧 Network adapters
  ▲ 🔲 Other devices
      🔲 Nexus 5
  ▷ 🖧 Portable Devices
  ▷ 🖳 Ports (COM & LPT)
  ▷ 🖨 Print queues
  ▷ 🖥 Processors
  ▷ 🖩 Software devices
  ▷ 🔊 Sound, video and game controllers
  ▷ ⟺ Storage controllers
```

Debugging your work

The Android Device Monitor equips you with the necessary tools to find those pesky bugs, allowing you to go behind the scenes as your app is running to see the state of its hardware, such as the wireless radio. But wait — there's more! The Device Monitor also simulates actions normally reserved for physical devices, such as sending global positioning system (GPS) coordinates manually, simulating phone calls, or simulating text messages. Get all the Device Monitor details at `http://d.android.com/tools/help/monitor.html`.

Trying out the API and SDK samples

The API and SDK samples are provided to demonstrate how to use the functionality provided by the API and SDK. If you're ever stuck and can't figure out how to make something work, visit `http://d.android.com/samples/` to find samples of almost *anything,* from using Bluetooth to making a two-way text application or a 2D game.

You also have a few samples in your Android SDK. Simply open the Android SDK and navigate to the `samples` directory, which contains various samples that range from interacting with services to manipulating local databases. Spend some time playing with the samples — the best way to learn to develop Android applications is to look at existing working code bases and then experiment with them in Android Studio.

Giving the API demos a spin

The API demos inside the `samples` folder in the SDK are a collection of apps that demonstrate how to use the included APIs. You can find sample apps with a ton of examples, such as

- Notifications
- Alarms
- Intents
- Menus

  ✔ Search

  ✔ Preferences

  ✔ Background services

If you get stuck or you simply want to prepare yourself for writing your next spectacular Android application, check out the complete details at `http://d.android.com/samples/`.

Part II
Building and Publishing Your First Application

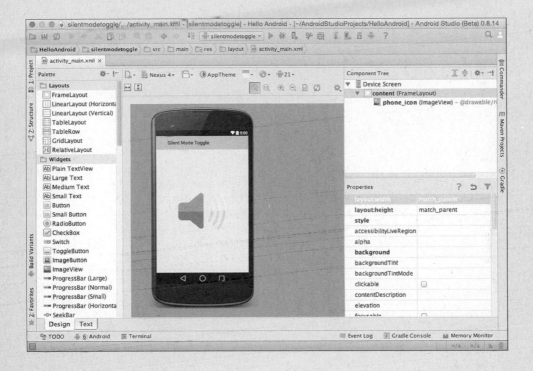

Learn how to test your Android app online at www.dummies.com/extras/androidappdevelopment

In this part . . .

Part II walks you through developing a useful Android application. You start with the basics of the Android tools and then delve into developing the screens and Home screen widgets that users will interact with. When the application is complete, you sign your application digitally so that you can publish it. You finish by publishing your application to the Google Play Store.

Chapter 3

Your First Android Project

*B*efore you start creating that next blockbuster Android application, I walk you through creating your first Android application to help solidify a few key aspects in the Android project-creation process. In this chapter, you create a simple "Hello Android" application that requires no coding whatsoever. What — no coding? How is that possible? Follow along as I show you.

Starting a New Project in Android Studio

First things first: Start Android Studio. You should see a screen that looks similar to the one shown in Figure 3-1. Now you're ready to start cooking with Android.

If you haven't set up your development environment yet, turn to Chapter 2. It shows you how to set up all the tools and frameworks necessary to develop Android applications.

Android Studio 0.8.14 Build 135.1538390. Check for updates now.

Figure 3-1:
The Android
Studio
development
environ-
ment.

Follow these steps to create your first Android application project:

1. **In Android Studio, choose File⇨New Project.**

   The Create New Project Wizard opens, as shown in Figure 3-2.

2. **Enter** Hello Android **as the application name.**

   The application name is the name of the application as it pertains to
   Android. When the application is installed on the emulator or physical
   device, this name appears in the application launcher.

3. **Enter** dummies.com **as the Company Domain.**

   Your Package name should autocomplete to `com.dummies.helloandroid`.
   This is the name of the application ID, which will generally be the same as
   your Java package. (See the nearby sidebar "Java package nomenclature.")

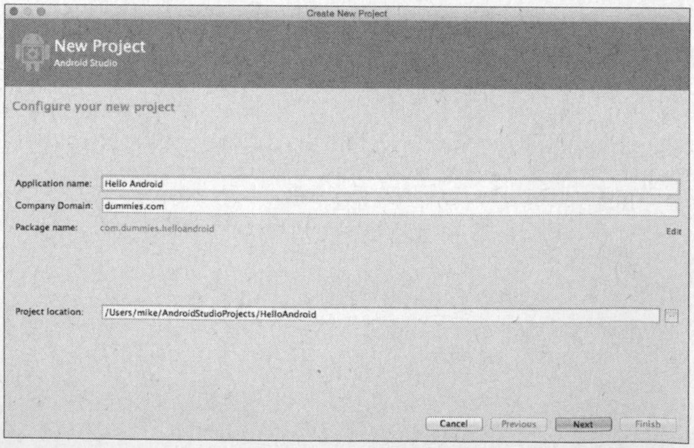

Figure 3-2:
The Create
New Project
Wizard.

Java package nomenclature

A *package* in Java is a way to organize Java classes into namespaces similar to modules. Each package must have a unique name for the classes it contains. Classes in the same package can access one another's package-access members.

Java packages have a naming convention defined as the hierarchical naming pattern. Each level of the hierarchy is separated by periods. A package name starts with the highest-level domain name of the organization; then the subdomains are listed in reverse order. At the end of the package name, the company can choose what it wants to call the package. The package name `com.dummies.helloandroid` is the name used in this example.

Notice that the highest-level domain is at the front of the package name (`com`). Subsequent subdomains are separated by periods. The package name traverses through the subdomains to get to the final package name of `helloandroid`.

A great example of another use for a package is having a Java package for all your web-related communications. Any time you need to find a web-related Java class, you can open that Java package and work on your web-related Java classes. Packages allow you to keep your code organized.

4. **Choose a location for your project.**

   The default location will probably be fine. Click Next.

5. **Select Phone and Tablet, choose a Minimum SDK version of API 21: Android 5.0 Lollipop, and click Next.**

   The Minimum SDK drop-down list identifies which application programming interface (API) you want to develop for this project. Always set the Build Target SDK to the latest version that you've tested your app on. When you select Lollipop, you build and test your app on devices going up to Lollipop. Doing so allows you to develop with the Lollipop APIs, which include new features such as the Material Design look and feel. If you had selected Android 2.2 as the target, for example, you wouldn't be able to use any features introduced in Lollipop (or 2.3, 3.1, and so on).

6. **In the Create Activity box, choose Blank Activity and click Next.**

   The Add an Activity screen appears, as shown in Figure 3-3.

7. **Enter MainActivity in the Activity Name box, `activity_main` in the Layout name, MainActivity in the Title, and `menu_main` as the Menu Resource Name.**

   The New Blank Activity screen defines what the initial activity is called — the entry point to your application. When Android runs your application, this activity is the first one to be accessed.

   The Layout name is the name of the file that will contain the layout of your activity's user interface.

8. Click the Finish button.

You're done! You should see Android Studio think for a few moments, and then create a new project with your new blank activity, ready for you to populate (see Figure 3-4).

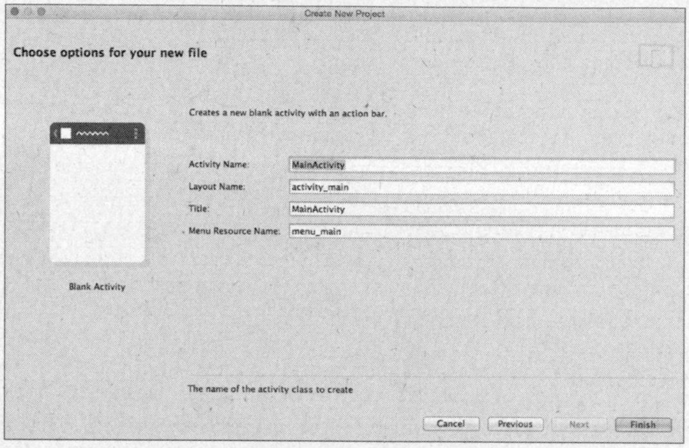

Figure 3-3: Set up your new activity.

Understanding Android versioning

Version codes aren't the same as version names. (Huh?) Android has version names and version codes. Each version name has a single version code associated with it. The following table outlines the version names and their respective version code. You can also find this information in the Build Target section of the New Android Project dialog box.

Platform Version	API Level	Codename
4.0	14	Ice Cream Sandwich
4.0.3	15	Ice Cream Sandwich
4.1	16	Jelly Bean
4.2	17	Jelly Bean
4.3	18	Jelly Bean
4.4	19	Kit Kat
4.4W	20	Wearables
5.0	21	Lollipop

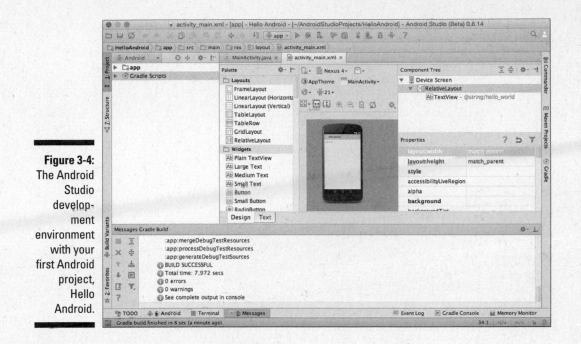

Figure 3-4:
The Android
Studio
develop-
ment
environment
with your
first Android
project,
Hello
Android.

Responding to Errors

The Android project generated by Android Studio is a fresh, clean project
with no compiled binary sources. You will need to understand what happens
under the hood of Android Studio at a high level. Click the `MainActivity`
`.java` tab in Android Studio, then change `package com.dummies.`
`helloandroid` to **org.dummies.helloandroid**, like in Figure 3-5.

You may notice a little red square on the upper right-hand side of the window
(refer again to Figure 3-5). That icon is Android Studio's way of letting you
know that something is wrong with the project in the workspace. If you look
carefully, you'll see a red line below it that indicates exactly where in the file
the error was detected.

Now choose Navigate⇨Next Highlighted Error. The editor jumps your
cursor to the location of the error so you can fix it. If you keep selecting
it, you can jump from error to error. Once all the errors are fixed, Android
Studio then jumps you from warning to warning until you fix all those as
well. Eventually, once all your problems are fixed, the icon will turn a very
satisfying green.

The red square indicates an error.

The red underlined code shows the error location.

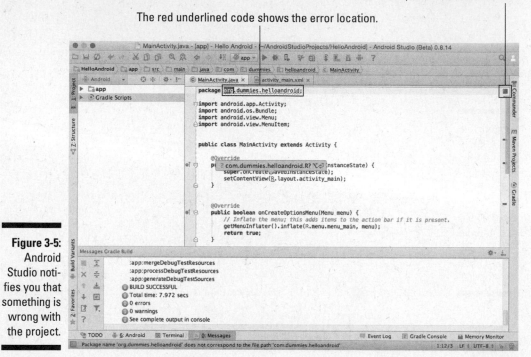

Figure 3-5:
Android
Studio noti-
fies you that
something is
wrong with
the project.

Now put your text cursor back on org.dummies.helloandroid. If you look
carefully in the lower left-hand corner of the screen, Android Studio gives you
some assistance to fix the problem (Figure 3-6). Here it says:

Figure 3-6:
Package
name org.
dummies.
helloan-
droid
does not
correspond
to the file
path com.
dummies.
helloan-
droid.

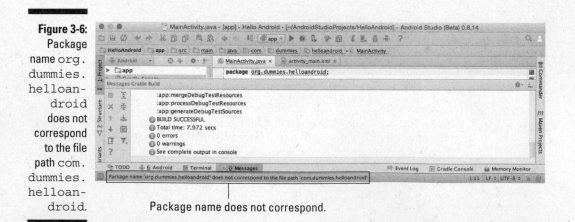

Package name does not correspond.

```
Package name "org.dummies.helloandroid" does not correspond to the file path
                "com.dumies.helloandroid"
```

If you don't see it, you can choose View➪Error Description to see the message. With your text cursor still on the error, press Alt+Enter to view a couple Quick Fix options for this error. You want to change the package name back to what it should be, so choose Set package name to com. dummies.helloandroid.

Setting Up an Emulator

You're almost ready to run your Hello Android application! The next step is to set up an emulator.

An emulator (also known as an AVD) is an Android Virtual Device that looks, acts, walks, and talks (well, maybe not walks and talks) like a physical Android device. AVDs can be configured to run just about any particular version of Android.

Follow these steps to create your first AVD:

1. **Choose Tools➪Android➪AVD Manager.**

   The AVD Manager dialog box opens.

2. **Click Create a Virtual Device, then click the Nexus 5 item and click Next, as in Figure 3-7.**

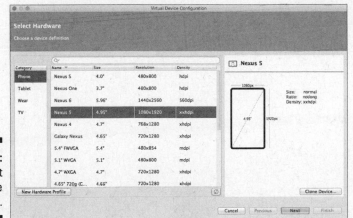

Figure 3-7: The Select Hardware dialog box.

3. **In the System Image dialog box, select the Lollipop x86 item as in Figure 3-8, then click Next.**

4. **In the Configure AVD dialog box, use the default AVD name or change it to a haiku.**

   Leave everything else alone, as in Figure 3-9.

5. **Click the Finish button.**

   Figure 3-10 shows the completed AVD Manager dialog box. You should now see your new AVD listed under Your Virtual Devices.

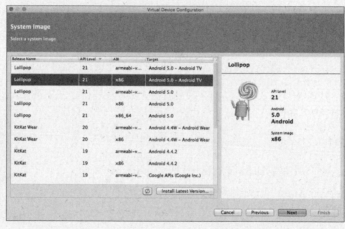

Figure 3-8:
The System
Image
dialog box.

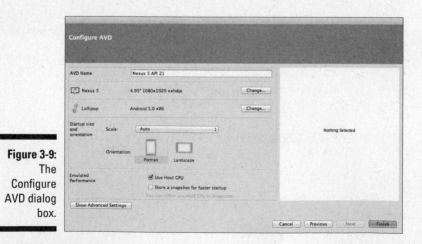

Figure 3-9:
The
Configure
AVD dialog
box.

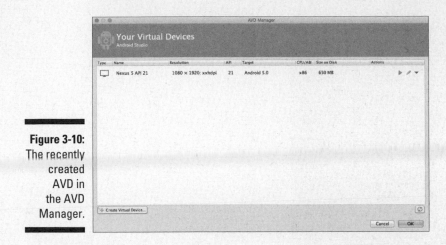

Figure 3-10:
The recently
created
AVD in
the AVD
Manager.

Running the Hello Android App

Understanding the basics of how to get an Android application up and running is a simple but detailed process. You're now ready to see your hard work in action. You've created an Android Virtual Device; now it's time to get the application running. Finally!

Running the app in the emulator

Starting your application is as simple as choosing Run⇨Run 'app'. At this point, Android Studio will compile your app. When it's done, choose Launch Emulator and select the emulator you just created. Check Use same device for future launches, and click OK. Android Studio compiles your application, deploys it to the emulator, and then runs it, as shown in Figure 3-11.

Look for "HAX is working and emulator runs in fast virt mode" in the Run app log at the bottom of Android Studio, as in Figure 3-12.

If you don't see this, then your emulator will likely run much slower than it could. To fix this, you will want to enable the

- ✔ Graphics acceleration
- ✔ Intel HAXM virtual machine acceleration

Visit `http://d.android.com/tools/devices/emulator.html#acceleration` for more information about how to enable these two features to speed up your emulator.

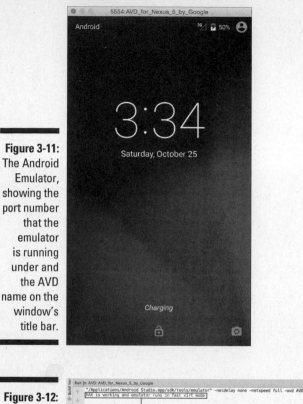

Figure 3-11:
The Android
Emulator,
showing the
port number
that the
emulator
is running
under and
the AVD
name on the
window's
title bar.

Figure 3-12:
HAX is
working and
emulator
runs in fast
virt mode.

Look for this message

Help! If your emulator never loads and stays stuck on the ANDROID screen(s), there's no need to worry, comrade. The first time the emulator starts, it can take many minutes to finish loading because you're running a virtual Linux system in the emulator. The emulator has to boot up and initialize. The slower your computer, the slower the emulator is in its boot process.

You can save valuable time by leaving the emulator running. The emulator doesn't have to be loaded every time you want to run your application. After the emulator is running, you can change your source code and then rerun your application. Because you checked the Use same device for future launches option, Android Studio will reuse it when running your app.

When the emulator finishes loading, you see your app running with the words "Hello world!" like in Figure 3-13.

Figure 3-13:
The Hello
Android
applica-
tion in the
emulator.

You've just created and started your first Android application.

Checking app logs

You can view the logs of your application in the Android tool window, as shown in Figure 3-14. This tool window should have popped up automatically when you ran your app, but if it didn't, you can access it by choosing View⇨Tool Windows⇨Android.

Inside the Android view, you'll see your app's log output in the logcat tab. Here's an example log that you might see:

```
1885-1885/com.dummies.helloandroid I/art: Not late-enabling
          -Xcheck:jni (already on)
1885-1898/com.dummies.helloandroid I/art: Profiler disabled.
          To enable setprop dalvik.vm.profiler 1
1885-1885/com.dummies.helloandroid W/Resources: Preloaded drawable resource
          #0x1080093 (android:drawable/sym_def_app_icon) that varies with
          configuration!!
1885-1885/com.dummies.helloandroid I/am_on_resume_called: [0,com.dummies.
          helloandroid.MainActivity]
```

Figure 3-14:
The Android
Tool
window
displaying
logs from
your app.

The logcat view provides valuable information on the state of your application. It lets you know it's launching an activity, shows which device you're connected to, and shows warnings and errors. In the previous example, you can see that the `com.dummies.helloandroid.MainActivity`, the activity you just wrote, was run and its `on_resume` was called:

```
1885-1885/com.dummies.helloandroid I/am_on_resume_called:
          [0,com.dummies.helloandroid.MainActivity]
```

I'll explain what `on_resume` means later in the book, but for now just know that your activity was started up as expected.

Understanding Project Structure

You've created your first application. You even did it without coding. It's nice that Android Studio provides you with the tools to fire up a quick application, but it won't write your next blockbuster application for you. The beginning of this chapter walked you through how to create a boilerplate Android application by using the New Android Project Wizard. The rest of this chapter shows you how to use the file structure that the Wizard created for you.

The following sections aren't ones you should skim (they're vital!), because you'll spend your entire Android development time navigating these folders. Understanding what they're for and how they got there is a key aspect of understanding Android development.

Navigating your app's folders

In Android Studio, the Project View expands to show the Hello Android project, as shown in Figure 3-15. If you don't see the Project view, choose View➪Tool Windows➪Project to turn it on. Then click on Android in the upper left and select Project to view the Project view.

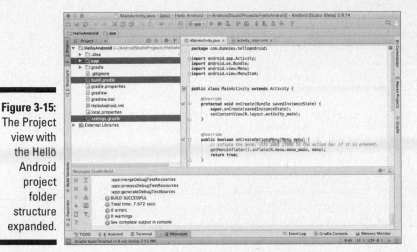

Figure 3-15:
The Project view with the Hello Android project folder structure expanded.

The Project view and Android views are both very useful. Try switching back and forth between them both to see which you prefer. For more information about the Android view, visit `https://developer.android.com/sdk/installing/studio-androidview.html`.

After the Hello Android project is expanded, you'll see a few directories and files. The important ones are

✔ app: Where your main app code is placed.

✔ build.gradle: Your top-level build file. It's not the only build.gradle file in your project, but it's the one at the top. It tells gradle, the Android build system, how to build the various subdirectories in your project.

✔ settings.gradle: This file doesn't have much in it right now, but it does contain the list of subdirectories that gradle needs to build. In this case, it just lists app.

Go ahead and open up the app directory and look what's inside. Some of the interesting folders and files here include

✔ Another build.gradle: The build.gradle file in this directory is different from the one at the top level. This build.gradle file includes the real meat of what's necessary to compile your app. You'll examine it in more detail later.

✔ build: This directory isn't something you normally look at. It contains temporary and generated files that are built by the Android build system during the course of compiling your app.

- ✔ libs: This directory is also something you won't normally look at. If you need to add third-party libraries to your project, you can download the jars and put them into this libs directory to include in your app. However, more commonly you add them as dependencies into your build.gradle file. You'll find out more about how to add dependencies to your Android projects in Chapter 9.

- ✔ src: This directory is the most interesting one here. It contains all the source files necessary to build and test your app.

Go ahead and open up the src directory now. You'll see two directories:

- ✔ androidTest: This directory is where you'll put all your test cases to test your app.

- ✔ main: Your app's source code is inside the main folder.

If you open the main folder, you'll see three things:

- ✔ AndroidManifest.xml
- ✔ java
- ✔ res

The AndroidManifest.xml file tells Android what's inside your app. Android uses this information to find and load the various components of your app. You'll find out more about AndroidManifest.xml in Chapter 9.

To learn how to use the androidTest folder to create automated test cases for your app, read the articles online about testing at www.dummies.com/extras/androidappdevelopment.

The following sections discuss the other folders.

Java Source (java) folder

The Java source folder — known as the java folder in Android projects — includes your stub MainActivity.java file, which you created in the New Android Project Wizard earlier in this chapter. If you open the java folder, you'll see the com.dummies.helloandroid package, with the MainActivity.java file inside.

You aren't limited to a single package in your Android applications. In fact, separating the different pieces of your app into separate packages is considered to be a best practice. For example, your application might have Customer objects that represent a customer, and those customers are retrieved via a web API. To make that easy, you might also have some http classes that represent your API. One way you might organize these classes is to use packages like the following:

- ✔ `com.dummies.helloandroid.models`
- ✔ `com.dummies.helloandroid.http`

These packages contain their respective Java components. `com.dummies.helloandroid.models` contains the domain model Java classes (such as your `Customer` object), and `com.dummies.helloandroid.http` contains the HTTP-related Java classes used to access your web APIs.

Resources (res) folder

The `res` folder contains the various resources that your application will use. Classic examples of resources include text strings, images, and layout files, but there are many other kinds of less-common resources that you might include with your app. See Table 3-1 for a more complete list.

Android allows you to define the same resource multiple times in different folders. For example, if you open up `res/values/strings.xml`, you'll see that the `hello_world` string is defined to be the text "Hello world!" If you wanted to, you could define the same `hello_world` string in `res/values-es/strings.xml` and give it the value of `"¡Hola Mundo!"` Android would then automatically choose the Spanish translation when the app runs on a Spanish device, and the English translation when it runs on an English device. You can use the same trick to use different layouts on different sized devices.

You can access your resources in code via resource IDs that are generated by Android Studio in the `R` class. (See "The mysterious build/generated folder," later in this chapter.)

You should place each resource in a specific subdirectory of your project's `res` directory. Table 3-1 lists the subdirectories that are the most common types of resource folders under the parent `res` directory.

That is a lot of drawable directories! Don't worry, you do not need to supply images and icons for every possible resolution device that your app runs on. In general, you should provide drawables for the highest resolution you expect to need (usually `xxhdpi`), and the device will scale them down to other resolutions. For performance reasons and to avoid any scaling artifacts, you may decide to scale them down yourself and put them into the appropriate drawables directory, and that's why Android gives you so many different drawable directories to choose from.

A full discussion of the powerful resource mechanism inside Android could fill its own book, but this book covers the basics to get you up and running.

Table 3-1	Supported Subdirectories of the res Directory
Directory	*Resource Type*
`anim/`	XML files that define animations.
`color/`	XML files that define a list of colors.
`drawable/`	Bitmap files (`.png`, `.9.png`, `.jpg`, `.gif`) or XML files that are compiled into drawable resources. Typically you would use one of the other drawable directories instead of using this one directly.
`drawable-xxhdpi/`	Drawables for screens with extra-extra-high resolution, approximately 480 dpi.
`drawable-xhdpi/`	Drawables for screens with extra-high resolution, approximately 320 dpi.
`drawable-hdpi/`	Drawables for high-resolution screens, approximately 240 dpi.
`drawable-ldpi/`	Drawables for low-resolution screens, approximately 120 dpi.
`drawable-mdpi/`	Drawables for medium-resolution screens, approximately 160 dpi.
`layout/`	XML files that define a user interface layout.
`menu/`	XML files that represent application menus.
`raw/`	Arbitrary files to save in their raw form. Files in this directory aren't compressed by the system and can be accessed by `Resources.openRawResource()`.
`values/`	XML files that contain simple values, such as strings, integers, and colors. Whereas XML resource files in other `res/` folders define a single resource based on the XML filenames, files in the `values/` directory define multiple resources for various uses. You should follow a few filename conventions, outlined in the nearby sidebar "Naming resources in the values directory," for the resources you can create in this directory.

Naming resources in the values directory

You should follow a few filenaming conventions for the resources you can create in the `values` directory:

- ✔ `arrays.xml` for resource arrays (storing like items, such as strings or integers, together).

- ✔ `colors.xml` for resources that define color values; accessed via the `R.color` class.

- ✔ `dimens.xml` for resources that define dimension values (20px equals 20 pixels,

for example); accessed via the `R.dimen` class.

- ✔ `strings.xml` for string values; accessed via the `R.string` class.

- ✔ `styles.xml` for resources that represent styles; accessed via the `R.style` class. A style is similar to a cascading style sheet in HTML. You can define many styles and have them inherit from one another.

The resource mechanism can help with internationalization (enabling your app for different languages and countries), device size and density, and even resources for the mode that the phone may be in. To dive into the ocean of resources, review the "Providing Resources" section of the Dev Guide in the Android documentation, at `http://d.android.com/guide/topics/resources/providing-resources.html`.

The mysterious build/generated folder

Ah, you finally get to witness the magic that is the `generated` folder. When you create an Android application, before the first compilation, the `generated` folder doesn't exist. Upon the first compilation, Android Studio generates the `generated` folder and its contents. To see it, make sure Project Tool window is set to Project view instead of Android view.

The `generated` folder contains source files generated by Android Studio. One particular file it creates is the `R.java` file (I will tell you more about that topic in a moment). The `generated` folder contains items generated from the `res` directory. Without a proper understanding of what the `res` folder is and what it contains, you have no clue what the `generated` folder is for. But because you're already an expert on the `res` folder, you can dive right into the `generated` folder.

When you write Java code in Android, you reach a point when you need to reference the items in the `res` folder. You do this by using the `R` class. The `R.java` file is an index to all resources defined in your `res` folder. You use this class as a shorthand way to reference resources you've included in your project. This is particularly useful with the code-completion features of Android Studio because you can quickly identify the proper resource via code completion.

Go to the `app/build/generated/source/r/debug/com/dummies/helloandroid` folder in the Hello Android project. Now open the `R.java` file by double-clicking it. You can see a Java class that contains nested Java classes. These nested Java classes have the same names as some of the `res` folders defined in the preceding `res` section. Under each of those subclasses, you can see members that have the same names as the resources in their respective `res` folders (excluding their file extensions). The Hello Android project's `R.java` file should look similar to the following code:

```
/* AUTO-GENERATED FILE.  DO NOT MODIFY.
 *
 * This class was automatically generated by the
 * aapt tool from the resource data it found.  It
 * should not be modified by hand.
 */

package com.dummies.helloandroid;

public final class R {
    public static final class attr {
    }
    public static final class dimen {
        public static final int activity_horizontal_margin=0x7f040000;
        public static final int activity_vertical_margin=0x7f040001;
    }
    public static final class drawable {
        public static final int ic_launcher=0x7f020000;
    }
    public static final class id {
        public static final int action_settings=0x7f080000;
    }
    public static final class layout {
        public static final int activity_main=0x7f030000;
    }
    public static final class menu {
        public static final int main=0x7f070000;
    }
    public static final class string {
        public static final int action_settings=0x7f050000;
        public static final int app_name=0x7f050001;
        public static final int hello_world=0x7f050002;
    }
    public static final class style {
        /** Customize your theme here.
```

```
        */
        public static final int AppTheme=0x7f060000;
    }
}
```

Whoa — what's all that 0x stuff? Android Studio generates this code for you so that you don't have to worry about what's happening behind the scenes. As you add resources and the project is rebuilt, Android Studio regenerates the R.java file. This newly generated file contains members that reference your recently added resources.

 You should never edit the R.java file by hand. If you do, your application may not compile, and then you're in a world of hurt. If you accidentally edit the R.java file and can't undo your changes, you can delete the gen folder and build your project. At this point, Android Studio will regenerate the R.java file for you.

Viewing the application's manifest file

You keep track of everything you own and need through lists, don't you? Well, that's similar to what the Android manifest file does. It keeps track of everything your application needs, requests, and has to use in order to run.

The Android manifest file is stored in your src/main directory and is named AndroidManifest.xml. Every application must have an Android manifest file.

What the Android manifest file contains

The application manifest file provides essential information to the Android system — information that it must have before it can run any of your application's code. The application manifest file also provides

- ✔ The name of your application ID for the application, which is the unique identifier for your application in the Android system as well as in the Google Play Store
- ✔ The icon for your application
- ✔ The components of the application, such as the activities and background services
- ✔ The declaration of the permissions your application requires to run

Permissions

Assume that your application needs to access the Internet to retrieve some data. Android restricts Internet access by default. For your application to have access to the Internet, you need to ask for it.

Table 3-2	Commonly Requested Application Permissions
Permission	*What It Means*
Internet	The application needs access to the Internet.
Write External Storage	The application needs to write data to the Secure Digital card (SD card).
Camera	The application needs access to the camera.
Access Fine Location	The application needs access to the global positioning system (GPS) location.
Read Phone State	The application needs to access the state of the phone (such as ringing).

In the application manifest file, you must define which permissions your application needs to operate. Table 3-2 lists some commonly requested permissions.

Viewing the build.gradle file

The `build.gradle` file tells Android Studio how to build your app.

You can also compile your app using the command line instead of Android Studio if you want. Simply choose View➪Tool Windows➪Terminal (or open your own terminal) and `cd` to the `HelloAndroid` directory. Then type **./ gradlew assembleDebug** to build your app into `app/build/outputs/apk`. Type **./gradlew tasks** for a list of valid build targets you can use. And visit `http://d.android.com/sdk/installing/studio-build.html` for more information about using Gradle with Android.

Your `build.gradle` file might start off like the following:

```
apply plugin: 'com.android.application'

android {
    compileSdkVersion 21
    buildToolsVersion "21.1.2"

    defaultConfig {
```

```
        applicationId "com.dummies.helloandroid"
        versionCode 1
        versionName "1.0"
        minSdkVersion 21
        targetSdkVersion 21
    }
    ...
```

The following further explains this code:

- ✔ The `compileSdkVersion` tells Android Studio what version of the Android SDK you are compiling against. This version is set based off the choices you made when you went through the New Activity Wizard earlier in this chapter.

- ✔ The `buildToolsVersion` tells Android Studio what version of the build tools to use (which is the version of the tools that you installed on your computer).

- ✔ The `applicationId` must match the package that you set in your `AndroidManifest.xml` file.

Version code

The *version code* is an integer value that represents the version of the application relative to other versions of your application. The Google Play Store uses it as a basis for identifying the application internally and for handling updates.

You can set the version code to any integer value you want, but you must make sure that each successive release has a version code greater than the previous one.

Typically, on the first release, you set the version code to 1. Then you monotonically increase the value with each release, whether the release is major or minor. This means that the version code doesn't have a strong resemblance to the application release version that's visible to the user, which is the version name. (See the next section.) The version code typically isn't displayed to your users.

You must increase the version code with every version of the app that you publish to the Google Play Store. The Google Play Store does not accept an app that has the same version code as one that has previously been uploaded.

Version name

The *version name* is a string value that represents the app's version as it should display to the user. The value is a string that can be anything, but it typically follows a common release-name nomenclature that describes the application version:

```
<major>.<minor>.<optional point>
```

An example of this release-name nomenclature might be 2.1 or 3.2.4.

The Android system doesn't use this value for any purpose other than to display it to users. Android uses the version code rather than the version name internally.

The version name may be any other type of absolute or relative version identifier. The Foursquare application, for example, uses a version-naming scheme that corresponds to the date. An example of the version application name is 2012.05.02, which clearly represents a date. The version name is left up to you. You should plan ahead and make sure that your versioning strategy makes sense to you and your users.

Understanding the Compile SDK, Minimum SDK, and Target SDK Versions

This section discusses three very important parameters you should understand about supporting different versions of Android in your app. Reviewing this section will help you determine what settings to use to support users who are running your app on older versions of Android.

Compile SDK Version

The *Compile SDK Version* is the version of Android in which you write code. If you choose 5.0, you can write code with all the APIs in version 21. If you choose 2.2, you can write code only with the APIs that are in version 2.2 or earlier. You can't use the Wi-Fi Direct APIs in version 2.2, for example, because they weren't introduced until version 4.0.

Minimum SDK Version

Android operating system (OS) versions are backward-compatible. If your minSdkVersion is set to Android version 4.0, for example, your application can run on Android 5.0, 4.4, 4.3, 4.2, 4.1, and 4.0. The benefit of choosing the 4.0 framework is that your application is exposed to a much larger market share. Your app can be installed on devices going back to 4.0 (and on future versions, too!). Selecting an older version isn't free of consequences, however. By targeting an older framework, you're limiting the functionality you have access to.

You should set the `minSdkVersion` to the oldest version of Android that you are willing to support. For this app you will simplify your development life by supporting only the latest version of Android, but see Chapter 17 for more information about supporting older versions of Android.

If your Minimum SDK Version is not the same as your Compile SDK Version, you must take great care! For example, you might set your Compile SDK Version to 5.0 in order to use the latest APIs and your Minimum SDK Version to 16 to support devices running Android 4.1, but your app will crash if you use 5.0 APIs and run it on an Android 4.1 device (because Android 4.1 did not have any of 5.0's APIs).

The Google Play Store decides which users to show your app to based on your `minSdkVersion`. If you're having trouble deciding which version to set as your minimum, the current version distribution chart can help you decide: `http://d.android.com/about/dashboards`.

The `minSdkVersion` is technically optional, but you should always set it! If you don't know what to set it to, then set it to the same value as your `compileSdkVersion`.

It's up to you to test your app on all the versions of Android between your Minimum SDK Version and the latest Android SDK version! To help automate your testing, visit the book's website and read the articles online at `www.dummies.com/extras/androidappdevelopment`.

Target SDK Version

Compile SDK Version and Minimum SDK Version are arguably the most important SDK version settings that you need to understand. However, there's a third SDK version called `targetSdkVersion` that's often misunderstood and equally important to understand.

You should set the `targetSdkVersion` to the most recent version of Android that you have tested on. In this case, I am building and testing against Lollipop, so that's what I'll set my `targetSdkVersion` to.

Whenever a new version of Android comes out, you will want to update the `targetSdkVersion` to the latest Android version and test your app to fix any problems. If you don't update the `targetSdkVersion`, Android devices will assume that your app wasn't tested on the latest version of Android, so they may introduce some backward-compatibility behavior for your app to make sure your app still looks and feels the way you designed it for that older version of Android. It gets a little tricky, so the best policy is to always keep your `targetSdkVersion` up to date with the latest versions of Android.

What's up next

You're now done examining the guts of your Hello World! app. Next, you are going to create another app with a little more functionality, which you'll upload to the Google Play Store so that your mom and her friends can download it to their Android phones.

Chapter 4

Creating the User Interface

. . . .

. . . .

*I*n Chapter 3, you discover what Android is and how to build your first application. Chapter 4 helps you delve into the fun stuff: building a real application and publishing it to the Google Play Store.

The application you build in this chapter allows the user to toggle the ringer mode on the phone by simply pressing a button. This application seems simple, but it solves a real-world problem.

Creating the Silent Mode Toggle Application

Create the new application by choosing File⇨New Module from inside the project you created in Chapter 3. Choose Phone and Tablet Application from the list, and then click Next. Use Table 4-1 for your module settings.

On the Add an Activity page, choose Blank Activity and click Next. Use the settings in Table 4-2 to create your activity.

Now click Finish. You should now have the Silent Mode Toggle application in your Project view, as shown in Figure 4-1.

Table 4-1	Project Settings for Silent Mode Toggle
Setting	*Value*
Application Name	Silent Mode Toggle
Module Name	Silent Mode Toggle
Package Name	`com.dummies.silentmo-detoggle`
Minimum Required SDK	API 21: Android 5.0 Lollipop

Table 4-2	Settings for Blank Activity
Setting	*Value*
Activity Name	MainActivity
Layout Name	activity_main
Title	MainActivity
Menu Resource Name	menu_main

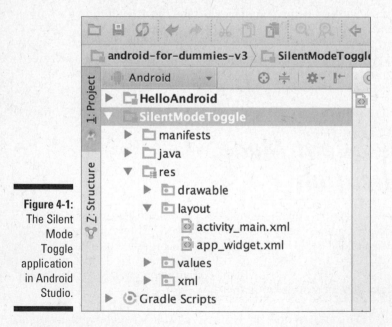

Figure 4-1:
The Silent
Mode
Toggle
application
in Android
Studio.

Laying Out the Application

When you have the Silent Mode Toggle application created inside Android Studio, it's time for you to design the application's *user interface,* the part of an application that users interact with.

Your application will have a single image centered in the middle of the screen to toggle silent mode. The image will also provide visual feedback to let the user know whether the phone is in silent mode or normal ringer mode. Figure 4-2 shows what the finished application will look like.

It's time to start developing the user interface. First, open the user interface layout file that you created when you created the new blank activity in the previous section. The file is called `activity_main.xml`, and you can find it by expanding `SilentModeToggle`, `res`, and `layout` as in Figure 4-1. Double-click it to open it.

Then make sure that you're in the Text tab of your layout by clicking the Text tab as in Figure 4-3.

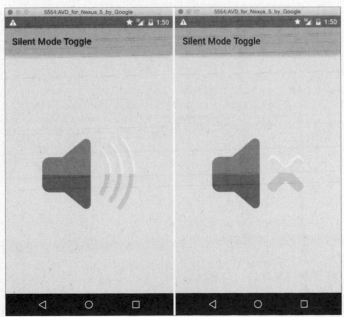

Figure 4-2:
The Silent
Mode
Toggle
application
in (left) nor-
mal ringer
mode and in
silent ringer
mode (right).

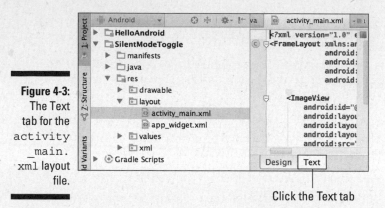

Figure 4-3:
The Text
tab for the
`activity`
`_main.`
`xml` layout
file.

Click the Text tab

When you're on the Text tab, delete the XML and replace it with the following. Your layout should now look like this:

```
<?xml version="1.0" encoding= encoding="utf-8"?>
<FrameLayout xmlns:android="http://schemas.android.com/apk/res/android"
            android:id="@+id/content"
            android:layout_width="match_parent"
            android:layout_height="match_parent" >



</FrameLayout>
```

A view occupies a rectangular space on the screen and is responsible for drawing and event handling. All items that can show up on a device screen are views. The `View` class is the superclass that all items inherit from in Android. This includes all layout classes, such as the `FrameLayout` used in this example.

The first line in every XML file provides the default XML declaration, letting text editors such as Android Studio and platforms such as Android know what type of file it is:

```
<?xml version="1.0" encoding="utf-8"?>
```

Working with views

As stated in the previous section, views in Android are the basic building blocks of user interface components. Any time you implement a user interface component in Android such as a layout or `TextView`, you're using a view. Every view must be configured, and the next sections explain the configuration you created for your `FrameLayout`. You can also see them summarized in Table 4-2.

Setting layout_width and layout_height values

Before a view can be presented to the screen, a couple of settings must be configured on the view so that Android knows how to lay out the view on the screen. The attributes that are required, `layout_width` and `layout_height`, are part of the `LayoutParams` in the Android SDK.

The `layout_width` attribute specifies the given width of a view, and the `layout_height` attribute specifies the given height of a view.

Setting match_parent and wrap_content values

The `layout_width` and `layout_height` attributes can take any pixel value or density-independent pixel value to specify their respective dimensions. However, two of the most common values for `layout_width` and `layout_height` are the `match_parent` and `wrap_content` constants.

The `match_parent` value informs the parent view to make this view the same width/height as itself. The `wrap_content` value informs Android to occupy only as much space as needed to show the view's content. As the view's content grows, as would happen with a `TextView` when text is added, the view's dimension grows (see Table 4-3).

Table 4-3	XML Layout Attributes
Layout	**What It Does**
`xmlns:android= "..."`	Defines the XML namespace for `android:...` that you will use in your XML elements. This will always be `http://schemas.android.com/apk/res/android`.
`android:id=" @+id/content"`	Sets the ID of this view to `id/content`. All references to resources in Android XML files start with the @ symbol. And because you are defining a new ID resource, you must also have a + symbol after the @.
`android:layout_ width="match_ parent"`	Informs the view that it should fill as much horizontal space as it can, up to the size of its parent, to make its own width the same as its parent's.
`android:layout_ height="match_ parent"`	Informs the view that it should fill as much vertical space as it can, up to the size of its parent, to make its own height the same as its parent's.

In general, you will set your view parameters in XML. If you're creating views dynamically via code, though, you can configure the layout parameters via Java code. To find out more about dynamic creation of views, see the API samples that come with the Android SDK.

Using Android layouts

When you create a user interface, you sometimes have to lay out components relative to each other, or in a table, or in a list or grid. Thankfully, the engineering geniuses at Google who created Android thought of all this and provided the necessary tools to create those types of layouts. Table 4-4 briefly introduces the common types of layouts available in Android.

Other, different types of layout tools exist, such as a TabHost for creating tabs and DrawerLayout for side "drawers" that hide and display views. Programmers tend to use these layout tools in special-case scenarios. The items in Table 4-4 outline the most commonly used layouts.

For now, this example uses the simplest layout, the FrameLayout. You'll use more advanced layouts in later chapters.

Table 4-4	Android SDK Layouts
Layout	*What It Does*
FrameLayout	Designed to block out an area on the screen to display a single item. You can add multiple children to a FrameLayout, but all children are pegged to the upper left area of the screen by default. Children are drawn in a stack, with the most recently added child at the top of the stack.
	This layout is commonly used as a way to lay out views on top of each other, or to lay them out relative to their parent.
LinearLayout	Arranges its children in a single row or column.
RelativeLayout	Lets the positions of the children be described in relation to each other or to the parent.
GridLayout	Arranges its children into a grid.

Adding an Image to Your Application

You will add a ringer icon to your app, so first you need to download the icon, of course. You can download the image from this book's source code, available from this book's website (at `http://www.dummies.com/go/androidappdevfd3e`), or you can use your own.

Adding images to a project is simple: Drag them from the folder where they're stored to the `src/main/res/drawable-xxhdpi` folder, as shown in Figure 4-4.

For the Silent Mode Toggle application, you need two ringer images: off and on. Be sure to put both images in the `src/main/res/drawable-xxhdpi` folder.

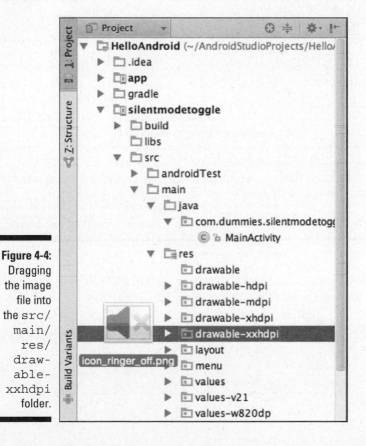

Figure 4-4:
Dragging
the image
file into
the `src/
main/
res/
draw-
able-
xxhdpi`
folder.

Why you should worry about density folders

Android supports various screen sizes and densities. Elsewhere in this chapter, we mention placing an image in the xxhdpi folder, which is for extra-high-density devices. What about low- and high-density devices? If Android cannot find the requested resource in the desired density, it uses whatever density resource it can find and scales it appropriately. If your device has a higher pixel density than Android can find, Android scales the image up to the necessary size, resulting in resize "jaggies." To avoid this problem, create multiple versions of your image to target multiple screen densities. For more information, see the Supporting Multiple Screens page in the Android documentation at http:// d.android.com/guide/practices/ screens_support.html. And to see a list of which are the most common screen densities, visit http://d.android.com/ about/dashboards/index.html.

To follow along in the rest of the chapter, be sure that the images are named this way:

- **Normal mode image:** ringer_on.png
- **Silent mode image:** ringer_off.png

If your images aren't named correctly, you can rename them now.

When you drag images into Android Studio, it regenerates the build/ generated folder, and the R.java file is updated to include a reference to the two new images you added.

You can use the references to these resources to add images to your layout in code or in XML definition. You declare them in the XML layout in the following section.

To add an image to the layout, type the following into the activity_main. xml file, overwriting the current content of the file:

```xml
<?xml version="1.0" encoding="utf-8"?>
<FrameLayout xmlns:android="http://schemas.android.com/apk/res/android"
             android:id="@+id/content"
             android:layout_width="match_parent"
             android:layout_height="match_parent"
             android:foreground="?android:attr/selectableItemBackground"
    >
```

```
    <ImageView
        android:id="@+id/phone_icon"
        android:layout_width="wrap_content"
        android:layout_height="wrap_content"
        android:layout_gravity="center"
        android:src="@drawable/ringer_on"/>

</FrameLayout>
```

This code adds the `ImageView` inside the `FrameLayout`. An `ImageView` allows you to project an image to the screen on the device.

Setting image properties

Your `ImageView` contains a few new parameter attributes:

✔ **The** `android:id="@+id/phone_icon"` **property:** The `id` attribute defines the unique identifier for the view in the Android system. You can find an in-depth explanation of the `android:id` value nomenclature at `http://d.android.com/guide/topics/ui/declaring-layout.html`.

✔ **The** `layout_width` **and** `layout_height` **properties:** You used `layout_width` and `layout_height` in your `FrameLayout`, but there you set them to `match_parent`. For the `ImageView`, we want the `ImageView`'s size to be the same as the image it's showing, so we'll set it to have a `layout_width` and `layout_height` of `wrap_content` to "wrap" the content inside the view. If we had set the height and width to be `match_parent`, Android would have scaled the image up much too large to take up the full screen. Try it!

✔ **The** `layout_gravity` **property:** This property defines how to place the view (both its x- and y-axes) with its parent. In this example, the value is defined as the `center` constant. Since the `ImageView` is smaller than the `FrameLayout`, using `layout_gravity=center` instructs the Android system to place the `ImageView` in the center of the `FrameLayout` rather than in the default location of the upper left. You can use many other constants, such as `center_vertical`, `center_horizontal`, `top`, `bottom`, `left`, `right`, and many more. See the `FrameLayout.LayoutParams` Android documentation for a full list.

✔ **The** `android:src="@drawable/ringer_on"` **property:** You use this property to set the image that you want to show up on the screen.

Notice the value of the `src` property — `"@drawable/ringer_on"`. You can reference drawable resources via XML by typing the "at" symbol (@) and the type and id of the resource you want.

Certain Android attributes begin with the `layout_` prefix — `android:layout_width`, `android:layout_height`, and `android:layout_gravity` are all examples. The `layout_` convention tells you that the attribute relates to the view's *parent*. Attributes that don't begin with `layout_` pertain to the view itself. So the `ImageView`'s `android:src` attribute tells the `ImageView` which image to use, but its `android:layout_gravity` tells the `ImageView`'s parent (the `FrameLayout`, in this case) to lay out the `ImageView` in the center of the parent.

Setting drawable resources

In your `ImageView`, you set your `image src` to `@drawable/ringer_on`. You don't type **@drawable-xxhdpi/ringer_on** for the drawable resource identifier, because it's Android's job (not yours) to figure out the correct size image for the current device's screen. At runtime, Android determines which density is correct for that device, and loads the closest matching drawables.

For example, if the app is running on a medium-density device and the requested drawable resource is available in the `drawable-mdpi` folder, Android uses that resource. Otherwise, it uses the closest match it can find. Support for various screen sizes and densities is a broad topic (and can be complex!). For an in-depth view into this subject, read the "Supporting Multiple Screens" article in the Android documentation at `http://d.android.com/guide/practices/screens_support.html`.

The `ringer_on` portion of the identifier identifies the drawable you want to use. The image filename is `ringer_on.png`. If you were to open the `R.java` file in the `build/generated` folder, you would see a static field with the name `phone_on`.

You can use code completion to see the available resources in Android Studio. Place the cursor directly after `@drawable/` in the `src` property of the `ImageView` in the Android Studio editor, and press Ctrl+spacebar. The code-completion window opens, as shown in Figure 4-5. The other resource names in the window are other options you could choose for the `src` portion of the drawable definition.

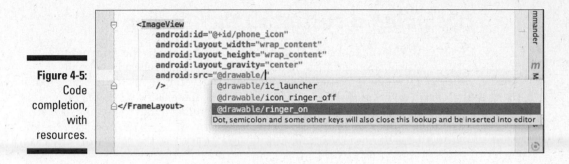

Figure 4-5:
Code
completion,
with
resources.

```
<ImageView
    android:id="@+id/phone_icon"
    android:layout_width="wrap_content"
    android:layout_height="wrap_content"
    android:layout_gravity="center"
    android:src="@drawable/"
    />
        @drawable/ic_launcher
        @drawable/icon_ringer_off
        @drawable/ringer_on
</FrameLayout>   Dot, semicolon and some other keys will also close this lookup and be inserted into editor
```

Creating a Launcher Icon for the Application

When your app is installed, its icon helps users identify its presence in the application launcher. When you create the Silent Mode Toggle application, Android Studio automatically includes a default launcher icon, as shown on the left in Figure 4-6.

original icon.png   new icon.png

Figure 4-6:
The default
icon (left)
and a
unique icon
(right).

You should change this icon to one of your own. You can create your own (as shown in the following section) or use the one from the downloaded source code at http://www.dummies.com/go/androidappdevfd3e.

Designing a custom launcher icon

Creating your own launcher icons is fairly easy, thanks to the Android project. The article "Iconography" in the Android documentation covers all aspects of icon design — a how-to manual for creating icons for the Android platform, a style guide, a list of do's and don'ts, materials and colors, size and positioning guidelines, and (best of all) icon templates that you can use. You can find useful resources for designing icons at `www.google.com/design/spec/style/icons.html` and `http://d.android.com/design/style/iconography.html`.

Working with templates

After you download the Android SDK, these icon templates and materials are available for you to use immediately on your computer's hard drive. Navigate to your Android SDK installation directory (see Chapter 2), and from there navigate to the `docs/shareables` directory. You'll find various `.zip` files that contain templates and samples. Open the templates in the image editing program of your choice, and follow the design guidelines in the documentation to create your next rockin' icon set.

Matching icon sizes with screen densities

Because every screen density requires an icon in a different size, you, as the designer, need to know how large the icon should be. Each density must have its own icon size to look appropriate (no pixilation, stretching, or compressing) on the screen.

Table 4-5 summarizes the finished icon sizes for each of the three generalized screen densities.

Table 4-5	Finished Icon Sizes
Screen Density	*Icon Size in Pixels*
Low-density screen (ldpi)	36 x 36
Medium-density screen (mdpi)	48 x 48
High-density screen (hdpi)	72 x 72
Extra-high-density screen (xhdpi)	96 x 96
Extra-extra-high density screen (xxhdpi)	144 x 144
Extra-extra-extra-high density screen (xxxhdpi) In general, xxxhdpi is not currently used for more assets. It's only used for providing extra-large launcher icons on some devices.	192 x 192

In general, you won't need to supply most of your assets in xxxhpi (triple-x). The only asset you should use xxxhdpi for is your launcher icon. Some Android devices use the additional resolution to provide an extra-large launcher icon. On these devices, adding an xxxhdpi launcher icon will make your app icon look pretty. But don't bother adding xxxhdpi assets for other images because the highest resolution that's currently used in devices is only xxhdpi (double-x).

Adding a custom launcher icon

To place your custom launcher icon into the project, follow these steps:

1. **Rename the image icon to** ic_launcher.png.

2. **Create the** drawable-xxxhdpi **folder in** src/main/res.

3. **Drag your icon into the** drawable-xxxhdpi **folder.**

   Android Studio asks whether you want to overwrite the existing ic_ launcher.png.

4. **Click Yes.**

   The ic_launcher.png file is now in the drawable-xxxhdpi folder.

You're not done yet! For the other drawable folders, you need to delete the other versions of ic_launcher.png or provide your own versions.

If you don't delete the icons of other densities in their respective folders, users who have a low- or high-density device receive the default launcher icon (refer to Figure 4-6), whereas the xxhdpi-density devices receive the new icon that you included in the project.

Previewing the Application in the Visual Designer

To take a look at what the layout looks like in the visual designer, click the Design tab to view it, as shown in Figure 4-7.

The visual designer has many different possible configurations.

Selecting the Devices drop-down list in the visual designer shows you which devices you can simulate your layout on. You can test out what your app will look like on many different kinds of phones and tablets.

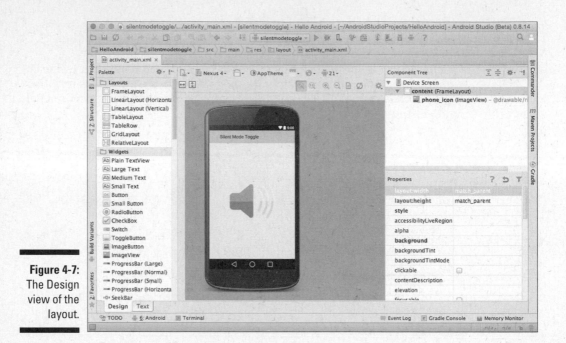

Figure 4-7:
The Design
view of the
layout.

Selecting the Orientation drop-down list allows you to see what your app looks like in portrait and landscape modes.

You can also preview what your app looks like in other languages, on older versions of Android (if you enabled backward compatibility), and on devices that have different default themes.

Using the visual designer allows you to quickly test out your app on various configurations so you can fix bugs quickly without having to load up an emulator for each and every one of those configurations. It's not a substitute for actually testing on a device, but it can make your development much quicker.

Try out a few other configurations!

Chapter 5

Coding Your Application

You're probably eager to start coding your application. In this chapter, you write the Java code, from soup to nuts. Before you can start banging out bits and bytes, though, you need a firm understanding of activities.

Understanding Activities and the Activity Lifecycle

An *activity* is a single, focused action that a user can take. You can think of an activity like a "page" in your app. For example, an activity might present a list of menu items that a user can choose from, or it might display photographs along with captions. An app may consist of only one activity or (more commonly) several. Though activities may work together to appear to be one cohesive application, they work independently from each other. Almost all activities interact with the user, so the Activity class creates for you the window in which you can place your user interface (UI).

An activity in Android is an important part of an application's overall lifecycle, and the way the activities are launched and put together is a fundamental aspect of the Android application model. Every activity is implemented as a subclass of the Activity base class.

The Activity lifecycle is one of the most important differences between Android and other phone operating systems. It's complicated, but it's an important set of concepts to grasp before you dive into developing Android apps.

The Activity lifecycle

Two important methods that almost all activities implement are

- ✔ onCreate: Where the activity is initialized. Most importantly, it's where you tell the activity which layout to use by using a layout resource identifier — considered the entry point of your activity.

- ✔ onPause: Where you deal with the user leaving your activity. Any changes made by the user should be committed at this point (if you need to save them).

Activities in the system are managed as an *activity stack*. When a new activity is created, it's placed on top of the stack and becomes the running activity. The previous running activity always remains below it in the stack and returns to the foreground only when the new activity exits.

To be a successful Android programmer, you must understand the importance of how and why the activity works behind the scenes. This will make you a better Android programmer and help you debug strange problems later.

An activity essentially has four states, as described in Table 5-1.

Table 5-1	Essential States of an Activity
Activity State	*Description*
Active/running	The activity is in the foreground of the screen (at the top of the stack).
Paused	The activity has lost focus but is still visible. (A new, non-full-size or transparent activity has the focus on top of your activity.) Because a paused activity is completely alive, it can maintain state and member information and remains attached to the window manager in Android.

Activity State	Description
Stopped	If an activity becomes obscured by another activity, it is stopped. It retains all state and member information, but isn't visible to the user. Therefore, the window is hidden and will often be killed by the Android system when memory is needed elsewhere.
Destroyed	When the activity is paused or stopped, the system can reclaim the memory by asking it to finish, or it can kill the process. When it displays the activity again to the user, it must be completely restarted and restored to its previous state.

Figure 5-1 shows the important paths of an activity — the *activity lifecycle*.

The rectangles represent callback methods you can implement to respond to events in the activity. The shaded ovals represent the major states of the activity.

The activity lifecycle is a large and complex topic, and the following sections cover only the basics. If you want to read more about activity lifecycles, check out the "Activity Lifecycle" article in the Android documentation at `http://d.android.com/reference/android/app/Activity.html`.

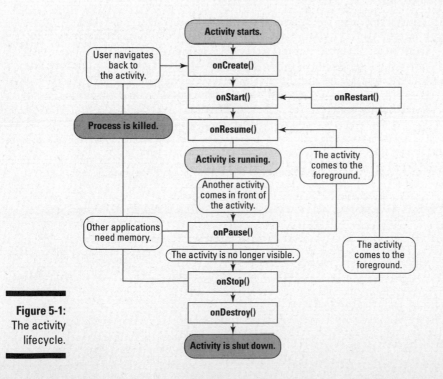

Figure 5-1:
The activity
lifecycle.

Important lifecycle loops

You may be interested in monitoring these three loops in your activity:

- ✔ The **entire lifetime** takes place between the first call to onCreate() and the final call to onDestroy(). The activity performs all global setup in onCreate() and releases all remaining resources in onDestroy(). For example, if you create a thread to download a file from the Internet in the background, it may be initialized in the onCreate() method. That thread can be stopped in the onDestroy() method.

- ✔ The **visible lifetime** of the activity takes place between the onStart() and onStop() methods. During this time, the user can see the activity onscreen (though it may not be in the foreground interacting with the user, which can happen when the user is interacting with a dialog box). Between these two methods, you can maintain the resources that are needed to show and run your activity. For example, you can create an event handler to monitor the state of the phone. The phone state can change, and this event handler can inform the activity of the phone entering Airplane mode and react accordingly. You would set up the event handler in onStart() and tear down any resources you're accessing in onStop(). The onStart() and onStop() methods can be called multiple times as the activity becomes visible or hidden to the user.

- ✔ The **foreground lifetime** of the activity begins at the call to onResume() and ends at the call to onPause(). During this time, the activity is in front of all other activities and is interacting with the user. An activity normally toggles between onResume() and onPause() multiple times, for example, when the device goes to sleep or when a new activity handles a particular event — therefore, the code in these methods must be fairly lightweight.

Viewing activity methods

The activity lifecycle boils down to these methods:

```
public class Activity extends ApplicationContext {
    protected void onCreate(Bundle savedInstanceState);
    protected void onStart();
    protected void onRestart();
    protected void onResume();
    protected void onPause();
    protected void onStop();
    protected void onDestroy();
}
```

All methods can be overridden, and custom code can be placed in all of them. All activities implement onCreate() for initialization and may also implement onPause() for cleanup. You should always call the superclass (base class) when implementing these methods.

Following an activity's path

The movement of an activity throughout its lifecycle looks like this:

✔ onCreate(): Called when the activity is first created. You initialize most of your activity's class-wide variables here. onStart() is always called next. Killable: No. Next: onStart().

✔ onRestart(): Called after your activity has been stopped before being started again. onStart() is always called next. Killable: No. Next: onStart().

✔ onStart(): Called when your activity is becoming visible to the user. Followed by onResume() if the activity is brought to the foreground or onStop() if it becomes hidden from the user. Killable: No. Next: onResume() or onStop().

✔ onResume(): Called when the activity will be available for interacting with the user. The activity is at the top of the activity stack at this point. Killable: No. Next: onPause().

✔ onPause(): Called when the system is about to resume a previous activity or if the user has navigated away to another portion of the system, such as by pressing the Home key. This stage is typically used to commit unsaved changes to data that needs to be persisted. If the activity is brought back to the foreground, onResume() is called; if the activity becomes invisible to the user, onStop() is called. Killable: Yes, but only on Honeycomb (3.0) or earlier. Next: onResume() or onStop().

✔ onStop(): Called when the activity is no longer visible to the user because another activity has resumed and is covering this one. This may happen because another activity has started or a previous activity has resumed and is now in the foreground of the activity stack. It's followed by onRestart() if this activity is returning to interact with the user or by onDestroy() if this activity is going away. Killable: Yes. Next: onRestart() or onDestroy().

✔ onDestroy(): The final call you receive before your activity is destroyed. This method gets called either because the activity is finishing (such as someone calling finish() on it) or because the system is temporarily destroying the activity to reclaim space. You can distinguish between these two with the isFinishing() method, which helps identify whether the method is finishing or the system is killing it. The `isFinishing()` method is often used inside `onPause()` to determine whether the activity is pausing or being destroyed. Killable: Yes. Next: Nothing.

The *killable* indicator at the end of each activity method description notes the activities the Android system can kill at any time and without notice. You should therefore use the `onPause()` method to complete any cleanup to write persistent data (such as user edits to data) to your storage mechanism.

Recognizing configuration changes

A configuration change is a change that's made to the screen orientation (for example, if the user moves the screen to the side and back or moves it from portrait to landscape mode or vice versa), the language, or an input device. A configuration change causes your activity to be destroyed while completing the normal activity lifecycle: `onPause()` followed by `onStop()` and then `onDestroy()`. After the `onDestroy()` method is called, the system creates a new instance of the activity to be created, which takes place because resources and layout files and other elements might need to change depending on the current system configuration. For example, an application may look completely different if the user is interacting with it in portrait mode, as compared to being displayed in landscape mode (on its side).

Creating Your First Activity

You may have already created the `MainActivity` class if you created a project using the New Android Project Wizard in Chapter 3. Open the `MainActivity.java` file in the Silent Mode Toggle module to enhance it in the following sections.

Starting with onCreate

The entry point into your application is the `onCreate()` method. The code for the `MainActivity.java` file already contains an implementation of the `onCreate()` method. It's where you start writing code! For now, your code should look like this:

```
public class MainActivity extends Activity {
    /** Called when the activity is first created. */
    @Override
```

```
public void onCreate(Bundle savedInstanceState) {
    super.onCreate(savedInstanceState);

    // Initialize our layout using the res/layout/activity_main.xml
    // layout file that contains our views for this activity.
    setContentView(R.layout.activity_main);    }
}
```

You write the initialization code directly below the `setContentView()` method.

Be sure to always include this method call to your `onCreate()` method:

```
super.onCreate(savedInstanceState);
```

It's required for the application to run. This line directs the base `Activity` class to perform setup work for the `MainActivity` class. If you omit this line of code, you receive a runtime exception.

Telling Android to display the user interface

By default, an activity has no idea what its user interface is. It can be a simple form that allows the user to type information to be saved. It can be a visual, camera-based, augmented, virtual reality application (such as Layar in the Google Play Store). Or it can be a drawn-on-the-fly user interface, such as in a 2D or 3D game. As a developer, it's your job to tell the activity which layout the activity should load.

To show the user interface onscreen, you have to set the content view for the activity, by adding this line of code:

```
setContentView(R.layout.activity_main);
```

`R.layout.activity_main` refers to the `activity_main.xml` file that's located in the `src/main/res/layouts` directory. It's the layout you defined in Chapter 4.

Handling user input

The Silent Mode Toggle application has little user interaction. The only user interaction that your application will have is a single button that the user taps to toggle Silent mode.

To respond to this tap event, you need to register an *event listener,* which responds to an event in the Android system. Though you find various types of events in the Android system, two of the most commonly used are keyboard events and touch events (also known as clicks).

Keyboard events

A *keyboard event* occurs whenever a particular keyboard key is pressed. For example, if the user presses the Alt+E hot key in your application, you may want the view to toggle into Edit mode. Responding to keyboard events allows you to do this. If you need to override the onKeyDown method to use your own keyboard event, do it this way:

```
@Override
public boolean onKeyDown(int keyCode, KeyEvent event) {
        return super.onKeyDown(keyCode, event);
}
```

You won't need to use onKeyDown for the examples in this book, but it's useful to know about it.

Touch events

A *touch event* occurs whenever the user taps a widget on the screen. The Android platform recognizes each tap event as a click event. Examples of views that can respond to touch events include (but aren't limited to)

- ✔ Button
- ✔ ImageButton
- ✔ EditText
- ✔ Spinner
- ✔ ListView Rows
- ✔ MenuItem

 All views in the Android system can react to a tap; however, some widgets have their *clickable* property set to false by default. You can override this setting in your layout file or in code to allow a view to be clickable by setting the clickable attribute on the view or the setClickable() method in code.

Writing your first click listener

For your application to respond to the click event of the user toggling Silent mode, you respond to the click event that's exposed by the button.

Add the method shown in Listing 5-1 to your `MainActivity` class. It demonstrates how to implement a click handler for `contentView`. The code consists of the entire `onCreate()` method with the new code. You can either fill in the button code (in bold) or overwrite your entire `onCreate` code.

Listing 5-1:   The Initial Class File with a Default Button OnClickListener

```
@Override
public void onCreate(Bundle savedInstanceState) {
    super.onCreate(savedInstanceState);
    setContentView(R.layout.activity_main);

    // Find the view with the ID "content" in our layout file.
    FrameLayout contentView =
            (FrameLayout) findViewById(R.id.content);

    // Create a click listener for the contentView that will toggle
    // the phone's ringer state, and then update the UI to reflect
    // the new state.
    contentView.setOnClickListener(new View.OnClickListener() {
        public void onClick(View v) {
            // TODO
        }
    });
}
```

This listing uses the `findViewById()` method, which is available to all activities in Android. This method allows you to find any view inside the activity's layout and do some work with it.

Be sure to cast the result of `findViewById()` to the appropriate type. If the type in your layout file is different from what you're casting it to (if you're trying to cast an `ImageView` in the layout file to `ImageButton`, for example), you'll crash your application.

Immediately following this line of code, you start setting up the event handler.

The event handling code is placed inline after you retrieve the `contentView` from the layout. Setting up the event handler is as simple as setting a new `View.OnClickListener`. This click listener contains an `onClick()` method that's called after the user taps the button. It's where you place the code to handle the Silent mode toggle.

What should the view do when it's clicked? You'll set that up shortly, but for now leave it empty.

Working with the Android Framework Classes

This section gets into the good stuff — the nitty-gritty of Android development and its Android framework classes! Yes, activities and views are integral parts of the system, but they're simply the "plumbing" that's required in any modern operating system (in one capacity or another). The real fun is just about to start.

The following sections describe how to check the state of the phone ringer to determine whether it's in Normal mode (ringing loud and proud) or Silent mode. At this point, you can begin to start toggling the phone's ringer mode.

Getting good service

To access the Android ringer, you'll need access to the `AudioManager` in Android, which is responsible for managing the ringer state, so you should initialize it in `onCreate()`.

All important initialization needs to happen in `onCreate()`.

You first need to create a field of type `AudioManager` by the name of `audioManager`. Type this name at the top of your class file, directly after the class declaration line, as shown in Listing 5-2.

Listing 5-2: Adding the Class-Level AudioManager Variable

```
package com.dummies.silentmodetoggle;

import android.media.AudioManager;                              →3

. . .

public class MainActivity extends Activity {

    AudioManager audioManager;                                  →9

    @Override
    public void onCreate(Bundle savedInstanceState) {
        // Always call super.onCreate() first.
        super.onCreate(savedInstanceState);
```

```
        // Get a reference to Android's AudioManager so we can use
        // it to toggle our ringer.
        audioManager = (AudioManager) getSystemService(AUDIO_SERVICE);        →18


        . . .

    }
}
```

This list briefly explains what the numbered lines denote:

→ **3**   The import statement that brings in the necessary package so
        that you can use AudioManager.

→ **9**   The AudioManager field. Because it's a field, you can have access
        to it in other parts of the activity.

→ **18**   Initializes the audioManager field by getting the service from the
        getSystemService() method in the Activity superclass.

Whoa! What's getSystemService()? By inheriting from the base
Activity class, MainActivity receives all the benefits of being an activity, including access to the getSystemService() method call. This method
returns the base Java Object class, so you have to cast it to the type of service you're requesting.

This call returns all available system services that you might need to work
with. All services that are returned can be found in the Context class in
the Android documentation, at http://d.android.com/reference/
android/content/Context.html. Popular system service types
include

✔ AUDIO_SERVICE

✔ LOCATION_SERVICE

✔ ALARM_SERVICE

Toggling Silent mode with AudioManager

After you have an instance of AudioManager, you can start checking the
state of the ringer and toggling the ringer. The code you need to add or
modify is in bold in Listing 5-3.

Listing 5-3:   Adding the Application Toggle to the App

```
package com.dummies.silentmodetoggle;

import android.app.Activity;
import android.media.AudioManager;
import android.os.Bundle;
import android.util.Log;
import android.view.View;
import android.widget.FrameLayout;
import android.widget.ImageView;

import com.dummies.silentmodetoggle.util.RingerHelper;

public class MainActivity extends Activity {

    AudioManager audioManager;

    /**
     * This method is called to initialize the activity after the
     * java constructor for this class has been called.  This is
     * typically where you would call setContentView to inflate your
     * layout, and findViewById to initialize your views.
     * @param savedInstanceState contains additional data about the
     *          saved state of the activity if it was previously shutdown
     *          and is now being re-created from saved state.
     */
    @Override
    public void onCreate(Bundle savedInstanceState) {
        // Always call super.onCreate() first.
        super.onCreate(savedInstanceState);

        // Get a reference to Android's AudioManager so we can use
        // it to toggle our ringer.
        audioManager = (AudioManager) getSystemService(AUDIO_SERVICE);


        // Initialize our layout using the res/layout/activity_main.xml
        // layout file that contains our views for this activity.
        setContentView(R.layout.activity_main);

        // Find the view named "content" in our layout file.
        FrameLayout contentView =
                (FrameLayout) findViewById(R.id.content);

        // Create a click listener for the contentView that will toggle
        // the phone's ringer state, and then update the UI to reflect
        // the new state.
        contentView.setOnClickListener(new View.OnClickListener() {
            public void onClick(View v) {
```

```
                    // Toggle the ringer mode.  If it's currently normal,
                    // make it silent.  If it's currently silent,
                    // do the opposite.
                    RingerHelper.performToggle(audioManager);

                    // Update the UI to reflect the new state
                    updateUi();
            }
        });
}


/**
 * Updates the UI image to show an image representing silent or
 * normal, as appropriate
 */
private void updateUi() {
    // Find the view named phone_icon in our layout.  We know it's
    // an ImageView in the layout, so downcast it to an ImageView.
    ImageView imageView = (ImageView) findViewById(R.id.phone_icon);

    // Set phoneImage to the ID of image that represents ringer on
    // or off.  These are found in res/drawable-xxhdpi
    int phoneImage = RingerHelper.isPhoneSilent(audioManager)
            ? R.drawable.ringer_off
            : R.drawable.ringer_on;

    // Set the imageView to the image in phoneImage
    imageView.setImageResource(phoneImage);
}


/**
 * Every time the activity is resumed, make sure to update the
 * buttons to reflect the current state of the system (since the
 * user may have changed the phone's silent state while we were in
 * the background).
 *
 * Visit http://d.android.com/reference/android/app/Activity.html
 * for more information about the Android Activity lifecycle.
 */
@Override
protected void onResume() {
    super.onResume();

    // Update our UI in case anything has changed.
    updateUi();
}
}
```

Now, create the file `src/main/java/com/dummies/silentmodetoggle/` `util/RingerHelper.java` and add the following to it:

```
package com.dummies.silentmodetoggle.util;

import android.media.AudioManager;

public class RingerHelper {
    // private to prevent users from creating a RingerHelper object
    private RingerHelper() {}

    /**
     * Toggles the phone's silent mode
     */
    public static void performToggle(AudioManager audioManager) {
        // If the phone is currently silent, then unsilence it.  If
        // it's currently normal, then silence it.
        audioManager.setRingerMode(
                isPhoneSilent(audioManager)
                        ? AudioManager.RINGER_MODE_NORMAL
                        : AudioManager.RINGER_MODE_SILENT);
    }

    /**
     * Returns whether the phone is currently in silent mode.
     */
    public static boolean isPhoneSilent(AudioManager audioManager) {
        return audioManager.getRingerMode()
                == AudioManager.RINGER_MODE_SILENT;
    }
}
```

`RingerHelper` is a simple Java class that has only static methods that help us deal with the `AudioManager` ringer. These methods are useful in `MainActivity` now, but they'll also be useful in other classes later, so that's why they're in a separate class.

Installing Your Application

You've done it — you've written your first Android app. Okay, your second, but your first one that does anything useful. In the next sections, you will install your app on the emulator and put that baby into action!

Running your app in an emulator

It's time to install this app on the emulator. Follow these steps:

1. **In Android Studio, choose Run⇨Run 'Silent Mode Toggle'.**

   You see the Choose Device window, shown in Figure 5-2.

Figure 5-2:
The Choose
Device
window.

Choose Device

○ Choose a running device

Device	Serial Number	State

⦿ Launch emulator

Android virtual device: | Nexus_5_API_21 ▲▼ | ... |

☑ Use same device for future launches

Cancel   OK

2. **If your emulator is already running, select it now.**

   Otherwise, select Launch Emulator and choose your desired emulator.

   Click the Use same device for future launches check box to avoid having to see the dialog box every time you launch your app.

3. **Wait for the emulator to load and launch your app.**

   Your application starts and the emulator runs your program, as shown in Figure 5-3.

   If your application doesn't start, try Step 1 again and watch the Android view to see the logcat output from your app. Refer to Chapter 3 for how to use the Android view.

TIP

Silent Mode Toggle

Figure 5-3:
The
emulator
running the
application.

4. **Click the Toggle Silent Mode button to see the image toggle, shown in Figure 5-4.**

    Notice the new icon on the notification bar — the Silent Notification icon.

5. **Return to the Home screen by clicking the Home button on the emulator.**

6. **Open the application (it's the center button at the bottom of screen).**

    You see the application launcher icon in the list of applications.

After the emulator is running, it's running on its own. The emulator has no dependencies on Android Studio. In fact, you can close Android Studio and still interact with the emulator.

Installing on a physical Android device

Installing an application on a device is no different from installing it on the emulator, except for having to make a few small adjustments to get it to work. If you're on a Windows machine, refer to Chapter 2 for how to install the necessary drivers. The remaining steps are straightforward:

Figure 5-4:
The app
in Silent
mode, with
the Silent
Notification
icon.

1. **From the Home screen of your phone, access the Settings panel.**

2. **Choose About Phone.**

   Tap on Build number seven times to unlock the developer options. You should see a message that says "You are now a developer!" If only you'd known that being an Android developer was so easy, you wouldn't have needed to buy this book!

3. **Go back to Settings and choose Developer Options, then select the USB Debugging option, as shown in Figure 5-5.**

   This step allows you to debug your application on a device. (You can find more about debugging later in this chapter, in the "Using the Android Studio debugger" section.)

4. **Connect your phone to the computer by using a USB cable.**

   The phone will ask you whether you want to allow USB debugging for this computer. Click the Always allow from this computer check box and click OK.

5. **When the phone is detected on your system, run the application by choosing Run⇨Run 'Silent Mode Toggle'.**

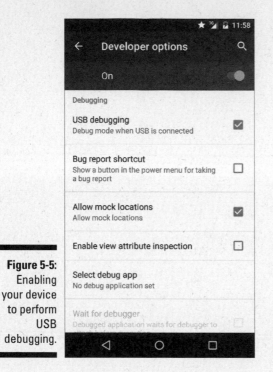

Figure 5-5:
Enabling
your device
to perform
USB
debugging.

Your device and any emulators that are currently running will show up in the device chooser (refer to Figure 5-2).

6. **Choose your phone from the list and click OK.**

This step sends the application to your phone, and it launches it just as it would on the emulator. In a few seconds, the app should show up on your phone.

You've now deployed the application to your phone.

If you change the app and you need to test it again, you have to reinstall it on your phone. It's a simple matter of plugging in your phone and choosing Run⇨Run 'Silent Mode Toggle'.

Material Design

Your app runs, it works great, and does what it says it will do. But does it feel right? You may have noticed that every time you click on the toggle button in the app, there's no visual acknowledgment of your click. Sure the image toggles, but is there more that you can do?

Android's visual design language, called *Material Design*, is all about making your phone's UI look like physical materials. Backgrounds should look like card stock paper; views set on top of the background should be elevated to cast a shadow onto the background; button clicks should cause ripples that expand out over the view like ripples on a pond. These are the little details that make your app a delight to use.

Visit `http://www.google.com/design/spec/material-design/` for more information about Material Design and how to use it to build a visually appealing app.

Your UI is quite simple right now, so there's no need to elevate one part of it over another. But what you do need is some sort of click animation.

Luckily, it's simple to add one. Go back to your `activity_main.xml` layout file, and change your `FrameLayout` to add the following line:

```
<FrameLayout xmlns:android="http://schemas.android.com/apk/res/android"
        android:id="@+id/content"
        android:layout_width="match_parent"
        android:layout_height="match_parent"
        android:foreground="?android:attr/selectableItemBackground">
```

The foreground attribute in the `FrameLayout` class allows you to overlay a drawable on top of whatever is inside the `FrameLayout`. By setting your foreground to `?android:attr/selectableItemBackground`, you are placing the Android-standard `selectableItemBackground` over your entire image. What does the `selectableItemBackground` do? It's a usually transparent drawable that when clicked displays a ripple animation across its view.

The question mark (?) in an attribute value means that you are referencing a value in the currently applied theme. If you change your app's theme or run your app on a phone with another version of Android, the app will look and behave slightly differently (as it should) because you are referencing values from the proper theme.

Go ahead and run your app again, and you will see the standard Android ripple animation when you click your `FrameLayout`.

You will learn how to use other aspects of Material Design, such as setting your view elevation, in Chapter 9.

Uh-Oh! (Responding to Errors)

You write perfect code, right? Even if it's perfect this time, though, the day will come when it isn't. When coding doesn't go as planned, you have to figure out the problem. To help developers facing application crashes, Android Studio provides valuable tools to help debug applications.

Using the Android view

Debugging is rarely fun. Thankfully, the Android Tool window provides the tools necessary to help you dig yourself out of a hole filled with bugs. One of the most commonly used features in the Android Tool window is the logcat viewer, which allows you to view the output of system log messages from your system, as shown in Figure 5-6.

This system log reports everything from basic information messages (which include the state of the application and device) to warning and error information. Seeing only an "Application Not Responding" or a force-close error message on the device doesn't clarify what has happened. Opening the Android view and reviewing the entries in logcat can help identify, down to the line number, where the exception is occurring.

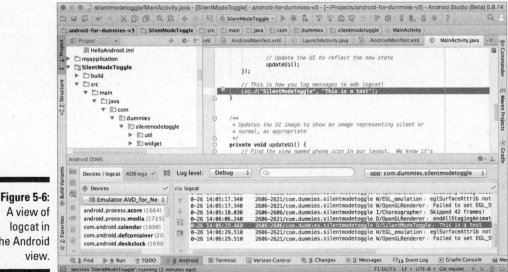

Figure 5-6:
A view of
logcat in
the Android
view.

Logging messages to logcat

Displaying log messages in the Android view is as simple as adding one line of code to your app. Open the `MainActivity.java` file, and at the bottom of the method, add a log entry, as shown in bold in Listing 5-4.

Listing 5-4:   The onCreate() Method

```java
import android.util.Log;

@Override
public void onCreate(Bundle savedInstanceState) {
    super.onCreate(savedInstanceState);

    . . .

    Log.d("SilentModeApp", "This is a test");                    →9
}
```

Line 9 demonstrates how to output a message into the system log. `SilentModeApp` is known as the `TAG` that you're giving to this log entry; the second parameter to the log call is the message you want to output. The tag helps filter messages while looking at them in Android Studio.

TIP

Declare a `TAG` constant in your code and use it instead of repeatedly typing the `TAG`, as in this example:

```java
private static final String TAG = "SilentModeApp";
```

Another common technique for dealing with tags is to use the class name:

```java
private static final String TAG = MainActivity.class.getSimpleName();
```

Notice the d in `Log.d` in Listing 5-4, indicating that this is a debug message. Other options are

- ✔ e: error
- ✔ i: info
- ✔ w: warning
- ✔ wtf: What a terrible failure (Yes, it's an option.)
- ✔ v: verbose

The various logging types exist for you to decide how various messages should be logged.

Viewing log messages in logcat

You can view log messages in the Android Studio Android view by choosing View⇨Tool Windows⇨Android.

Start the application by choosing Run⇨Run 'Silent Mode Toggle'. When your application is running, open the Android view and look for your log messages. It should look somewhat similar to the one shown in Figure 5-6.

By default, the Android view automatically filters the output for you to some sensible defaults. If you would like to explore other filters, try clicking the filter selector in the top right of the Android view and select No filter. You can also filter by log level, and you can search for specific log messages if you like.

Using the Android Studio debugger

Although the Android view might be one of your best allies, your number-one weapon in the battle against the army of bugs is the *Android Studio debugger,* which lets you set various breakpoints, inspect variables using the watch window, and much more.

Checking runtime errors

The *runtime error* is the Wicked Witch of the East — it comes out of nowhere and leaves everything a mess. Your application might be humming along and, all of a sudden, it crashes when you click a menu option or a button, for example. It can be very difficult to solve these kinds of problems just by looking at the source code.

The debugger can help in this situation because you can set a breakpoint at the start of onCreate() that allows you to inspect the values of the variables as the app is running.

Let's make your app crash! Listing 5-5 demonstrates one way to crash your app — commenting out the setContentView initialization will cause an exception to be thrown at runtime. Go ahead and do this now:

Listing 5-5:   Commenting Out the setContentView Initialization

```java
@Override
public void onCreate(Bundle savedInstanceState) {
    // Always call super.onCreate() first.
    super.onCreate(savedInstanceState);

    // Get a reference to Android's AudioManager so we can use
    // it to toggle our ringer.
    audioManager = (AudioManager) getSystemService(AUDIO_SERVICE);
```

```
    // Initialize our layout using the res/layout/activity_main.xml
    // layout file that contains our views for this activity.
    //setContentView(R.layout.activity_main);                        →12

    // Find the view named "content" in our layout file.
    FrameLayout contentView =
            (FrameLayout) findViewById(R.id.content);                →16

    // Create a click listener for the contentView that will toggle
    // the phone's ringer state, and then update the UI to reflect
    // the new state.
    contentView.setOnClickListener(new View.OnClickListener() {      →21
        public void onClick(View v) {
                          . . .
        }
    });
}
```

Listing 5-5 works this way:

→ 12   This code, which is intentionally commented out, is a bug and prevents our activity from getting a layout.

→ 16   findViewById won't be able to find R.id.content anymore, so it will return null.

→ 21   Calling contentView.setOnClickListener will throw a NullPointerException because contentView is null.

Attaching a debugger to your app allows you to track down the root cause of the error.

Creating breakpoints

You have a couple ways to create a breakpoint, which will pause your application mid-execution and let you examine its running state:

✔ Choose the line where you want to place the breakpoint by clicking it with the mouse. Choose Run➪Toggle Line Breakpoint.

✔ Click the left gutter in the Android Studio editor where you want to create a breakpoint.

Either method creates a small, round red icon in the left gutter of the Android Studio editor, as shown in Figure 5-7.

Figure 5-7:
A set break-
point in the
left gutter
of Android
Studio's
editor
window.

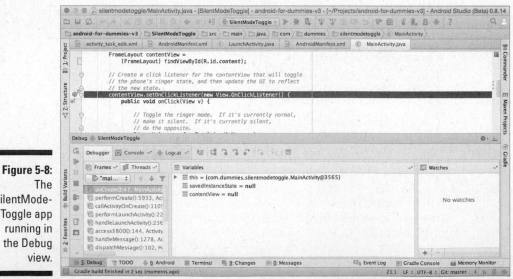

```
        // Create a click listener for the contentView that will toggle
        // the phone's ringer state, and then update the UI to reflect
        // the new state.
        contentView.setOnClickListener(new View.OnClickListener() {
            public void onClick(View v) {

                // Toggle the ringer mode.  If it's currently normal,
                // make it silent.  If it's currently silent,
                // do the opposite.
                RingerHelper.performToggle(audioManager);

                // Update the UI to reflect the new state
                updateUi();

            }
```

TODO   6: Android   Terminal   9: Changes   0: Messages
Gradle build finished in 3 sec (a minute ago)

To try debugging in Android Studio, set a breakpoint on the line with
`contentView.setOnClickListener`.

Starting the debugger

Follow these steps to debug your code:

1. **Choose Run⇨Debug 'Silent Mode Toggle'.**

   Android Studio installs the application on the emulator (or device) and
   then attaches the debugger to it. If your emulator is not running, you will
   have the option to start one now.

2. **Wait for the debugger to break at your breakpoint.**

   You're now at a breakpoint, as shown in Figure 5-8. You can hover the
   cursor over variables to see their values.

Figure 5-8:
The
SilentMode-
Toggle app
running in
the Debug
view.

3. **Hover the cursor over the `contentView` variable.**

   The variable is `null` because you commented out the code. Silly human, why did you do that?

   If you click the Resume button and look at your emulator, you can see that your application has now crashed, as shown in Figure 5-9.

4. **To disconnect the debugger, click the Stop button.**

Go back to `MainActivity.java` and remove the comment you added to ensure that the application runs successfully.

Figure 5-9:
The app
crash dialog
box opens
after an
exception.

Thinking Beyond the Application Boundaries

At times, the device may perform extraneous work that can affect your application, such as downloading a large file in the background while playing music from an online radio application. Will these heavy network-bound activities affect the application in any way? It depends. If your app needs a connection to the Internet and for some reason cannot connect, will it crash? What will happen? Knowing the answers to these questions means that you're thinking beyond your application boundaries.

Not all apps are created equal — some good ones are out there, along with some *bad* ones. Before building or releasing your first Android application, ensure that you know the ins and outs of your application and anything that can affect it. Be sure that the app doesn't crash when users perform routine tap events and screen navigation.

Building applications on embedded devices is very different than building them on a PC or Mac, and the reason is simple: The resources (battery, memory and processor, for example) are limited. If the Android device is a phone, its main purpose is to perform phone-like duties, such as recognizing an incoming call, maintaining a signal, and sending and receiving text messages.

If a phone call is in progress, the Android system treats that process as vital, whereas a downloading file in the background is considered non-vital. If the phone starts to run out of resources, Android kills all non-vital processes to keep the vital ones alive. A file can be downloaded again, but when a call is lost, it's lost forever — you have to make that call again, which would only frustrate the user if the main purpose for purchasing the device was to have a phone. Your app might download a file in the background and the process gets killed — this is a scenario that you need to test. It can also happen if your phone encounters an area with a poor or non-existent wireless signal. If the connection gets dropped, your file isn't downloaded.

Test for all possible solutions and have a safety guard for them. Otherwise, your app will be prone to runtime exceptions, which can lead to poor reviews from users at the Google Play Store.

Interacting with your application

To ensure that your app works, fire it up and play with its features. While your app is running, start another app, such as the browser. Visit a few sites, and then return to your app. Click any buttons related to your app to see what happens. Try all kinds of things to see whether you find outcomes that you didn't consider. What happens if a user is interacting with your app and receives a phone call? Are you saving the necessary state in `onPause()` and restoring it in `onResume()`?

Android handles the difficult task management for you, but it's ultimately your responsibility to manage the state of your application.

The most common errors come from Android developers failing to save their state properly in onPause and restore it in onResume. Remember that Android can kill your activity at any time, and it's up to you to make sure you properly save your activity's state so it can be re-created later if necessary! See Chapter 10 for more information about saving and restoring your activity state.

Testing whether your application works

In the emulator or on your device, open the Silent Mode Toggle application from the launcher. You've already performed the first step in the testing process — making sure that the app starts!

After the app is open, check to see whether the phone is in Silent mode by looking for the small star icon on the notification bar (refer to Figure 5-3).

Click the Silent Mode Toggle button to toggle the ringer mode. Did the application's image change? Try various actions to ensure that your application works as expected. If you find a flaw, use the debugging tools featured in this chapter to help identify the issue.

Are you having difficulty turning Silent mode off again? You may have been hit by a bug introduced in Android 5.0. Visit https://code.google.com/p/android/issues/detail?id=78652 for more details.

What about automated testing?

With the rise of agile methodologies over the past decade, it's only a matter of time before you start to wonder how to perform automated testing in Android. The SDK installs Android unit-testing tools that you can use to test not only Java classes but also Android-based classes and user interface interactions. You can read more about unit testing in the Android documentation at http://d.android.com/guide/topics/testing/testing_android.html.

Here are some tools at your disposal:

✔ **JUnit:** The Android SDK includes JUnit 3.x integration. You can use JUnit, a popular unit-testing framework that's used in Java, to perform unit testing or interaction testing, and you can find more information about JUnit at www.junit.org. To make your development life easier, Android Studio has built-in tools to help facilitate testing in JUnit through Android Studio.

✔ **Monkey:** The user interface and application exerciser known as Monkey runs on your emulator or device and generates pseudorandom streams of user events, including taps, gestures, touches, clicks, and a number of system events. Monkey, which is installed with the Android SDK, is a helpful way to stress-test an application.

✔ **UI Automator:** The UI Automator testing framework lets you test your user interface (UI) efficiently by creating automated functional UI test cases that can be run against your app on one or more devices.

✔ **Espresso:** The Espresso library makes unit testing Android significantly easier than using straight JUnit. It uses a simple and concise style to write Android unit tests. Beginning with 2.0, Espresso is now distributed as part of the Android SDK.

To learn more about how to use Espresso to create automated tests for your app, visit the book's online website at www.dummies.com/extras/androidappdevelopment to read the articles on testing.

Chapter 6

Understanding Android Resources

Resources are mentioned in detail throughout this book, so you might wonder why an entire chapter is devoted to them. Discussing resources and their use in Chapters 3 and 4 is necessary to help you understand the basic structure of the resource directory and the use of resources to build a simple application. One compelling reason to use resources in your application — localization — is covered in this chapter.

Understanding Resources

Resources are additional static content that are an intrinsic part of your app but aren't part of your Java code. The most common resources are

- Layout
- String
- Image
- Dimension
- Style
- Theme
- Value
- Menu
- Color

Earlier chapters in this book introduce you to layouts, strings, and images because they're the most common types of resources that you use in everyday Android application development. The remaining resources may need some explanation, so the following few sections will clear them up.

Dimensions

In an Android resource, a *dimension* is a number followed by a unit of measurement, such as 10px, 2.5in, or 5sp. You use a dimension when specifying any property in Android that requires a numeric unit of measure. For example, you may want the padding of a layout to be 10px. Android supports the following units of measure:

- **density-independent pixel (dp or dip):** This is the most commonly used dimension. Dp is based on the physical density of the screen. These units are relative to a screen measuring 160 dots per inch (dpi); therefore, 1 dp is equivalent to 1 pixel on a 160-dpi screen. The ratio of dp to pixels changes with screen density, but not necessarily in proportion.

  The dp concept is complex; you will want to support multiple screen densities, so check out the "Supporting Multiple Screens" article at `http://d.android.com/guide/practices/screens_support.html`.

- **scale-independent pixel (sp or sip):** This unit resembles the dp unit but is scaled according to the user's font-size preference. Use sp dimensions when specifying font sizes in your application.

- **pixel (px):** A pixel corresponds to a pixel on the screen. This unit of measure isn't recommended for most cases. Your app may look great on a medium-density device but look distorted and out of place on a high-density screen (and vice versa) because the dpi differs.

- **point (pt):** A point is $1/72$ inch, based on the physical size of the screen. Like px, pt is not recommended.

- **millimeter (mm):** This unit is based on the size of the screen. Like px, mm is not recommended.

- **inch (in):** This unit is based on the physical size of the screen. Like px, in is not recommended.

Styles

Styles in Android are similar to Cascading Style Sheets (CSS) in the web development realm: You use styles to (you guessed it) style an application. A *style* is a collection of properties that can be applied to an individual view (within the layout file) or to an activity or to your entire application (from within the manifest file). Styles support inheritance, so you can provide a basic style and then modify it for each particular use case in your application. Style `property` attribute examples include text size, text color, and background.

Themes

A *theme* is a style applied to an entire activity or application, rather than an individual view. When a style is applied as a theme, every view in the activity and/or application inherits the style settings. For example, you can set all `TextView` views to a particular font, and all views in the themed activity or application then display their text in that font.

Values

The value resource can contain many different types of value type resources for your application, including

- ✔ **Bool:** A Boolean value defined in XML whose value is stored in an arbitrary filename in the `res/values/<filename>`.xml file, where *<filename>* is the name of the file. An example is `bools.xml`.

- ✔ **Integer:** An integer value defined in XML whose value is stored with an arbitrary filename in the `res/values/<filename>`.xml file. An example is `integers.xml`.

- ✔ **Integer array:** An array of integers defined in XML whose set of values is stored with an arbitrary name in the `res/values/<filename>`.xml file, where *<filename>* is the name of the file. An example is `integers.xml`. You can reference and use these integers in your code to help define loops, lengths, and other elements.

- ✔ **Typed array:** An array used to create an array of resources, such as `drawables`. You can create arrays of mixed types. Therefore, the arrays aren't required to be homogeneous — however, you must be aware of the data type so that you can appropriately cast it. As with other resources, the filename is arbitrary in the `res/values/<filename>`.xml file. An example is `types.xml`.

Menus

Whether your app is using the action bar or a menu, Android treats them both the same and you'll define them the same way. A menu can be defined via either code or XML. The preferred way to define one is via XML; therefore, the various menus you create should be placed into the menu/ directory. Each menu has its own .xml file.

Colors

The colors file, typically located in the values/colors.xml file, lets you name colors, such as login_screen_font_color. This might depict the color of the text you're using on the logon page, for example. Each color is defined as a hexadecimal value.

Working with Resources

You may have worked with resources a few times in this book, and at this point you're likely familiar with using the R class to access resources from within your application. If you're rusty on resources and the generated R file, see Chapter 3.

Moving strings into resources

As you become an experienced programmer, you may start to take shortcuts to get your project built and working. Say that initially you forget to move strings into resources, and you have to come back at a later time to do it. You can extract a string into a resource using the built-in tools.

The long way

Here's one way to extract a string into a resource:

1. **Create a new string resource.**
2. **Copy its name.**
3. **Replace the string value in your layout with the resource identifier.**

This way is fine. It's not a huge pain, but it does take a little time.

The fast way

You can cut the time to create a string resource to fewer than 15 seconds. If you do this 30 times a day (which is feasible in an 8-hour day), you can save 15 minutes of just copying and pasting. That's five hours a month doing the copy-and-paste dance!

Follow these steps:

1. **In Android Studio, open a random layout file such as** `activity_main.xml` **in the** `layouts` **directory.**

2. **Add a new** `TextView` **element that looks like the following:**

```
<TextView
    android:layout_width="wrap_content"
    android:layout_height="wrap_content"
    android:text="I need a kombucha refill, please"/>
```

3. **Place your cursor on the boldface line with the hardcoded text string and press Alt+Enter.**

   A menu opens with various options.

4. **Choose the Extract String Resource option.**

   The Extract String Resource dialog box opens, as shown in Figure 6-1, and you can set various options for the resource.

Figure 6-1:
The Extract
Android
String dialog
box.

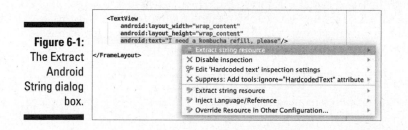

5. **Choose a name for your resource such as** `kombucha_refill`**, leave the other options set to their defaults, and click OK.**

   You can now see that the layout file has been modified. The text `"I need a kombucha refill, please"` has been replaced with `"@string/kombucha_refill"`.

   If you open the `strings.xml` file in the `res/values` folder, you can see your new string resource.

That's pretty cool! You can see that doing this 20 or 30 times a day can add up and save you a lot of time.

Wrestling the image beast

One of the most difficult parts about resources can be images. They might look great on medium-density devices but look like garbage on high-density devices. This is where multiple-density folders come into play. These density-specific drawable folders are explained in Chapter 3.

Battling pixelation and compression

The issue you'll most likely encounter is pixelation and compression/expansion (moving from higher- to lower-density devices and vice versa). To work around this issue, design your graphics at a high density, such as 640 dpi in large-size format. For example, if you're building the launcher icon, build it at 512px high and 512px wide to upload to Google Play. Although the xxxhdpi folder might need an image of only 192px high x 192px wide (the largest in use), it doesn't mean that in two or three months a higher resolution device won't be released.

This situation can be painful because working with large image files in image editing programs is difficult if you don't have a computer with decent capabilities. But you have to trust us on this one: Having a large raw-image file that's high density is much easier to mold and shape into the correct densities you'll need.

Downsizing a high-resolution image doesn't distort its quality (other than losing its fine edges and detail), but upscaling does because it creates pixelation. Starting with a large file reduces the chance that you'll ever have to upscale, which means that your app graphics will always look crisp. If possible, working with vector files will make this even easier.

Using layers

If you're creating graphics in an image editing tool that supports layers, place each item in your graphic on a different layer. The reasons are many, but here are the key factors:

- **Changes:** At some point, you will need to change something in your graphic — its background, font, or logo, for example. If you have all these items in different layers, you can make the change without affecting the rest of the graphic.

- **Localization:** An example from an earlier section in this chapter talks about various strings in different languages, and graphics are no different. Many times as you develop applications, you will encounter graphics with stylized text in the graphic itself. If your application is being translated into Japanese and your graphics contain stylized English text, you can create a Japanese version of those graphics and place them in a Japanese drawable region folder, such as res/drawable-ja. The Android platform recognizes which region it's in (in this case, Japan). If the region's resource folders (res/drawable-ja, res/values-ja, and so on) are available, Android uses them in the application. That being said, it's always easier to keep your text in text resources and your images in image resources. Translating text resources is easier than making new copies of your images for every new language.

: FLAWN
: Chan, Peter

:
3906513755
7136
Transited:
February 12,
2018 11:06

with resources

...hone in U.S. market share in the ... world are developing Android- ...re potential users for your apps.

...loper is that Android is a ...ng to be tapped. Though this ...advantage of it requires that ...ffect the usability of your apps. ...uses your app and it was written ...esources or not), the user can ...string values into your views and ...ese version, you have to rewrite ...you use resources, you can have ...rawables into the region you're

...-readable strings, images, and view- ...an reference. You can create various resource... differing sizes, languages (strings and drawables), and layout op... as landscape and portrait. Landscape and portrait layouts come into play when a user rotates the device 90 degrees in either direction.

If you want your apps to be available on as many Android devices as possible around the world, you should use resources at all times. Always put all strings into the `strings.xml` file because, someday, someone from another country will want your application in another language. To transport your application to another language, you simply need a translator to translate your `strings.xml` file into her language, and then you can create various `values` folders to hold the appropriate region's values. Android takes care of the hard work. For example, if the user is in China and his phone is set to the Chinese Locale, Android looks for the values folder named `values-cn`, which is where Chinese values are stored — including the Chinese version of the `strings.xml` file. If Android cannot find such a folder, the platform defaults to the `values` folder, which contains the English version of the `strings.xml` file. (For more on strings, see the section, "Moving strings into resources," earlier in this chapter.)

When it comes down to it, having a translator update your strings and creating a new folder with the new `strings.xml` file located within are simple tasks. Expand this concept to other languages and tablets and televisions and you can see the potential. You're no longer looking at mobile users as your target audience. You're looking at *Android users*, and with the options being released, you could be looking at *billions* of users. Using resources correctly can make your expansion into foreign markets that much easier.

Looking to have your app translated? You have a few options. Visit `http://translate.google.com/toolkit` to learn how to upload your `strings.xml` file and have it automatically translated by a computer. For higher quality results, you should look at `http://d.android.com/distribute/tools/localization-checklist.html` to learn how to upload your app and have it translated by a professional translator.

Designing your application for various regions is a big topic. You can find more in-depth information in the "Localizing with Resources" article of the SDK documentation at `http://d.android.com/guide/topics/resources/localization.html`.

You're not forced into releasing your application to all countries at once — Google Play will allow you to release your app only to specific countries. Therefore, if you have written an application for the Berlin bus route system in Germany, it probably doesn't make sense to have a Chinese version, unless you want to cater to Chinese tourists as well as to German residents.

Different Strokes for Different Folks: Using Resource Qualifier Directories

As discussed in Chapter 3, you can use different drawable directories to create different resources for higher and lower resolution devices. This is an example of using *resource qualifiers*, and it turns out that you can use the same trick to do many other things.

Using default resources

By default, when you place a resource into your drawable, layout, menu, value, or other directory in the `res` folder, you're supplying a *default resource*. This is the resource that will be used if no other resources are specified. You've done this already with drawables, layouts, and strings.

These default resources will be used if there are no other specific resources overriding them. To override a resource for special cases, you create files in directories that have special names. The next sections will go over some common ways you might want to override resources.

Localizing to another language

Let's say that you want to translate the Silent Mode Toggle app into Spanish. As covered in Chapter 3, you can do that by creating a `values-es` directory, and placing a new `strings.xml` file into that directory that "overrides" the default values that are in `values/strings.xml`. Whenever your app is opened on a device that is set to use Spanish as the default language, your app automatically displays the strings from `values-es/strings.xml` rather than the default English values.

This works with any of Android's supported languages, not just Spanish. You can use *fr* for French, *de* for German, and so on.

In addition, Android allows you to subdivide languages by region. So you can provide Portuguese translations for Portugal in `values-pt`, and in `values-pt-rBR` for Brazil (which also speaks Portuguese).

Visit `http://developer.android.com/guide/topics/resources/localization.html` for more information about how to localize your app to different languages and regions.

You don't necessarily need to override every value in your `strings.xml` files. For example, if you have a `values/strings.xml` using U.S. English and a `values-en-rGB/strings.xml` for U.K. English, you only need to supply translations for those few things that mean different things in the U.S. and the U.K. (such as *pants*).

But be careful if you supply selective translations! The above might make sense for U.S. and U.K. English, but it does not make sense for a French translation file. If you provide only some French translations, then some of your app will be in English and some in French!

Handling different screen sizes

Resource qualifier directories can be a key tool in your battle to handle the hundreds of different screen sizes and resolutions out there in the Android world.

There are two main techniques you will want to use: selecting resources based on screen density or based on screen size.

Screen density (pixel density)

Android devices come in many different pixel densities. Older phones came in mdpi- or ldpi-pixel densities. These days, most newer phones come in hdpi-or-above pixel densities. But some tablets may still come in mdpi densities. Here is the list of densities Android supports:

- ldpi (low): ~120 dpi (dots per inch)
- mdpi (medium): ~160 dpi
- hdpi (high): ~240 dpi
- xhdpi (extra-high): ~320 dpi
- xxhdpi (extra-extra-high): ~480 dpi
- xxxhdpi (extra-extra-extra-high): ~640 dpi

As described in Chapter 3, you can use these densities as qualifiers in your drawables directory to provide different images for different density screens. For example, you can provide different sizes of assets for different devices by putting the image files in `drawables-mdpi`, `drawables-xxhdpi`, and so on.

In addition, you can use them as qualifiers on your values directories to utilize slightly different values for things like margin, padding, and text size on different sized devices. These values are typically put into a `dimens.xml` file in the corresponding `values` directory.

Remember, you do not necessarily have to provide all your images for all densities. A good rule of thumb is to provide the xxhdpi assets for all your images and rely on Android to automatically scale them down to the other sizes as necessary. But if there are some images that don't look great when scaled down (such as a company's logo for example), you may want to provide that asset at all densities.

Layouts

You may want to use different layouts for different sized screens. For example, a tablet has much more screen real estate than a phone, so you will likely want to lay out some of your screens differently on a tablet than on a phone.

Android provides the `smallestWidth` qualifier to help you distinguish between a phone and tablet. "Smallest width" means the smaller of your height of width, regardless of which orientation your device is in. So if your phone is 600dp x 800dp, the smallest width would be 600.

This is very handy for distinguishing between phones and tablets. In general, the common consensus is that a smallest width of 600dp or more is a tablet, whereas anything less is a phone.

The way to use the `smallestWidth` qualifier is to provide your default phone layouts in `res/layouts`, and then put any tablet-only layouts that you need in `res/layouts-sw600dp`. Android will then pick the correct layout file depending on whether the user is using a phone or a tablet.

See Part IV for more information about how to use different layouts for tablets versus phones.

Portrait versus landscape orientations

Similarly, you may want to provide a different layout if the phone is in portrait mode or landscape mode. This can be handy for showing multi-pane layouts when in landscape mode, but collapsing them to a single pane when in portrait.

Put all your default layouts into `res/layout`. These are used regardless of which orientation your phone is in. If you want to have landscape-only layouts, put them in `res/layout-land`. Similarly, portrait-only layouts should go in `res/layout-port`.

Handling old Android versions

You can also use resource qualifiers to supply alternate resources for when your app is running on different versions of Android. For example, older versions of Android use different styles and colors, so perhaps you want your app to use a slightly different color when running on Android 4.1 rather than Android 5.0.

To do this, you can put your regular colors in `res/values/colors.xml`, and then put your Android 4.1 colors into `res/values-v16/colors.xml` (for platform level 16, or Android 4.1).

See Chapter 17 for more information about backward compatibility and handling older versions of Android.

Qualifier name rules

Now that you know the basics, there are some additional things that can be helpful to know about using resource qualifiers:

 ✔ You can specify multiple qualifiers for a single set of resources, separated by dashes. For example, `drawable-en-rUS-land` applies to US-English devices in landscape orientation.

✔ If you use multiple qualifiers, they must be in a special order that you can find here: `http://d.android.com/guide/topics/resources/providing-resources.html#table2`. For example:

- Wrong: `drawable-hdpi-port/`

- Correct: `drawable-port-hdpi/`

✔ Only one value for each qualifier type is supported. For example, if you want to use the same drawable files for Spain and France, you cannot have a directory named `drawable-rES-rFR`.

There are many other things you can customize by using resource qualifiers! Visit `http://d.android.com/guide/topics/resources/` for more information.

Chapter 7

Turning Your Application into an App Widget

*U*sability is the name of the game in regard to all disciplines of application development: If your application isn't easy to use, users simply won't use it.

If you've followed the first six chapters of this book to build the Silent Mode Toggle application, it undoubtedly works well. But it still requires launching an app to use. To make this application even easier to use, simply turn it into a Home screen widget. A Home screen widget allows you to place a view on the user's Home screen, which they can use to interact with your app without having to open the app.

In this chapter, you build an app widget for your application. An app widget normally is a small icon or tiny view on the Home screen. Users can interact with your application by simply tapping this widget to toggle their phone's Silent mode. This chapter introduces you to these classes:

✔ `Intent`

✔ `BroadcastReceiver`

✔ `AppWidgetProvider`

✔ `IntentService`

Each of these classes plays a vital role in Android as well as in the app widget framework.

Working with App Widgets in Android

An *app widget* in Android is a special kind of view that can be embedded on your device's Home screen. An app widget can accept user input via click events, and it can update itself regularly. A user can add an app widget to the Home screen by tapping the Applications button and then selecting Widgets. The result is shown in Figure 7-1.

To make the Silent Mode Toggle application more usable, build an app widget for it so that users can add the widget to the Home screen. Tapping the widget changes the phone's ringer mode without having to open the application. The widget also updates its layout to indicate what state the phone is in, as shown in Figure 7-2.

Working with remote views

When you develop apps in Android, remember that it's based on the Linux kernel. Linux comes supplied with its own idioms about security, and the Android platform inherits them. For example, the Android security model is heavily based around the Linux user, file, and process security model.

Figure 7-1:
Adding a widget to the Home screen.

Phone is in regular mode   Silent mode is enabled

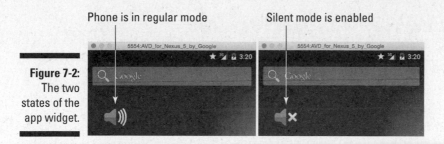

Figure 7-2:
The two
states of the
app widget.

Because every Android application is (usually) associated with its own unique user, Android prevents applications from modifying the files of other applications. This prevents developers from injecting malicious code into other apps.

Because the Home screen (also known as the Launcher) is its own application and thus has its own unique user, developers such as yourself aren't allowed to directly run your application code on the Home screen for security reasons. To provide a way to access the Home screen and modify the contents of a particular area on it from an application, Android provides the RemoteViews architecture: It lets you run code inside your application, in a separate process from the Home screen application, but it still allows a widget's view to be updated on the Home screen. This architecture protects the Home screen app from buggy or malicious apps, because no third-party app code needs to run in the Home screen app.

Suppose that a user taps the Home screen app widget (in this case, an icon she added to the Home screen). This action sends a request — addressed to *your* application — to change the ringer mode. Android routes the request to your application, and the application processes the request, instructing the Android platform to change the ringer mode and update the app widget on the Home screen with a new image. None of this code is run in the Home screen application — it's all run remotely in your application, with Android routing the message to the appropriate application. These messages are called *intents* in Android.

A *remote view* combines a little magic with innovative engineering. Known as the RemoteViews class on the Android platform, it allows your application to programmatically supply a remote user interface to the Home screen in another process. The app widget code isn't an activity (as in earlier chapters), but is an implementation of an AppWidgetProvider. When Android routes an intent to your application from the Home screen, the message is handled in your implementation of the AppWidgetProvider class.

Using AppWidgetProviders

The AppWidgetProvider class allows the developer to programmatically interact with the app widget on the Home screen. When this interaction takes place, messages are sent from the Home screen app widget to your application via broadcast events. Using these broadcast events, you can respond when the app widget is updated, enabled, disabled, or deleted. You can also update the look and feel of the app widget on the Home screen by providing a new view. Because this view is located on the Home screen and not within your running application, you use RemoteViews to update the app widget layout. All the logic that determines what should happen is contained in an implementation of AppWidgetProvider and initiated by an intent.

Picture the app widget framework (AppWidgetManager) as the translator of a conversation between two entities. If you need to speak to someone who knows Italian, but you don't know how to speak Italian, you would find a translator who would accept your input, translate it into Italian, and relay the message to the native Italian speaker. The same process applies to the app widget framework: This framework is your translator.

When the Italian native (AppWidgetHost, which is the Home screen, in this case) needs to let you know that something has happened (such as a user tapping a button), the translator (the app widget framework in the Android system) translates the action into a message (intent) that you can understand (tapping a particular button). At that time, you can respond with the action you want to take (such as change the app widget background color to lime green), and the translator (the app widget framework) relays the message to the native Italian speaker (AppWidgetHost; that is, the Home screen via the Android system). The Home screen then updates the background color of the view.

App widgets can only accept input from tap-type events. When you're working within an app widget, you have no access to other basic input views, such as an editable text box or drop-down lists.

Working with Intents and Pending Intents

When the user needs to interact with your application, she communicates by tapping the app widget using the Android messaging architecture (as described earlier), and you aren't immediately notified. However, this doesn't mean you *can't* be notified about a click event on your app widget — it's just done a little differently than regular views.

App widget click events contain instructions for what to do when a click event happens via the `Intent` class in the Android framework.

Understanding the Android intent system

An `Intent` object in Android is a message telling Android to make something happen. When you turn on a light using a wall switch, the action of your intent is to turn on the light, so you flip the switch to the On position. In Android, this action correlates to creating an instance of the `Intent` class with an action in it specifying that the light is to be turned on:

```
Intent turnLightOn = new Intent("TURN_LIGHT_ON");
```

This intent is fired off using `startActivity()` in the Android messaging system (as described in Chapter 1), and the appropriate activity handles the `Intent`. (If multiple activities respond, Android lets the user choose one to do the work.) However, in the physical world, an electrical connection is made by positioning the switch to the On position, resulting in illuminating the light. In Android, you have to provide code, In the form of an activity, to make this happen. This activity (which could hypothetically be named `TurnLightOnActivity`) responds to the `turnLightOn` intent. If you're working with an app widget, you must handle the intent in a `BroadcastReceiver` rather than in an activity. `AppWidgetProvider` is a subclass of a `BroadcastReceiver` with a few extra bells and whistles that configure a lot of the app widget framework for you. A `BroadcastReceiver` is responsible for receiving broadcast intents.

The `AppWidgetProvider` (a `BroadcastReceiver`) handles the intent from the Home screen and responds with the appropriate result that you determined, using your code, inside your custom `AppWidgetProvider`.

An *intent* is a message that can carry a wide variety of data describing an operation that needs to be performed. An intent can be addressed to a specific activity or broadcast to a generic category of receivers known as `BroadcastReceivers` (which includes `AppWidgetProvider`). The `Intent`, `Activity`, and `BroadcastReceiver` system is reminiscent of the message bus architecture, where a message is placed on a message bus and any of the endpoints on the bus respond to the message if (and only if) they know how. If no endpoint knows how to respond to the message, or if the message wasn't addressed to the endpoint, the app will crash.

An intent can be launched into the message bus system in a couple of ways:

✔ **Start another activity:** Use the `startActivity()` call, which accepts an `Intent` object as a parameter.

✔ **Notify any interested `BroadcastReceiver` components:** Use the `sendBroadcast()` call, which also takes an intent as a parameter.

✔ **Communicate with a background service:** Use the `startService()` or `bindService()` call, which both accept intents as parameters.

An intent is the glue that binds together the various components of the application. It provides a mechanism that allows you to communicate within your app, as well as communicate with other apps.

Understanding intent data

An intent's data consists of these elements:

✔ **Action:** The general action to be performed. A few common actions include `ACTION_VIEW`, `ACTION_EDIT`, and `ACTION_MAIN`. You can also provide your own custom action.

✔ **Data:** The data to operate on, such as a record in a database or a uniform resource identifier that should be opened, such as a URL.

Table 7-1 demonstrates a few action and data parameters for `Intent` objects and their simple data structure.

Table 7-1   **Intent Data Examples**

Action	Data	Result
`ACTION_VIEW`	`tel:123`	Display the dialer with the given number (123) filled in.
`ACTION_DIAL`	`content://contacts/people/1`	Display the dialer showing the phone number from the contact with the ID of 1.
`ACTION_EDIT`	`content://contacts/people/1`	Edit the information about the person whose given identifier is 1.
`ACTION_VIEW`	`http://www.example.org`	Display the web page of the given intent.
`ACTION_VIEW`	`content://contacts/people`	Display a list of all people in the Contacts system.

Intents can also carry an array of other data that include these elements:

- ✔ **category:** Gives additional information about the action to execute. As an example, if `CATEGORY_LAUNCHER` is present, the application should show up in the application launcher as a top-level application. Another option, `CATEGORY_ALTERNATIVE`, can provide alternative actions that the user can perform on a piece of data.

- ✔ **type:** Specifies a particular type (MIME type) of intent data. For example, when you're setting the type to `audio/mpeg`, the Android system recognizes that you're working with an MP3 file. Normally, the type is inferred by the data itself. By setting the type, you override the inferred type by explicitly setting the type in the intent.

- ✔ **component:** Specifies an explicit component name of the class on which to execute the intent. Normally, the component is inferred by inspection of other information in the intent (action, data/type, and categories), and matching components can handle it. If this attribute is set, none of that evaluation takes place, and this component is used exactly as specified (likely the most common use case in your applications). You can provide another activity as the component — this instructs Android to interact with that specific class.

- ✔ **extras:** A bundle of additional, key-based information that's used to provide extra information to the receiving component. For example, if you need to send an email address, you use the extras bundle to supply the body and subject and other components of the email.

Evaluating intents

In the Android system, intents are evaluated either explicitly or implicitly.

Explicitly

The intent has specified an explicit component or the exact class that will execute the data in the intent. (Again, this is likely the most common way to address intents.) This type of intent often contains no other data because it's a means to start other activities within an application. You find out later in this chapter how to use an explicit intent in an application.

An example of an explicit intent would be `new Intent(...,  MainActivity.class)` to create an intent that would explicitly launch your `MainActivity`.

Implicitly

The intent hasn't specified a component or class. Instead, the intent must provide enough information about the action that needs to be performed with the given data for the Android system to determine which available components can handle the intent — sometimes referred to as an *address* and a *payload*.

An example is setting up an email intent that contains email fields (To, CC, Subject, and Body) and an email MIME type. Android interprets it as an email and gives the user of the device the opportunity to choose which application should handle the intent. Possibilities include Gmail or Exchange or a POP email account. The user determines which email program to use. The Android capability to identify possible matches for the given intent is known as *intent resolution*.

To create an implicit email intent, you would do something like the following:

```
new Intent(Intent.ACTION_SENDTO,
           Uri.parse("mailto:taylor.swift@gmail.com"));
```

Using pending intents

A `PendingIntent` is used for something different than regular intents: A `PendingIntent` is created by your application and given to another, completely different application. By giving another application a `PendingIntent`, you're granting the other application the right to perform the operation you have specified as though the application were your own application. When the other application deems that the given work needs to take place, it executes the `PendingIntent`, which is sent back to your application to perform the necessary work.

For the purpose of the Silent Mode Toggle application, you use the `PendingIntent.getBroadcast()` call to create a `PendingIntent`. This call returns a `PendingIntent` that you can use to wrap a regular intent that instructs the Silent Mode Toggle app to toggle Silent mode. The call takes these four parameters:

- ✔ `Context`: The context in which this `PendingIntent` should perform the broadcast.

- ✔ `RequestCode`: The private request code for the sender. Not currently used in this app; therefore, a zero is passed in.

- ✔ `Intent`: The intent to be broadcast.

- ✔ `Flags`: A set of optional information used to configure the intent when it's started.

Avoiding the dreaded Application Not Responding (ANR) error

Because all the work that happens in the `AppWidgetProvider` takes place on the main thread of the user interface, you must complete all your work as quickly as possible. If your `AppWidgetProvider` takes too long to respond, your code holds up the UI thread and causes your application to display an Application Not Responding (ANR) dialog box because the Android system believes that the application is frozen and not responding. An example is network communication to download status updates from a service such as Twitter. If downloading the statuses takes too long (which can be much shorter than you might expect), Android shows the ANR dialog box letting the user know that the app widget isn't responding; at that point, the user can force-close the application.

One way to avoid the ANR error is to implement a separate service that performs its work in a background thread. The `IntentService` that you implement in the following sections helps you avoid ANR errors and allows the widget to remain very fast.

The `Intent` object is wrapped inside a `PendingIntent` because a `PendingIntent` is used for inter-process communication. When the `PendingIntent` is fired off, the real work that needs to be done is wrapped up in the broadcast `Intent` object.

That's a lot of information! Now that you understand the basics of the Android intent system, it's time to implement the guts of the application inside this app widget.

Creating the App Widget

The process of sending messages between the Home screen app widget and your application is handled via the Android messaging system, the `PendingIntent` class, and the `AppWidgetProvider`. In this section, you build each component to get your first app widget up and running on the Home screen.

Implementing the AppWidgetProvider

Implementing the `AppWidgetProvider` is fairly straightforward: Open Android Studio and open the Silent Mode Toggle application.

To add a new class to the `com.dummies.silentmodetoggle` package and provide a name, such as `AppWidget.java`, follow these steps:

1. **Right-click `com.dummies.silentmodetoggle` in the `src/` folder and choose Package, then create a package named `widget`.**

2. **Right-click `com.dummies.silentmodetoggle.widget` in the `src/` folder and choose New⇨Java Class.**

3. **Name the class `AppWidget` and click Finish.**

   The new class is added to the selected package.

Communicating with the app widget

The `AppWidget` class has no code in it at first — it's an empty shell. In the code file you just created, type the code shown in Listing 7-1 into the editor.

Listing 7-1:   The Initial Setup of the App Widget

```
/**
 * The main class that represents our app's widget.
 * Dispatches to a service to do all of the heavy lifting.
 */
public class AppWidget extends AppWidgetProvider {                    →5

    @Override
    public void onUpdate(Context context, AppWidgetManager           →8
            appWidgetManager, int[] appWidgetIds) {

        context.startService(new Intent(context, AppWidgetService.class)); →11
    }
}
```

This list briefly describes the numbered lines:

→5   The `AppWidget` class extends from `AppWidgetProvider`. Remember that `AppWidgetProvider` is a `BroadcastReceiver`, so it can receive broadcasted intents.

→8   Overrides the `onUpdate` method in `AppWidgetProvider`. `onUpdate` is called when the widget is first created. It is also called periodically at a set interval that you will define later in `widget_provider.xml`.

→11   Starts a service so the service can take on the responsibility of updating the widget without you having to worry about how long the responses take to generate. This is necessary for any widgets that do any sort of I/O (network, disk, and so on). Our widget doesn't do I/O, so using a service is not strictly speaking necessary, but it's a very common pattern and it's important to know.

The `AppWidgetProvider` does all the work of responding to events from the `RemoteViews`, but how so? Recall that `AppWidgetProvider` is a subclass of `BroadcastReceiver`. At a high level, a `BroadcastReceiver` is a component that can receive broadcast messages from the Android system. When a user taps a clickable view in the `RemoteViews` on the Home screen (such as a button), the Android system broadcasts a message informing the receiver that the view was clicked. After the message is broadcast, the `AppWidgetProvider` can handle that message.

Note that because these messages are *broadcast,* they're sent system-wide. If the payload of the message and the destination address information are vague enough, various `BroadcastReceiver` objects might handle the message. This is similar to walking into a room full of building contractors and asking whether any of them can do some work for you — everyone would respond. You have a vague message address and payload. However, if you ask the same group for a small electronics electrician contractor by the name of Bob Smith, only one might respond. You have a specifically addressed message with a detailed address and payload information.

Building the app widget's layout

The app widget needs to have a layout for Android to know what to display on the Home screen. The widget layout file defines what the widget will look like while on the Home screen. Earlier in this chapter, Figure 7-2 showed the app widget running in the emulator.

To create the widget layout, create an XML layout file in the `res/layout` directory. Create one now and name it `app_widget.xml`.

The contents of `app_widget.xml` are shown in Listing 7-2.

Listing 7-2:   The Contents of app_widget.xml

```
<?xml version="1.0" encoding="utf-8"?>
<ImageView xmlns:android="http://schemas.android.com/apk/res/android"
        android:id="@+id/phone_state"                                    →3
        android:layout_height="wrap_content"                             →4
        android:layout_width="wrap_content"
        android:src="@drawable/icon_ringer_on"                           →6
        android:contentDescription="@string/toggle_silent_mode"/>        →7
```

This layout should be nothing new. It's simply a single `ImageView` with an image that will represent whether the phone is in Silent mode or not.

Here's what the code is doing:

→ 3   Sets the ID of the image to `phone_state` so that it can be referenced later in the Java code. The + tells Android that this is a new ID and to create it.

→ 4   The height and width of this view is set to wrap the image.

→ 6   Sets the initial icon for the `ImageView`. You will write the code to update this icon based on the ringer state of the phone later. You can download `icon_ringer_on` from the sample source code on the book's website.

→ 7   A simple text string that describes what the image is. This is provided for accessibility. It's a good practice to include `contentDescription` text for any images you supply in your app. Go ahead and create a string resource for this string in your `res/values/strings.xml` file. Name it `toggle_silent_mode` and set its value to something like `"Toggle Silent Mode"`.

Doing work inside an AppWidgetProvider

After the `PendingIntent` has started your `AppWidgetProvider`, you perform some work on behalf of the calling application (in this case, the Home screen application). In the following sections, you perform time-sensitive work on behalf of the caller.

The work that your app does to update the widget is divided into two parts: The `AppWidgetProvider`, which must finish processing its work quickly, and the `IntentService`, which can take as long as it wants to finish.

Most widgets will have an `AppWidgetProvider` that does a little bit of light work, but passes all the heavier work to an `IntentService` to execute in the background. Anything that involves I/O (such as reading or writing from a network, database, or disk) or a lot of CPU processing, should be done on a background thread in something like an `IntentService`.

Understanding the IntentService

Any code that executes for too long without responding to the Android system is subject to the Application Not Responding (ANR) error. App widgets are especially vulnerable to ANR errors because they're executing code in a remote process, and because app widgets execute across process boundaries that can take time to set up, execute, and tear. The Android system watches app widgets to ensure that they don't take too long to execute. When they do, the calling application (the Home screen) locks up and the device is unusable. Therefore, the Android platform wants to ensure that you're never capable of making the device unresponsive.

Because app widgets are expensive in regard to CPU and memory, judging whether an app widget will cause an ANR error is difficult. If the device isn't doing any other expensive tasks, the app widget would probably work just fine. However, if the device is in the middle of expensive CPU or I/O operations, the app widget can take too long to respond — causing an ANR error. To work around this problem, move any CPU- or I/O-intensive work of the app widget into an `IntentService` that can take as long as it needs to complete — which in turn doesn't affect the Home screen application.

Unlike most background services, which are long-running, an `IntentService` uses the work queue processor pattern, which handles each intent in turn using a worker thread, and it stops when it runs out of work. In layman's terms, the `IntentService` simply runs the work given to it as a background service, and then stops the background service when no more work needs to be done.

The `AppWidget` in this example isn't doing any I/O and isn't CPU intensive, so technically it probably doesn't need to use an `IntentService`. But it's more common that your widgets will be doing some amount of I/O, so it's an important design pattern for you to understand.

Implementing the IntentService

Create a new class called `AppWidgetService` in `com.dummies. silentmodetoggle.widget`, then type the code in Listing 7-3 into your code editor.

Listing 7-3:   The AppWidgetService

```
public class AppWidgetService extends IntentService {            →1

    private static String ACTION_DO_TOGGLE = "actionDoToggle";   →3

    AudioManager audioManager;

    public AppWidgetService() {
        super("AppWidgetService");                               →8
    }

    @Override
    public void onCreate() {                                     →12
        // Always call super.onCreate
```

(continued)

Listing 7-3 *(continued)*

```
        super.onCreate();

        audioManager = (AudioManager) getSystemService(        →16
              Context.AUDIO_SERVICE);
    }

    @Override
    protected void onHandleIntent(Intent intent){             →21

        if( intent!=null && intent.getBooleanExtra(           →23
              ACTION_DO_TOGGLE,false)) {
            RingerHelper.performToggle(audioManager);
        }

        AppWidgetManager mgr = AppWidgetManager.getInstance(this);   →28
        ComponentName name = new ComponentName(this, AppWidget.class);  →30
        mgr.updateAppWidget(name, updateUi());
    }


    private RemoteViews updateUi() {                          →35
        RemoteViews remoteViews = new RemoteViews(getPackageName(),  →36
              R.layout.app_widget);

        int phoneImage = RingerHelper.isPhoneSilent(audioManager)   →39
              ? R.drawable.icon_ringer_off
              : R.drawable.icon_ringer_on;
        remoteViews.setImageViewResource(R.id.phone_state, phoneImage);  →42

        Intent intent = new Intent(this, AppWidgetService.class)   →44
              .putExtra(ACTION_DO_TOGGLE,true);

        PendingIntent pendingIntent =                         →47
              PendingIntent.getService(this, 0, intent,
                    PendingIntent.FLAG_ONE_SHOT);

        remoteViews.setOnClickPendingIntent(R.id.widget, pendingIntent);  →51

        return remoteViews;
    }
}
```

The following list briefly explains the purpose of the major sections of code:

→ 1   The service that handles all your widget's operations. The intent sent to the service will tell it what you it want to do.

This service is an instance of IntentService. An IntentService is a convenient way to handle things that need to be done on background threads. Whenever a new intent is received, `onHandleIntent` executes in a background thread. This allows you to perform whatever operations you want to in the background — no matter how long they might take — without blocking the foreground UI thread (which would cause the app to hang).

→ 3   A flag that you set in your intent whenever you want to indicate that you want to toggle the phone's silent setting.

→ 8   All `IntentServices` need to have a name. Ours is called `AppWidgetService`.

→ 12   `onCreate` is called when the service is initialized, after the object's Java constructor.

→ 16   Just like in the activity, you'll get a reference to Android's `AudioManager` so you can use it to toggle our ringer.

→ 21   `onHandleIntent` is called on a background thread. This is where all your heavy processing happens. All `IntentServices` must override `onHandleIntent`.

→ 23   Checks the intent. If it says `ACTION_DO_TOGGLE`, then it toggles the phone's Silent mode. If it doesn't say `ACTION_DO_TOGGLE`, then this is just an update request, so it updates the UI.

→ 28   Gets a reference to Android's `AppWidgetManager`, which is used to update the widget's state.

→ 30   Updates the widget's UI. First, find the name for your widget, then ask the `AppWidgetManager` to update it using the views that you'll construct in `updateUi()` in line 35.

→ 35   Returns the `RemoteViews` that is used to update the widget. Similar to `updateUi()` in `MainActivity`, but appropriate for use with widgets.

→ 36   Inflates the `res/layout/app_widget.xml` layout file into a `RemoteViews` object, which communicates with the widget.

→ 39   Determines which image to use in the widget.

→ 42   Sets the appropriate image.

→ 44   Creates an intent to toggle the phone's state. This intent specifies `ACTION_DO_TOGGLE=true`, which you look for in `onHandleIntent` on line 23.

→ 47   Wraps the intent in a `PendingIntent`, which gives someone in another process permission to send you an intent. In this case, the widget is actually running in another process (the device's launcher process), so it must have a pending intent to communicate back into your service.

You should specify `FLAG_ONE_SHOT` to this intent to ensure it is used only once. There are some situations where a `PendingIntent` can be automatically retried on your behalf, and you want to ensure that you don't accidentally do a few extra toggles. See `http://d.android.com/reference/android/app/PendingIntent.html` for more information about pending intents.

→ 51   Gets the layout for the app widget and attaches an on-click listener to the button.

Working with the app widget's metadata

After you've written the code to handle the updating of the app widget, you might wonder how to list it on the Widgets menu. This fairly simple process requires you to add a single XML file to your project. This file describes basic metadata about the app widget so that the Android platform can determine how to lay out the app widget on the Home screen. Follow these steps:

1. **In your project, right-click the `res` directory and choose New⇨Android resource directory.**

2. **Name the folder `xml`, select XML as the Resource type, and click Finish.**

3. **Right-click the new `res/xml` folder, and choose New⇨XML Resource File.**

4. **In the New Android XML File Wizard, type `widget_provider.xml` for the filename.**

5. **After the file opens, open the XML editor and type the following code into the `widget_provider.xml` file:**

```xml
<?xml version="1.0" encoding="utf-8"?>
<appwidget-provider
    xmlns:android="http://schemas.android.com/apk/res/android"
    android:minWidth="40dp"
    android:minHeight="40dp"
    android:updatePeriodMillis="1800000"
    android:initialLayout="@layout/app_widget"/>
```

The `minWidth` and `minHeight` properties are used for setting the minimum amount of space that the view needs on the Home screen. 40dp represents the size of one widget "cell," which is all we need for this widget.

Your app widget can occupy one Home screen cell or many cells. This app widget is occupying only one. Your `minWidth` and `minHeight` should be set to `70dp*N - 30dp`, where *N* is the number of cells you want to occupy. For example, a widget that is one cell tall and two wide would be 40dp x 110dp.

The `updatePeriodMillis` property defines how often the app widget should attempt to update itself. You will want the widget to update itself periodically in case the user changes the state of the ringer using some other mechanism. Therefore, this value is set to 1800000 milliseconds — 30 minutes. Every 30 minutes, the app attempts to update itself by sending an intent that executes the `onUpdate()` method call in the `AppWidgetProvider`.

The `initialLayout` property identifies what the app widget looks like when the app widget is first added to the Home screen, before any work takes place. The initial layout is shown until the widget finishes updating itself.

An example of a longer delay is an app widget that checks Twitter for status updates. The `initialLayout` is shown until updates are received from Twitter. Inform the user in the `initialLayout` that information is loading to keep him aware of what's happening when the app widget is initially loaded on the Home screen. You can do this by providing a `TextView` with the contents of `"Loading . . ."` while the `AppWidgetProvider` does its work.

Registering your new components with the manifest

Anytime you add an activity, a service, or a broadcast receiver (or certain other items) to your application, you need to declare them in the application manifest file. The application manifest presents vital information to the Android platform — namely, the components of the application. The system doesn't recognize the `Activity`, `Service`, and `BroadcastReceiver` objects that aren't declared in the application manifest.

To add your `AppWidgetProvider` and `IntentService` to your application manifest file, open the `AndroidManifest.xml` file and type the code shown in Listing 7-4 into the already existing file. Bolded lines are newly added lines for the new components.

Listing 7-4:   An Updated AndroidManifest.xml File with New Components Registered

```
<<?xml version="1.0" encoding="utf-8"?>
<manifest xmlns:android="http://schemas.android.com/apk/res/android"
        package="com.dummies.silentmodetoggle">

    <application
        android:icon="@drawable/ic_launcher"
        android:label="@string/app_name"
        android:allowBackup="true">
```

(continued)

Listing 7-4 *(continued)*

```
        <activity
            android:name=".MainActivity"
            android:label="@string/app_name">
            <intent-filter>
                <action android:name="android.intent.action.MAIN"/>
                <category android:name="android.intent.category.LAUNCHER"/>
            </intent-filter>
        </activity>

        <receiver
            android:name="com.dummies.silentmodetoggle.widget.AppWidget"
            android:label="@string/app_name">                              →21

            <intent-filter>
                <action android:name=                                      →24
                "android.appwidget.action.APPWIDGET_UPDATE"/>
            </intent-filter>

            <meta-data
                android:name="android.appwidget.provider"
                android:resource="@xml/widget_provider"/>                  →29
        </receiver>

        <service android:name=                                             →32
            "com.dummies.silentmodetoggle.widget.AppWidgetService"/>

    </application>
</manifest>
```

The following list briefly describes each section:

→ 21   The opening element registers a BroadcastReceiver as part of this application. The name property identifies the name of the receiver — in this case, .widget.AppWidget, which correlates to the AppWidget.java file in the application. The name and label help identify the receiver.

→ 24   Identifies what kind of intent (based on the action of the intent in the intent filter) the app widget automatically responds to when the particular intent is broadcast. Known as an IntentFilter, it helps the Android system understand what kind of events your app should be notified of. In this case, your application is concerned about the APPWIDGET_UPDATE action of the broadcast intent. This event fires after the updatePeriodMillis property has elapsed, which is defined in the widget_provider.xml file. Other actions include enabled, deleted, and disabled.

→ 29   Identifies the location of the `widget_provider.xml` file that you recently built into your application. Android uses the `widget_provider` to help determine defaults and to lay out parameters for your app widget.

→ 32   The `<service>` element registers the `AppWidgetService` with your application. This is the background service that does most of the work for your widget.

At this point, your application is ready to be installed and tested. To install the application, choose Run⇨Run 'Silent Mode Toggle'. It should show up on the emulator. Return to the Home screen by pressing the Home key. You can now add to the Home screen the app widget that you recently created.

Placing Your Widget on the Home Screen

Adding a widget to your Home screen is easy — follow these steps:

1. **Open the application list on the Home screen of the emulator.**

2. **When the list of applications is visible, select Widgets.**

3. **Choose Silent Mode Toggle, as shown in Figure 7-1, and drag it to your Home screen.**

You have now added the Silent Mode Toggle widget to the Home screen. You can tap the icon to change the ringer mode and the icon changes accordingly. (Refer to Figure 7-2.)

Chapter 8

Publishing Your App to the Google Play Store

The Google Play Store is the official application distribution mechanism for Android. Publishing your application to the store enables your application to be downloaded, installed, and used by millions of users across the world. Users can also rate your application and leave comments about it, which helps you identify possible use trends and problematic areas that users might be encountering.

The Google Play Store also provides a set of valuable statistics that you can use to track the success of your application.

In this chapter, you publish your application to the Google Play Store. You find out how to provide a couple of screen shots, a promotional screen shot, and a short description of your application.

Creating a Distributable File

So you have a great idea, and it has led you to develop the next hit application or game for the Android platform. Now you're ready to put the application into the hands of users. The first thing you need to do is package your application so that it can be placed on their devices. To do so, you create an Android package file, or *APK* file, which you will do in the following sections.

Choosing your tools

You can build an Android APK file in numerous ways:

- ✔ Android Studio
- ✔ Command line with Gradle
- ✔ Automated build process, such as a continuous integration server

Really, these are just three different ways to kick off your gradle build.

In this book you will use Android Studio to create a signed APK file. Android Studio provides an array of tools that compile, digitally sign, and package your Android application into an APK file.

 Other options, such as using Gradle and continuous integration to build signed APKs, are used in more advanced scenarios. You can find more information about setting up a command-line build process in the Android documentation at `http://d.android.com/tools/publishing/app-signing.html`.

Digitally signing your application

The Android system requires all installed applications to be digitally signed with a certificate that contains a public/private key pair. The private key is held by the developer. The certificate that's used to digitally sign the application identifies developer and establishes the trust relationships between applications.

You need to know some key information about signing Android applications:

- ✔ All Android applications *must be signed.* The system won't install applications that aren't signed. By default, your apps are signed by a debug key generated by the Android SDK.
- ✔ You can use self-signed certificates to sign your applications; a certificate authority isn't needed.
- ✔ When you're ready to release your application to the store, you must sign it with a private release key. You cannot publish the application

with the debug key that signs the APK file when debugging the application during development.

✔ The certificate has an expiration date, and it's verified only at install time. If the certificate expires after the application has been installed, the application continues to operate normally.

✔ If you don't want to use Android Studio to generate the certificate, you can use standard JDK tools such as `keytool` or `jarsigner` to sign your APK files.

You can create modular applications that can communicate with each other if the applications were signed with the same certificate. This arrangement allows applications to run within the same process, and the system can, if requested, treat them as a single application. Using this methodology, you can create your application in modules, and users can update each module as they see fit — for example, to create a game and then release update packs to upgrade it. Users can decide to purchase only the updates they want.

The certificate process is outlined in detail in the Android documentation at `http://d.android.com/tools/publishing/app-signing.html`.

Creating a keystore

A *keystore* in Android (and in Java) is a container in which your private certificates reside. You can use a couple of tools in Android to create a keystore file:

✔ **Android Studio Generate Signed APK Wizard:** Creates a keystore and a key that will be used to sign your app APK.

✔ **Keytool application:** Lets you create a self-signed keystore via the command line. Keytool, located in the Java bin directory, provides many options via the command line.

Safeguarding your keystore

The keystore file contains your private certificate, which Android uses to identify your application in the Google Play Store. Back up your keystore in a safe location because if you happen to lose it, you cannot sign the application with the same private key. Neither can you upgrade your application because the Google Play Store platform recognizes that the application isn't signed by the same key and restricts you from upgrading it — the store sees the file as a new Android application. This also happens if you change the package name of the app; Android doesn't recognize it as a valid update because the package and/or certificate are not the same.

Keep your keystore safe! If your source code is open source, do not check your keystore into your source code. You don't want the whole Internet to have access to your keystore and be able to modify your app in the Google Play Store whenever it wants. If you ever lose your keystore, you will not be able to update app in the Play Store, and Google would not be able to help you even if they wanted to.

Creating the APK file

To create your first APK file, follow these steps:

1. Choose Build⇨Generate Signed APK.

2. Select the Silent Mode Toggle module and click Next.

The Generate Signed APK Wizard, shown in Figure 8-1, opens with the current project name filled in.

● ● ● Generate Signed APK Wizard
Module: 🗀 SilentModeToggle ⬍
? Cancel   Previous Next

Figure 8-1:
The Generate Signed APK Wizard.

3. Press the Create New button (as shown in Figure 8-2).

Or, if you already have a keystore, press the Choose Existing button instead.

4. Choose the location of your keystore.

Find your project directory (the directory above SilentModeToggle) and create a keystore there named `release.jks`, as in Figure 8-3. For example: `/Users/mike/Projects/android-for-dummies-v3/release.jks`.

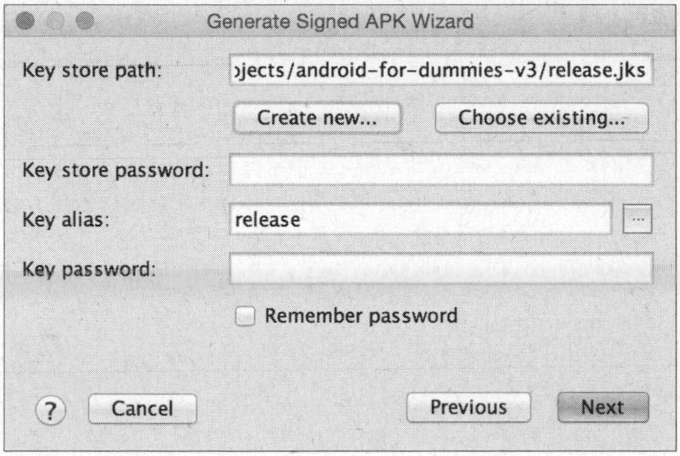

Figure 8-2:
The
Keystore
Selection
screen.

Figure 8-3:
The Key
Creation
screen.

5. **Enter a password that you'll remember, and reenter it in the Confirm field.**

   If using an existing keystore, you won't need to confirm your password.

   Your keystore file has been created, but now you need to create a key.

6. **Fill out the following fields:**

   • **Alias:** A simple name that you use to identify the key. Call it **release**.

   • **Password and Confirm:** The password that will be used for the key. You can use the same password that you used for the key-store, or you can use a different password.

   • **Validity:** Indicates how long this key will be valid. Your key must expire after October 22, 2033.

7. **Complete the certificate issuer section, filling out at least one of these fields:**

   • First and Last Name

   • Organization Unit

   • Organization

   • City or Locality

   • State or Province

   • Country Code (XX)

8. **Click OK.**

   You'll return to the Generate Signed APK Wizard dialog box, but this time the fields should be filled as in Figure 8-4.

9. **Optionally check the Remember password check box so that you don't have to retype it every time, and click Next.**

   If you don't have a Master Password configured for Android Studio, you may be prompted to set one so that Android Studio can remember your password securely.

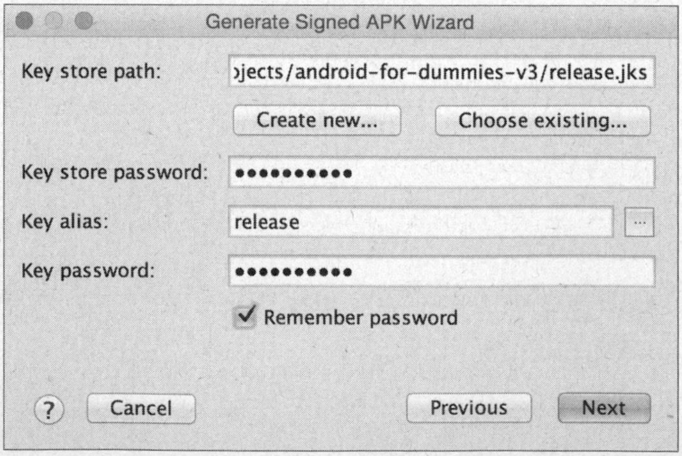

Figure 8-4:
The
Generate
Signed APK
Wizard
screen with
fields
filled out.

10. **Choose the APK destination folder and the Build Type as in Figure 8-5.**

    The location should be set to the `SilentModeToggle` directory, and the Build Type should be `release`.

11. **Click Finish.**

    The `.apk` file is created in your chosen location as well as a keystore in the location you chose in Step 4. Open these locations, and you can see a `.jks` file as well as an `.apk` file.

You have created a distributable APK file and a reusable keystore for future updates.

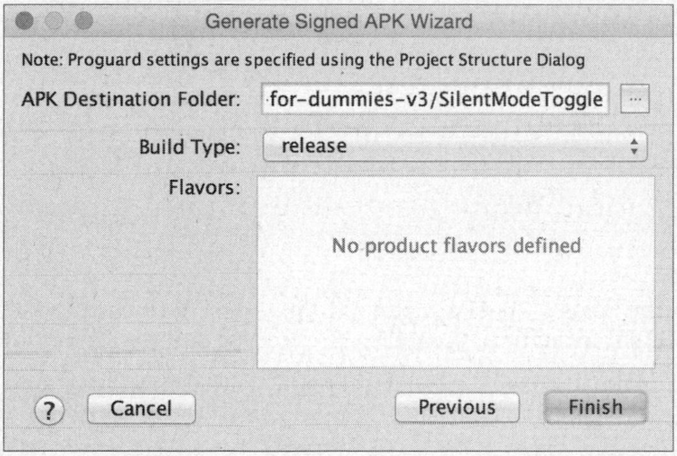

Figure 8-5:
Providing a
destination
for the
APK file.

Creating a Google Play Developer Profile

After you have created an APK file, you can release the application on the Google Play Store. To do so, you create a Google Play developer profile. To create this profile, you first need a Google account. Any Google-based account, such as a Gmail account, works. If you have no Google account, you can open a free one by navigating to `www.google.com/accounts`.

To create the Google Play developer profile, follow these steps:

1. **Open your web browser and navigate to** `http://play.google.com/apps/publish`.

2. **Sign in to your Google account.**

    If you're already signed in to your account, you go straight to Step 3 to fill in your developer profile.

3. **Check "I agree" to accept the terms of the developer agreement (Figure 8-6), and then click Continue to Payment.**

   If you don't pay the developer fee, you cannot publish applications.

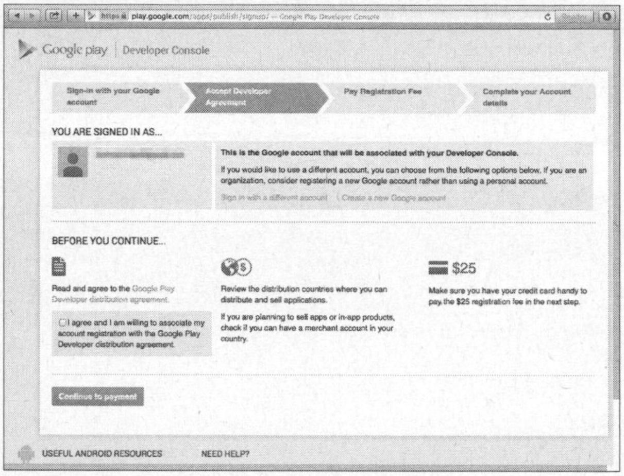

Figure 8-6:
The Google
Play
Developer
Console.

4. **On the Secure Checkout page, fill in your credit card details and billing information, then click the Accept and Continue button.**

   If you already have a credit card on file with Google, you may not see the page in Figure 8-7. If you already have a card set up, select one and continue.

5. **Fill out the following fields to complete your developer profile, as shown in Figure 8-8:**

   • **Developer Name:** The name that appears as the developer of the applications you release, such as your company name or your personal name. You can change it later, after you've created your developer profile.

   • **Email Address:** The email address to which users can send email with questions or comments about your application.

   • **Phone Number:** A valid phone number at which to contact you to discuss problems with your published content.

6. **Scroll down and click the Complete Registration button.**

   Congratulations, you are now a registered Android developer! The Android developer home page opens, as shown in Figure 8-9, where you can upload your application or set up a merchant account (which you need, if you'll be charging a fee for your apps). See the nearby "Google Wallet merchant accounts" sidebar.

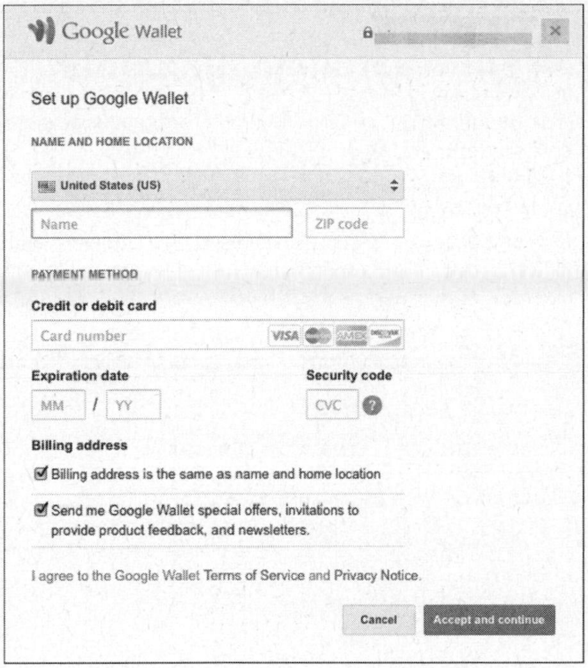

Figure 8-7:
Pay with
Google
Wallet.

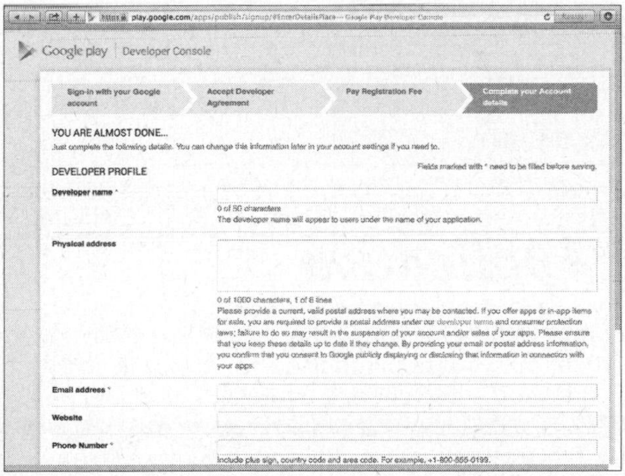

Figure 8-8:
Developer
listing
details.

Google Wallet merchant accounts

To have a paid application on the Google Play Store, you must set up a Google Wallet merchant account. To set it up, choose Setup Merchant Account from the Google Play developer console (refer to Figure 8-9) and provide these types of information:

✔ Personal and business name

✔ Tax identity (personal or corporation)

✔ Expected monthly revenue ($1 billion, right?)

After you have set up a Google Wallet merchant account, you can sell your applications.

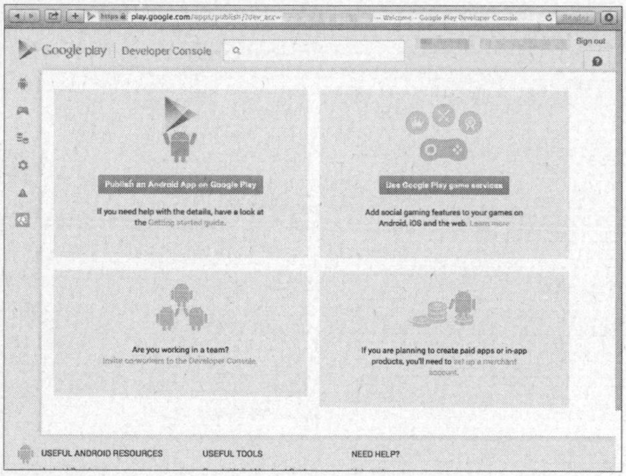

Figure 8-9: The Google Play Developer Console.

Pricing Your Application

So you have created an APK file and you're a registered Android developer. Now you're ready to put your app into users' hands. (Finally!) But you must answer one last question — is your app a free app or a paid app?

Make this decision before you release your app, because its price has psychological consequences for potential customers or users and monetary consequences for you. If yours is a paid application, you have to determine your price point. Only you can make this decision, so check out similar applications in the Play Store, and their price points, to determine your pricing strategy. The majority of apps are priced between $0.99 and $9.99. Keeping the pricing of your app competitive with your market is a game of economics that you have to play to determine what works for your application.

The paid-versus-free discussion is an evergreen debate, and both sides can be profitable. You only have to figure out what works best for your application, given your situation.

Choosing the paid model

If you choose the paid model for your app, you generally start seeing money in your pocket within 24 hours of the first sale (barring holidays and weekends). However, your paid application probably won't receive many active installs.

Users who download your app from the Google Play Store get a free, 2-hour trial period to try out your paid application. During the trial period, users can experiment with the fully functional application, and if they don't like it, simply uninstall it for a full refund. The trial period is extremely useful because users aren't penalized for taking your app for a brief test-drive.

Choosing the free model

If you choose to take the free route, users can install the application for free. Between 50 and 80 percent of the users who install your free app will keep the application on the device; the others will uninstall it. The elephant in the room now is the question of how to make money by creating free apps.

As the age-old saying goes, nothing in life is free, and the saying applies to making money on free apps. You have two basic options:

- ✔ **In-app purchases:** You identify different "upgrades" that users can buy when using your app, which are then managed via the Google Play Store.
- ✔ **Advertising:** Various mobile advertising agencies provide third-party libraries to display ads on your mobile application.

The top mobile advertising company is Google (`https://developer.android.com/google/play-services/ads.html`). Google offers useful SDKs and walks you through the steps to run ads on your native Android applications. Google pays on a net-60-day cycle, so you may have to wait a few months to receive your first check.

Getting Screen Shots for Your Application

Screen shots are a vital part of the Google Play Store ecosystem because they allow users to preview an application before installing it. Allowing users to view a couple of screen shots of your application can be the determining factor in installing your application. If you've spent weeks (or months) creating detailed graphics for a game that you want users to play, you want potential users and buyers to see them so that they can see the overall look of your app.

To grab real-time shots of your application, you use an emulator or a physical Android device. To grab screen shots with an emulator, follow these steps:

1. **Open the emulator.**

2. **In Android Studio, choose View⇨Tool Windows⇨Android.**

3. **Click the Screenshot button to take a screen shot.**

   After the screen shot is taken, save the file somewhere on your computer.

Uploading Your Application to the Google Play Store

You've finally reached the apex of Android application development: You're ready to publish the application. To publish your app, you'll need to collect the following information:

✔ The signed APK

✔ Your screen shots

✔ A description and promotional text for your application

✔ A promotional image used to advertise your app if it's featured in the Google Play Store

Publishing an application is easy — follow these steps:

1. **On the Android developer's home page (refer to Figure 8-9), click the Publish an Android App on Google Play button.**

   The Add New Application page opens, as shown in Figure 8-10.

2. **Click Upload APK, and choose the .apk file that you created earlier in this chapter.**

   No two applications can have the same package name in the Google Play Store. Therefore, if you try to upload the Silent Mode Toggle application at this point, you see this error message:

```
The package name of your apk (com.dummies.silentmodetoggle) is the same as
        the package name of another developer's application. Choose a
        new package name.
```

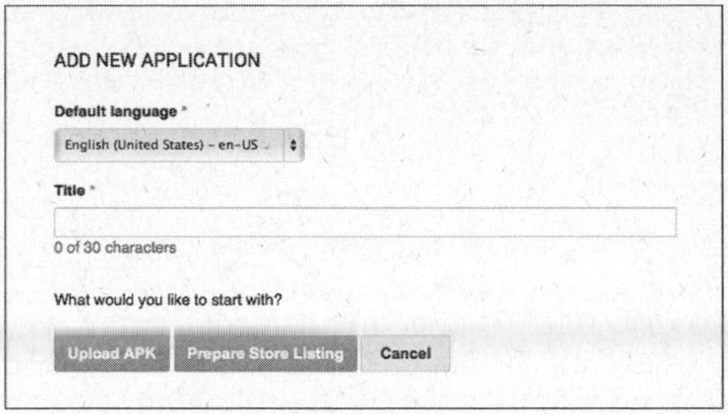

Figure 8-10:
The Add
New
Application
page.

When you upload an application that you've created, you don't see this message.

3. **Click Store Listing, and set the description for your application (see Figure 8-11).**

   Users see this description when they inspect your application to determine whether to install it. All this text is indexed for the Google Play Store search engine.

4. **Scroll down to the Screenshots section and add two screen shots from your application.**

   Apps with screen shots have higher install rates than apps without them. These screen shots allow users to preview your application in a running state without having to install your application.

5. **Add a promotional shot.**

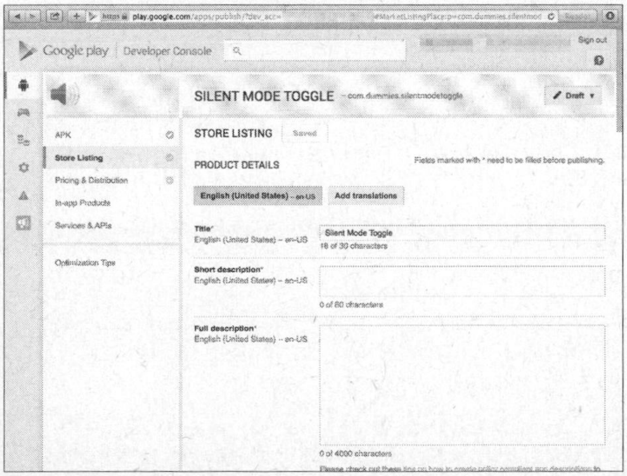

Figure 8-11:
The Store
Listing.

The promo shot is not a screen shot but rather an advertisement used for random promotions that Android chooses to showcase.

6. Upload a high-resolution app icon image.

Refer to Chapter 6 for instructions on how to create a 512-x-512-high resolution app icon.

7. Set the promotional text of your application.

Promotional text is used when your application is featured or promoted in the Google Play Store. Getting your application featured is likely based on the popularity of your application. If it's chosen to be featured in the promotional area of the Google Play Store (usually in the upper area of the screen of each category), the promo text shows up as the promotional component for it.

8. Set the application type, category, and content rating.

This app falls into the Applications type; if you have a game app, choose the Games type.

The Category is based on your application type.

The Content Rating helps to prevent kids from seeing things that are too mature for them.

9. Fill out the Web Site and E-Mail fields (and Phone, if you want).

These fields are used to contact you for various reasons, including app feature requests and bug reports. If you fill in the Phone field, remember that users can call to speak with you. If you're writing an app for one company and publishing it under your developer account, you can change the Web Site, E-Mail, and Phone fields so that users can't contact you.

10. Click Save, then click Pricing and Distribution (see Figure 8-12).

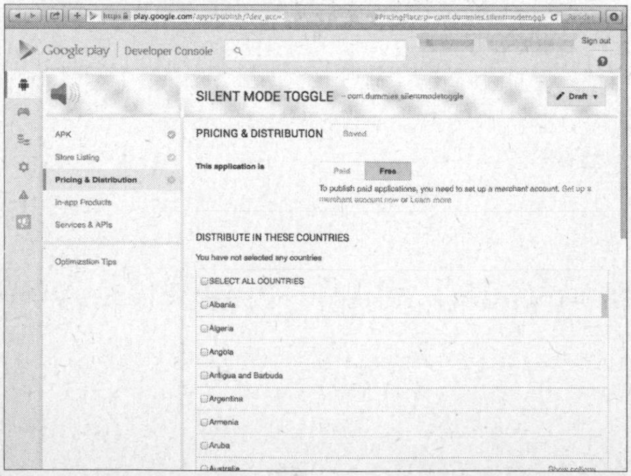

Figure 8-12:
The Pricing and Distribution page.

11. **Select the list of countries where the application should be visible.**

    For example, if your application is meant for an Italian audience, dese-lect All Locations and select Italy as the destination location, to ensure that only devices in the Italy region can see it in the store. If you leave All Locations enabled, all locations can (you guessed it) see your app in the store.

12. **Verify that your application meets the Android content guidelines and that you have complied with applicable laws by selecting the perti-nent check boxes.**

13. **Click Save, then click Publish.**

    Your application is published to the Google Play Store.

Figure 8-13 shows an application in the Google Play Store.

You've probably noticed a certain highlight in this process: It has no app-approval process (like a certain other platform does). You can create an app now and publish it, and users can install it within a few minutes or hours. You can then complete a quick release cycle and get new features out the door as quickly as you finish them — very cool.

Figure 8-13: The appli-cation is released in the Google Play Store.

Watching the Number of Installs Soar

You've finally published your first application. Now it's time to watch those millions start rolling in, right? Kind of. You might be an independent developer who's releasing the next standout first-person shooter game, or you might be a corporate developer who's pushing out your company's Android application. Regardless, to be aware of the user experience on various devices, you can identify how your application is doing in various ways using the Google Play developer console:

- ✔ **Five-star rating system:** The higher average rating your app receives, the more likely people will install it.

- ✔ **Comments:** Give people the courtesy of reading the comments they leave. You might be surprised at the outstanding ideas people provide to you for free. Users get excited about new features and return to the store to update their comments with a much more positive ratings boost.

- ✔ **Error reports:** Users who were gracious enough to submit error reports want to let you know that the app experienced a runtime exception for an unknown reason. Open these reports in the Google Play developer console, examine the error, review the stack trace, and fix the problem. An app that's reported to force-close frequently can quickly receive lots of bad reviews.

- ✔ **Installs versus active installs:** Though this comparison isn't the best metric for identifying user satisfaction, it's an unscientific way to determine whether users who install your app will tend to keep it on their devices. Users who keep your app probably like it.

- ✔ **Direct email:** Users will return to the Google Play Store to find your email address or website address and ask questions about features or send comments about their user experience. They may also send you ideas about how to improve your app or ask you to create another app that does something they cannot find at the Google Play Store. Reply if you have the time! Though maintaining an active dialogue with users is difficult if your app has a million active users, it makes users happy to know that they can contact you about issues with your app.

Staying in touch with your user base is a large task in itself, but doing so can reap the reward of dedicated, happy customers who refer their friends and family to your application.

Like the Google Play Store, the Amazon App Store for Android (one of the largest non-Google app stores for Android devices) offers applications for users to buy and install. Developers can sell their applications and receive a competitive rate for their apps from Amazon, or post free apps. Amazon also provides great sales metrics for developers and marketers. Find out more at http://developer.amazon.com. You can find out how to port your app to the Amazon App Store in Chapter 20.

Part III
Creating a Feature-Rich Application

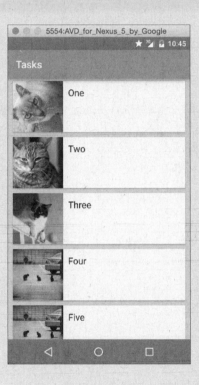

In this part . . .

Part III expands on the knowledge that you acquire in Part II by demonstrating how you can build a feature-rich application from scratch. By the end of Part III, you will have an advanced app that interacts with a local database, send notifications, and writes its settings to preferences.

Chapter 9

Designing the Tasks Application

*B*uilding Android applications is fun, but building truly in-depth applications is exciting because you dive into the guts of the Android platform. This chapter introduces you to the Tasks application, which you build in the next few chapters.

The Tasks application lets users create a list of tasks that can each have a reminder associated with them.

Reviewing the Basic Requirements

The Tasks application has a few basic requirements:

✔ Users must be able to add, edit, and delete tasks.

✔ Tasks must be easy to manage.

✔ Every task must have a reminder date and time when the user will be reminded of the task.

This application invites lots of interaction between the user and the Android system. The following sections delve into the features that you need to build in order to meet the above requirements.

Storing data

The task data and alarms needed to make the Tasks app work are stored in these locations:

- **Task data:** In a `ContentProvider` backed by an SQLite database. Android uses SQLite as its database. You will create a SQLite database to contain your task data, and you will then create a `ContentProvider` to access that database.

- **Alarm info:** In the `AlarmManager` after being pulled from the `ContentProvider`.

Scheduling a reminder script (That's alarming!)

For the Tasks application to work well, you need to implement a reminder system. The first thing that comes to mind is a scheduled task, or `cron` job. In the Windows operating system, you create a scheduled task to handle the execution of code and scripts at a given time. In the world of Unix and Linux, you use `cron` (short for the Greek word *chronos,* which means *time*) to schedule scripts or applications.

Because Android is running the Linux kernel, you might assume that Android uses `cron` to schedule tasks. Unfortunately, Android doesn't have `cron`, but instead it has the `AlarmManager` class, which accomplishes the same thing. The `AlarmManager` class lets you specify when things should happen, even if your app is not currently running. An alarm can be set as a single-use alarm or repeating. The Tasks application uses `AlarmManager` to remind users of pending tasks.

Notifying the user

After an alarm fires, the app has to notify the user of the alarm. You have two ways to grab the user's attention:

- **Toast:** A small view that contains a brief message for the user. The message is usually available for only a few seconds — a toast never receives focus. Because it shows up only briefly, it's good for showing users a message when you already have their attention, but it's bad at getting their attention when they're doing something else. The Tasks app uses a toast not for *reminding* users but instead for notifying users when their changes have been saved.

- **Notification Manager:** The `NotificationManager` class notifies a user that events have taken place. They can appear on the status bar at the top of the screen. Notification items can contain various views and are identified by icons you provide. The user can slide down the notification list to view notifications. The Tasks application uses the `NotificationManager` class to handle reminders. (See Chapter 1 if you're unsure how the notification area works.)

Creating the Application's Screens

The Tasks application needs two different screens to perform all its basic functions — create, read, update, and delete (CRUD) tasks:

- A list view that displays all the tasks in the application. This view also allows the user to delete a task by long-pressing the item.
- An edit view to allow the user to view or create a task, read a task's full details, or update a task.

Each screen eventually interacts with a database for changes to be persisted over the long-term use of the application.

Each screen consists of a single Android fragment that contains most of the user interface for the screen, and that fragment is contained in an activity. See Chapter 1 for more information about fragments.

You use fragments to reuse UI code between multiple activities. You will reuse the fragments you create here when you build tablet support into your app in Part IV.

Starting the new project

To get started, choose File⇨New Module and create a new module in your project. (If you're unfamiliar with how to create an Android project, see Chapter 3.) Choose Phone and Tablet as the module type, and use the settings in Table 9-1:

If you download the source code from this book's website, you can also open the Tasks example.

Table 9-1	Module Settings for Tasks
Setting	*Value*
Application Name	Tasks
Module Name	Tasks
Package Name	`com.dummies.tasks`
Minimum Required SDK	21

Choose Blank Activity when asked to add an activity, and use the following settings for the activity:

Table 9-2	Activity Settings for Tasks
Setting	*Value*
Activity Name	`TaskListActivity`
Layout Name	`activity_task_list`
Title	Tasks
Menu Resource Name	`menu_task_list`

Cleaning up the TaskListActivity

The `TaskListActivity` class that Android Studio generated for you is just a template, so you'll want to do a few things to fix it up before you go any further:

✔ **Change the package to** `com.dummies.tasks.activity`: Edit the `TaskListActivity.java` file, and change the package on the first line of the file to be `com.dummies.tasks.activity`. This will cause an error in the editor. Click on the error, and then press Alt+Enter to open the Quick Fix dialog box (see Chapter 3 to remind yourself how to use the Quick Fix dialog box). Choose Move to package `com.dummies.tasks.activity` to move the file to the proper directory. If you are given a choice between multiple directories, make sure you choose the directory path that contains `main` as in Figure 9-1. You may also need to update the entry for `TaskListActivity` in your `AndroidManifest.xml`.

✔ **Remove the menus:** Remove the `onCreateOptionsMenu` and `onOptionsItemSelected` methods. Also remove the `res/menu/menu_task_list.xml` file. You won't need them in this activity.

Your new `TaskListActivity` class now looks like Listing 9-1.

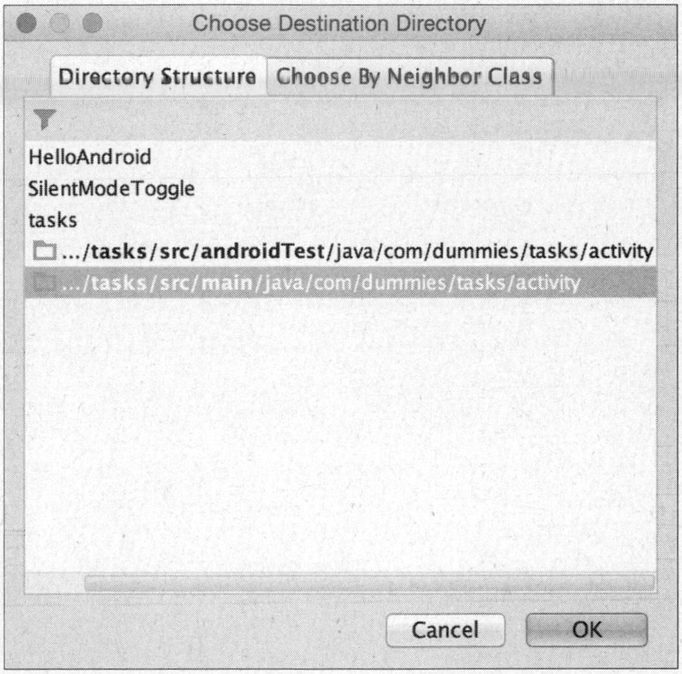

Figure 9-1:
Changing an activity's package.

Listing 9-1:   The ReminderListActivity Class

```
public class TaskListActivity extends Activity {

    @Override
    protected void onCreate(Bundle savedInstanceState) {
        super.onCreate(savedInstanceState);
        setContentView(R.layout.activity_task_list);
    }

}
```

Run it now and you will see the familiar "Hello world!" displayed on your device.

Editing the activity_task_list.xml layout file

Now that your activity runs, you will need to edit its layout file. The `TaskListActivity` will have a very simple layout consisting of a toolbar and a fragment. Open up `activity_task_list.xml` and edit the file to match Listing 9-2:

Listing 9-2:   The activity_task_list.xml Contents

```
<?xml version="1.0" encoding="utf-8"?>

<LinearLayout xmlns:android="http://schemas.android.com/apk/res/android"      →3
          android:orientation="vertical"
          android:layout_width="match_parent"
          android:layout_height="match_parent">

    <Toolbar                                                                   →8
        style="?android:actionBarStyle"
        android:layout_width="match_parent"
        android:layout_height="wrap_content"
        android:title="@string/app_name"
        android:id="@+id/toolbar"/>

    <fragment                                                                  →15
        android:layout_width="match_parent"
        android:layout_height="match_parent"
        android:id="@+id/fragment"
        android:name="com.dummies.tasks.fragment.TaskListFragment"/>           →19

</LinearLayout>
```

There are several things to be aware of in the previous layout file:

→ 3   The top-level layout for this activity. It is a vertically oriented linear layout that will contain the toolbar and the fragment.

→ 8   The toolbar for the activity. It won't be styled automatically, so set its style to the theme's `actionBarStyle`. Also, set its title to the app's name. Its id is set to `@+id/toolbar` so that it can be referenced later in the code.

→ 15   The fragment. A fragment of type `TaskListFragment` will be created using the default constructor, and attached to this layout. It is named `@+id/fragment` so that we can reference it later from the code.

> → **19** The `com.dummies.tasks.fragment.TaskListFragment` class
> does not exist yet, but you will create it in a subsequent section.

Setting the action bar

You need to tell Android how to find the action bar for the activity. Open up
the `TaskListActivity.java` file and modify your `onCreate` method to
add the line in bold:

```
@Override
protected void onCreate(Bundle savedInstanceState) {
    super.onCreate(savedInstanceState);
    setContentView(R.layout.activity_task_list);
    setActionBar((Toolbar) findViewById(R.id.toolbar));
}
```

This tells Android how to find the toolbar that you created in your layout,
and use it as your activity's action bar.

An action bar is a special case of a toolbar. You can have multiple toolbars in
your activity, but only one may be your activity's action bar. The action bar
is generally at the top of your activity.

Then open `res/values/styles.xml` and change your app's theme to be
the following:

```
<resources>

    <!-- By default, most apps for Lollipop and later should use
         some variant of android:Theme.Material.NoActionBar -->
    <style name="AppTheme"
           parent="android:Theme.Material.NoActionBar">
    </style>

</resources>
```

If there are any other `styles.xml` files in other `values` directories in your
module, delete them now. There should be only one, located in `res/values`.
So for example, if the New Blank Activity Wizard created a second `styles.`
`xml` in `res/values-21/`, you should delete it.

Creating the TaskListFragment

Fragments are the parts of your activities that are meant to be reused
throughout your application. Most activities have one or two fragments.

The list activity needs a fragment to display the list of tasks, so right-click on `tasks` (under `com/dummies`) in the Project view and add a new package named `fragment`. Then right-click on `fragment` and add a new Blank Fragment. Use the settings in Table 9-3:

Table 9-3   **Fragment Settings for TaskListFragment**

Setting	*Value*
Fragment Name	`TaskListFragment`
Create Layout XML?	Yes
Fragment Layout Name	`fragment_task_list`
Include Fragment Factory Methods	No
Include Interface Callbacks	No

The resulting fragment should look like Listing 9-3.

Listing 9-3:   **The TaskListFragment**

```
package com.dummies.tasks.fragment;

import android.os.Bundle;
import android.app.Fragment;
import android.view.LayoutInflater;
import android.view.View;
import android.view.ViewGroup;
import com.dummies.tasks.R;

public class TaskListFragment extends Fragment {

    public TaskListFragment() {
        // Required empty public constructor
    }

    @Override
    public View onCreateView(
        LayoutInflater inflater, ViewGroup container,
        Bundle savedInstanceState) {
        // Inflate the layout for this fragment
        return inflater.inflate(R.layout.fragment_task_list, container, false);
    }

}
```

Fish Creek Library
Self Checkout
January,24,2017 17:48

39065137557136 · 2/14/2017
Android application development for dum
mies

Total **1 item(s)**

You have 0 item(s) ready for pickup

Knowing when to use activities or fragments

Both activities and fragments are central parts of your user interface (UI) code. So how then do you decide whether to put certain functionality into a fragment or an activity?

If activities are the lunchbox of UI code, fragments are its Tupperware. You can insert your UI code directly into your lunchbox, but like an egg salad sandwich it would make a big mess all over your lunchbox. Put your UI code into your fragment Tupperware instead, where you can shift it from lunchbox to lunchbox as you need to use it again.

If you're absolutely certain that the code you're writing is specific to a given activity, put it directly into an activity. But if you're unsure, put your UI code in a fragment. In most applications, fragments contain all your UI code, and your activities contain only the glue that binds the fragments together.

If you run your app now, you should see a slightly modified message that now says "Hello blank fragment."

Making your fragment show a list

The goal of the `TaskListFragment` is to show a list of items. There are three things that need to be done for this to happen: Add a `RecyclerView` to your layout, create a view that represents a task in your list, and add an adapter to supply these task views to your `RecyclerView`.

Adding a RecyclerView

A `RecyclerView` is a neat view that can display an infinite set of items on your tiny little phone's screen. Because your phone has a limited amount of memory, it won't always be possible to display your entire database of tasks on the screen at one time without running out of memory. A `RecyclerView` takes care of this for you by only loading into memory the items that can fit onto the screen at any given time. As you scroll through your infinite list, items that fall off the screen will be purged from memory, and items that come onto the screen will be loaded into memory.

To add a `RecyclerView` to your fragment, first open the `build.gradle` file in your `Tasks` directory and replace the `dependencies` section with the following (or add a `dependencies` section at the end if one doesn't exist):

```
// Libraries that our app will use
dependencies {
    // recyclerview, cardview, and palette are all google libraries
    // used to create Android Lollipop apps.
    compile 'com.android.support:recyclerview-v7:21.0.3'
    compile 'com.android.support:cardview-v7:21.0.3'
}
```

In the old days, if you needed to add a library to your app, you would have to go out and find the library, download it, and copy it into your `sourcetree`. Not anymore! With Gradle, all you need to do is specify the name of the dependency you want, and Gradle automatically downloads it for you. For more information about Gradle dependency management, visit `http://www.gradle.org/docs/current/userguide/dependency_management.html`.

Then edit `fragment_task_list.xml` and replace its contents with a single `RecyclerView`:

```
<?xml version="1.0" encoding="utf-8"?>

<!-- Our recyclerview, which shows a scrolling list of items -->
<android.support.v7.widget.RecyclerView
    xmlns:android="http://schemas.android.com/apk/res/android"
    android:id="@+id/recycler"
    android:layout_width="match_parent"
    android:layout_height="match_parent"
/>
```

Finally, add the `RecyclerView` to your fragment by making the following edits to `TaskListFragment.java`:

```
public class TaskListFragment extends Fragment {

    RecyclerView recyclerView;

    public TaskListFragment() {
        // Required empty public constructor
    }

    @Override
    public View onCreateView(LayoutInflater inflater,
                             ViewGroup container,
                             Bundle savedInstanceState) {
```

```
        final View v = inflater.inflate(R.layout.fragment_task_list,
            container, false);
        recyclerView = (RecyclerView) v.findViewById(R.id.recycler);    →16
        recyclerView.setHasFixedSize(true);                             →17
        recyclerView.setLayoutManager(
            new LinearLayoutManager(getActivity()));                    →19
        return v;
    }
}
```

Things to note from the previous changes:

→ 16   Finds the `RecyclerView` in the layout and assigns it to the `recyclerView` field in the class.

→ 17   If all of a `RecyclerView`'s items are going to be the same size, the `RecyclerView` can cut some corners and improve performance by not having to re-measure the layout after displaying every item. All the items will be the same size, so turn on `setHasFixedSize`.

→ 19   Every `RecyclerView` needs to have a `LayoutManager` that tells it how to lay out the views. Because this fragment is just display-ing a list, use a `LinearLayoutManager`, which knows how to lay things out linearly in a list. There are other `LayoutManagers`, such as the `GridLayoutManager`, which knows how to lay things out in a two-dimensional grid, but for now all you need is the `LinearLayoutManager`.

Creating the item view

Each task in your `RecyclerView` must have a view to display it.

First, create a layout that's going to represent an item in your list. Create a new file named `res/layout/card_task.xml`, and add the following to it:

```
<?xml version="1.0" encoding="utf-8"?>

<android.support.v7.widget.CardView                                     →3
    xmlns:android="http://schemas.android.com/apk/res/android"
    xmlns:card_view="http://schemas.android.com/apk/res-auto"
    android:id="@+id/card_view"
    android:layout_width="match_parent"
    android:layout_height="100dp" >

    <RelativeLayout
        android:layout_width="match_parent"
        android:layout_height="match_parent">
```

```
            <ImageView                                                        →14
                android:id="@+id/image"
                android:layout_width="100dp"
                android:layout_height="100dp"
                android:scaleType="centerCrop"
                android:layout_alignParentStart="true"/>

        <TextView                                                             →22
                style="@android:style/TextAppearance.Medium.Inverse"
                android:id="@+id/text1"
                android:layout_width="match_parent"
                android:layout_height="wrap_content"
                android:maxLines="1"
                android:ellipsize="end"
                android:padding="10dp"
                android:layout_alignTop="@id/image"
                android:layout_toEndOf="@id/image"/>

        <TextView                                                             →33
                style="@android:style/TextAppearance.Inverse"
                android:id="@+id/text2"
                android:layout_width="match_parent"
                android:layout_height="match_parent"
                android:maxLines="2"
                android:ellipsize="end"
                android:padding="10dp"
                android:layout_alignStart="@id/text1"
                android:layout_below="@id/text1"/>

    </RelativeLayout>

</android.support.v7.widget.CardView>
```

Here is some more information about the code you just put into
`card_task.xml`:

→ 3 The card into which you'll place your task information. The view
is the same width as the parent and a height of 100dp.

→ 14 The image for the task. It's a cropped square image that fills the
height of the card. It's aligned to the far left of the card (the far
right in languages that read right-to-left like Hebrew and Arabic).

→ 22 The title of the task. You made it a little larger (`Medium`) than normal
text. You also used the `Inverse` color because the theme (`Theme.
Material`) uses light text on a dark background by default, which
is what you want; but if you did that on the light-colored cards,
then you wouldn't be able to read the text. A `maxLines` of 1 is set

to prevent wrapping of the title, and you've ellipsized the end if it exceeds one line. You placed the title to the right and aligned it with the top of the task image. You also gave the title a little padding on all sides to make it look good within the card.

→ 33 The task notes. You limit the number of lines to two and place them below the title and aligned on the left with the title.

Now that you have a basic `CardView` layout, add a little style to it by adding the following lines in bold:

```
<android.support.v7.widget.CardView
    xmlns:android="http://schemas.android.com/apk/res/android"
    xmlns:card_view="http://schemas.android.com/apk/res-auto"
    android:id="@+id/card_view"
    android:layout_width="match_parent"
    android:layout_height="100dp"
    android:layout_marginTop="@dimen/task_card_half_spacing"
    android:layout_marginBottom="@dimen/task_card_half_spacing"
    android:layout_marginStart="@dimen/gutter"
    android:layout_marginEnd="@dimen/gutter"
    android:layout_gravity="center"
    android:elevation="@dimen/task_card_elevation"
    android:foreground="?android:attr/selectableItemBackground"
    card_view:cardCornerRadius="0dp" >
```

The lines in bold in the previous block of code make a few visual improvements to the `CardView`. You added a margin on the top and bottom to create an empty space between items in the list, and added a gutter on the left and right. You're using an elevation to add a subtle shadowing effect. You set the foreground drawable to Android's `selectableItemBackground` so that you get a nice click animation when the user clicks on the card. You also turned off the default rounded corners for the card.

Now edit `res/values/dimens.xml` to create some of the values you just used in your layout:

```
<?xml version="1.0" encoding="utf-8"?>
<resources>
    <!-- The gutter on the left and ride side of most of our pages -->
    <dimen name="gutter">10dp</dimen>

    <!-- Half of the spacing we'll add between task cards.  The full
         spacing will be double this number. -->
    <dimen name="task_card_half_spacing">5dp</dimen>

    <!-- The elevation of our task cards -->
    <dimen name="task_card_elevation">6dp</dimen>

</resources>
```

Adding an adapter

A `RecyclerView` isn't very interesting without a list of data to display. To use a `RecyclerView`, you must create an adapter which will supply it with views of your tasks. An *adapter* is a class that knows how to read from a list of data somewhere (whether in a database, file, or wherever), and creates a view that represents an item in that list.

Create a new file called `com/dummies/tasks/adapter/TaskListAdapter.java` and set its contents to the following:

```
public class TaskListAdapter
    extends RecyclerView.Adapter<TaskListAdapter.ViewHolder>                    →2
{
    static String[] fakeData = new String[] {                                   →4
        "One",
        "Two",
        "Three",
        "Four",
        "Five",
        "Ah ... ah ... ah!"
    };

    @Override
    public ViewHolder onCreateViewHolder(ViewGroup parent, int i) {             →14
        // create a new view
        CardView v = (CardView) LayoutInflater.from(parent.getContext())        →16
            .inflate(R.layout.card_task, parent, false);

        // wrap it in a ViewHolder
        return new ViewHolder(v);
    }

    @Override
    public void onBindViewHolder(ViewHolder viewHolder, int i) {                →23
        viewHolder.titleView.setText(fakeData[i]);
    }

    @Override
    public int getItemCount() {                                                 →28
        return fakeData.length;
    }

    static class ViewHolder extends RecyclerView.ViewHolder {                   →32
        CardView cardView;
        TextView titleView;
```

```
        public ViewHolder(CardView card) {
            super(card);
            cardView = card;
            titleView = (TextView)card.findViewById(R.id.text1);          →39
        }
    }
}
```

Here's what the `TaskListAdapter` is doing:

→ 2   The `TaskListAdapter` is a subclass of `RecyclerView.`
         `Adapter`. `RecyclerView.Adapter` takes a parameter which
         represents the kind of `ViewHolder` that will be used by this
         adapter. The `ViewHolder` you will use is `TaskListAdapter.`
         `ViewHolder`, which will be defined on line 32.

→ 4   In Chapter 13 you will create a SQLite database that will contain
         all your task data. But for now, just use some dummy data.

→ 14   Every `RecyclerView.Adapter` must override
         `onCreateViewHolder`, which will be called whenever a new
         `ViewHolder` is needed. You must do two things to create a new
         view holder. First, you must inflate a `card_task` view. This
         `card_task` view will be reused over and over to display new
         tasks as they scroll onto the screen. Second, you must create a
         `ViewHolder` to wrap this `card_task` view.

         The purpose of a `ViewHolder` is to improve performance.
         Every call to `findViewById` is relatively expensive. By using a
         `ViewHolder`, you only need to make your calls to `findViewById`
         when the view is created in `onCreateViewHolder`, rather than
         every time a view is recycled in `onBindViewHolder`. Because
         you will create only a handful of views, this can be a significant
         time savings if you're scrolling through a nearly infinite list of
         tasks.

→ 16   Inflates the `CardView` from `card_task.xml` using a
         `LayoutInflater`. The call to inflate takes as parameters
         the XML file to inflate, the parent view to instantiate the right
         `LayoutParams` subclass, and `false` to indicate that this view
         should not be automatically attached to the parent (because the
         `RecyclerView` takes care of attaching and detaching the views).

→ 23   There will be roughly as many `ViewHolders` created by
         `onCreateViewHolder` as can fit on the screen at any one time,
         and each of these `ViewHolders` will be reused whenever a new
         item needs to be displayed. `onBindViewHolder` is responsible
         for recycling one of these `ViewHolders` and updating it to

display the information for the item that's currently being shown on the screen. The only thing that must be done to update the `ViewHolder` is to set its `titleView` to display the appropriate string from our `fakeData`.

→ 28   Returns the count of items in the list.

→ 32   The `TaskListAdapter.ViewHolder` class is a subclass of `RecyclerView.ViewHolder`. The purpose of the `ViewHolder` is to make it quick and easy to access the subviews in your `CardView` without having to call `findViewById` all the time. The two subviews you'll need access to for now are the `cardView` itself, as well as the `titleView` that contains the title of the card.

→ 39   Finds the `titleView` of the card by calling `findViewById` on the `cardView`.

Now modify your `TaskListFragment.java file` to add the adapter:

```java
public class TaskListFragment extends Fragment {

    RecyclerView recyclerView;
    TaskListAdapter adapter;

    public TaskListFragment() {
        // Required empty public constructor
    }

    @Override
    public void onCreate(Bundle savedInstanceState) {
        super.onCreate(savedInstanceState);
        adapter = new TaskListAdapter();
    }

    @Override
    public View onCreateView(LayoutInflater inflater,
                             ViewGroup container,
                             Bundle savedInstanceState) {

        final View v = inflater.inflate(R.layout.fragment_task_list,
            container, false);
        recyclerView = (RecyclerView) v.findViewById(R.id.recycler);
        recyclerView.setAdapter(adapter);
        recyclerView.setHasFixedSize(true);
        recyclerView.setLayoutManager(
            new LinearLayoutManager(getActivity()));
        return v;
    }
}
```

Now run your app. You should see something like what's in Figure 9-2:

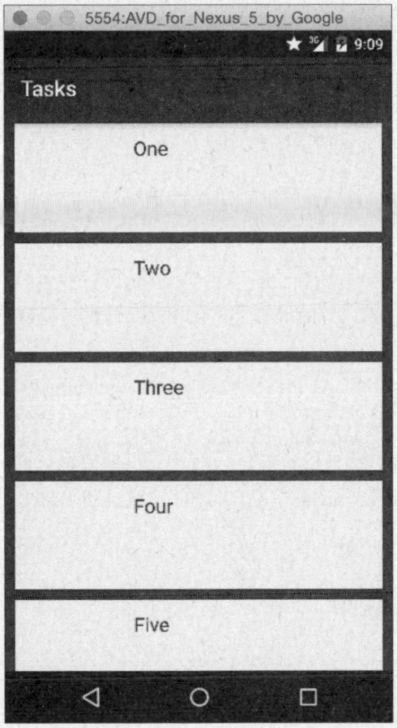

Figure 9-2:
The Tasks
app running
with fake
data.

The fragment lifecycle

Just like activities (see Chapter 5), fragments have their own lifecycle.

Like an activity, a fragment can exist in three states:

✔ **Resumed:** The fragment is visible in the running activity.

✔ **Paused:** Another activity is in the foreground and has focus, but the activity in which this fragment lives is still visible (the foreground activity is partially transparent or doesn't cover the entire screen).

✔ **Stopped:** The fragment is not visible. Either the host activity has been stopped, or the fragment has been removed from the activity but added to the back stack. A stopped fragment is still alive (all state and member information is retained by the system). However, it is no longer visible to the user and will be killed if the activity is killed.

(continued)

(continued)

Most of the fragment callbacks are very similar to the activity callbacks. However, there are some important differences. The three most common fragment callbacks are

✔ `onCreate`: Unlike an activity, fragments don't have a `setContentView()` method. Unlike activities, views are not created at all in a fragment's `onCreate()` method, so there is no way to manipulate views in `onCreate()`.

✔ `onCreateView`: To create a view in a fragment, override the `onCreateView()` method and inflate the view yourself, and then return it at the end of the function. See Listing 9-3 for an example. One important thing to note: Even though the views are created, they aren't fully constructed yet. If any saved state needs to be restored to the view (for example, if the activity was destroyed and re-created because of a screen rotation), that state isn't available until the next step.

✔ `onActivityCreated`: `onActivityCreated()` is the final step called before your fragment is fully created. At this point, your fragment is fully set up. Because of this, it's usually best to put most of the code involving views or saved state in `onActivityCreated()`.

Styling your activity

Now that you have a working list view for your tasks, it's time to make it a little bit prettier. Here's the list of changes you will make:

✔ Pick a color scheme for your app.

✔ Color the action bar, status bar, and navigation bar based on your scheme.

✔ Add an image to your cards.

Coloring your activity

Every Android app needs to have several colors defined:

✔ **Primary:** This is the main color of your app. You should set it to something distinctive that represents your app's brand. Your action bar will use this color to help users visually identify your app.

✔ **Primary Dark:** A slightly darker version of the primary color. Primary Dark will be used in the status bar above your action bar, as well as other places throughout your app.

✔ **Text Color Primary:** The main color for text in your app. There is also Text Color Primary Inverse for when you need to display text against a different colored background.

✔ **Accent:** An accent color that can be used to draw attention to things in your app. Typically, the accent color should be something bold and eye-catching.

✔ **Background:** The background color of your app.

You can see how these colors are used in a typical activity in Figure 9-3.

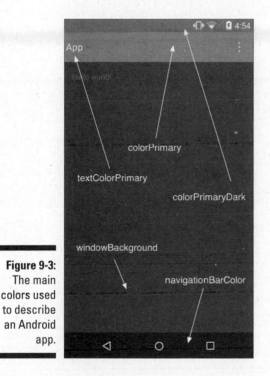

Figure 9-3:
The main colors used to describe an Android app.

Open the `res/values/styles.xml` file and edit it to look like the following:

```
<?xml version="1.0" encoding="utf-8"?>
<resources xmlns:android="http://schemas.android.com/apk/res/android">

    <!-- define your colors so that they can be referenced
        anywhere else you might need them -->
    <color name="primary">#1eabf2</color>                    →6
    <color name="primary_dark">#178acf</color>
    <color name="accent">#ffb936</color>
    <color name="window_background">#c1dae6</color>
```

```
        <!-- By default, most apps for Lollipop and later should use
            some variant of android:Theme.Material.NoActionBar -->
        <style name="AppTheme"
            parent="android:Theme.Material.NoActionBar">              →15

            <!-- your app's branding color (for the app bar) -->
            <item name="android:colorPrimary">@color/primary</item>

            <!-- darker variant of colorPrimary (for status bar, contextual
                app bars) -->
            <item name="android:colorPrimaryDark">@color/primary_dark</item>

            <!-- theme UI controls like checkboxes and text fields -->
            <item name="android:colorAccent">@color/accent</item>

            <!-- the background color of your windows -->
            <item name="android:windowBackground">
                @color/window_background
            </item>

            <!-- the background of the device's navigation bar (visible if the
                device doesn't have physical navigation buttons) -->
            <item name="android:navigationBarColor">@color/primary_dark</item>

            <!-- your primary and inverse text colors used in things like
                the actionbar.  These are commented out because we are
                happy with the default values. Uncomment and set your own
                colors if desired. -->
            <!--<item name="android:textColorPrimary">-->
                <!--@color/text_color_primary-->
            <!--</item>-->
            <!--<item name="android:textColorPrimaryInverse">-->
                <!--@color/text_color_primary_inverse-->
            <!--</item>-->
        </style>

</resources>
```

About this listing:

→ 6   First, you define the various colors that you will need to use
       throughout your app's theme.

→ 15   Now take the AppTheme you defined earlier in the chapter and
       update it to use the colors you defined in line 6.

Now run your app. You should see the same app as before, only now it will be using some prettier colors as in Figure 9-4:

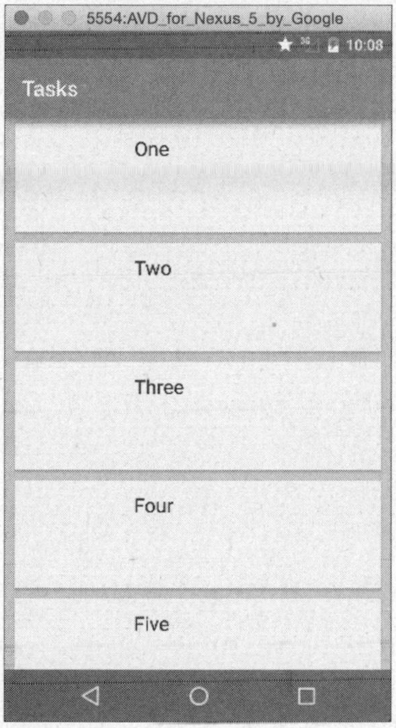

Figure 9-4:
The styled
Tasks app.

Adding an image

Most cards in a list view look better with an image. For now, there aren't any images for the tasks in the list, but you can add some dummy placeholder images and replace them later.

To do this, you will want to use a handy image library called Picasso. Add it to your project dependencies by opening `Tasks/build.gradle` and adding the lines in bold:

```
// Libraries that our app will use
dependencies {
    // recyclerview and cardview are google libraries
    // used to create Android Lollipop apps.
    compile 'com.android.support:recyclerview-v7:21.0.3'
    compile 'com.android.support:cardview-v7:21.0.3'
    // Picasso is a library from Square that makes downloading images easy
    compile 'com.squareup.picasso:picasso:2.4.0'
}
```

For more information on Picasso, visit `http://square.github.io/picasso/`

Now open up `TaskListAdapter.java` and add the lines in bold:

```
public class TaskListAdapter
    extends RecyclerView.Adapter<TaskListAdapter.ViewHolder>
{
...


    @Override
    public void onBindViewHolder(ViewHolder viewHolder, int i) {
        Context context = viewHolder.titleView.getContext();              →8

        viewHolder.titleView.setText(fakeData[i]);

        // set the thumbnail image
        Picasso.with(context)                                             →13
            .load(getImageUrlForTask(i))
            .into(viewHolder.imageView);
    }

...


    static class ViewHolder extends RecyclerView.ViewHolder {
        CardView cardView;
        TextView titleView;
        ImageView imageView;                                              →24

        public ViewHolder(CardView card) {
            super(card);
            cardView = card;
            titleView = (TextView)card.findViewById(R.id.text1);
            imageView = (ImageView)card.findViewById(R.id.image);
        }
    }
}
```

The new code does the following:

→ 8   Finds the context (the current activity) for the item in the list. Picasso will need the context later.

→ 13   Uses Picasso to load an image into the card's `ImageView`. All Picasso commands start with a `with()` clause, which instructs

Picasso which context to use to download the image. This generally is your current activity. Next, you tell Picasso which URL to load using the `load()` command. In this case, the URL comes from `getImageUrlForTask`, which hasn't been defined yet. Finally, you tell Picasso which `ImageView` to put the image into after it has been downloaded. Picasso then fires up an HTTP request on a background thread to download the image and displays it after it's available.

→ **24** Adds the `ImageView` to the `ViewHolder`. You previously defined the `ImageView` when you created `card_task.xml`, so all you have to do here is create a field for it and call `findViewById` to set it.

Because Picasso downloads images from the Internet, add the line in bold to your `AndroidManifest.xml` to give your app permission to access the Internet:

```xml
<?xml version="1.0" encoding="utf-8"?>
<manifest xmlns:android="http://schemas.android.com/apk/res/android"
    package="com.dummies.tasks" >

    <uses-permission android:name="android.permission.INTERNET"/>
```

This does everything that's necessary to display an image for each task. The only thing left to do is to determine *which* image to display.

Add the following method to `TaskListAdapter.java`:

```java
public static String getImageUrlForTask(long taskId) {
    return "http://lorempixel.com/600/400/cats/?fakeId=" + taskId;
}
```

This uses the `lorempixel.com` service to download a random 600-x-400-pixel cat image for the given `taskId`. Because cats. (If you prefer a different random image, you may also be interested in checking out `fillmurray.com`.)

You are now done styling your `TaskListActivity`! Run the app and you should see something like Figure 9-5:

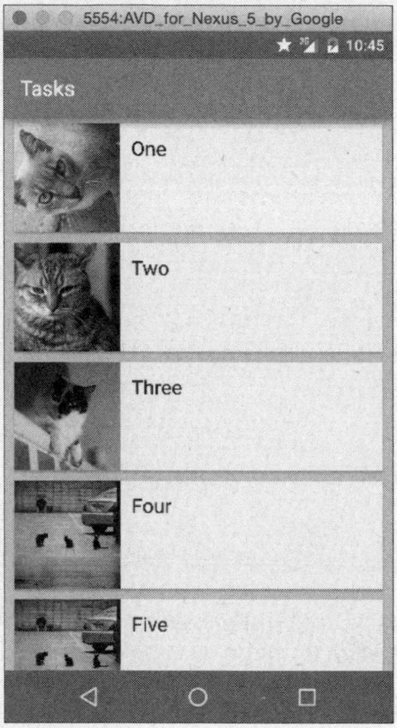

Figure 9-5:
The fully
styled
TaskList-
Activity.

Are you interested to learn more about how to style your Android app? There is a lot more information available on the web. Check out `http://android-developers.blogspot.com/2014/10/material-design-on-android-checklist.html` and `http://d.android.com/design` and `http://developer.android.com/training/material/index.html` for more information.

Chapter 10

Creating the Task Detail Page

● ●

In This Chapter

▶ Create the TaskEditActivity and TaskEditFragment

▶ Using the FragmentManager to start fragments

▶ Creating click listeners and starting activities

▶ Saving fragment state and restoring it later

▶ Transparent status, action, and navigation bars

▶ Using the Palette library

● ●

This chapter continues the Tasks app that you started in Chapter 9. You've already built a rudimentary list view for the app; now it's time to allow users to create and edit tasks.

This will require the following steps:

✔ Create a new activity and fragment to allow editing and updating tasks.

✔ Allow users to click on items in the list to open them in the editor.

Creating the TaskEditActivity

First things first, you will need a new activity to hold all this editing goodness. Right-click the `com/dummies/tasks/activity` folder and select New Blank Activity. Input the settings in Table 10-1:

After you've created the activity, delete the `onCreateOptionsMenu` and `onOptionsItemSelected` methods, as well as the `res/menu/menu_task_edit.xml` files. You won't be using them.

Table 10-1	Activity Settings for TaskEditActivity
Setting	**Value**
Activity name	`TaskEditActivity`
Layout name	`activity_task_edit`
Title	`Tasks`
Menu resource name	`menu_task_edit`
Launcher activity	`No`
Hierarchical parent	`com.dummies.tasks.` `activity.TaskListActivity`
Package name	`com.dummies.tasks.activity`

Add the lines in bold below, and your activity should now look like this:

```
public class TaskEditActivity extends Activity {

    public static final String EXTRA_TASKID = "taskId";                →3

    @Override
    protected void onCreate(Bundle savedInstanceState) {
        super.onCreate(savedInstanceState);
        setContentView(R.layout.activity_task_edit);
        setActionBar((Toolbar) findViewById(R.id.toolbar));            →9
    }

}
```

Some quick notes on the previous code:

→ 3 You use this constant later in the chapter, so add it in now to save yourself a little trouble later.

→ 9 Set the action bar for the activity to the toolbar in your layout. You will add a toolbar to your layout next. You may recognize this code from Chapter 9; you did the same thing there.

Now edit `res/layout/activity_task_edit.xml` and set it to the following:

```
<?xml version="1.0" encoding="uft-8"?>

<FrameLayout xmlns:android="http://schemas.android.com/apk/res/android"    →3
            android:layout_width="match_parent"
            android:layout_height="match_parent">
```

```
    <FrameLayout                                                →7
        android:layout_width="match_parent"
        android:layout_height="match_parent"
        android:id="@+id/container"/>

    <Toolbar                                                    →12
        android:layout_width="match_parent"
        android:layout_height="wrap_content"
        android:layout_marginTop="@dimen/status_bar_height"
        android:layout_gravity="top"
        android:id="@+id/toolbar"/>
</FrameLayout>
```

Some comments about the previous code:

→ 3   A view group that holds the fragment and your toolbar. Order is important: The first item in the `FrameLayout` is drawn first, and the last item drawn last. This means that the views at the top of the `FrameLayout` will be under the later views.

→ 7   This `FrameLayout` is an "anchor" into which the fragment is placed. It takes up the entire screen. Unlike `activity_task_list`, you do not use the `<fragment>` tag here because you do not want Android to auto-instantiate the fragment for you. Instead, you manually instantiate it so that you can pass in parameters to the non-default constructor (specifically, the ID of the task to be edited).

→ 12   This is the Toolbar view, which is placed at the top of the screen and in front of the fragment. Most of its styling settings are defined in the `AppTheme.TransparentActionBar` style in the `styles.xml` (which you set up later in this chapter). But you do need to add a little bit of buffer at the top of the screen to account for the status bar, because the status bar is translucent and content of the page has shifted up by a few pixels to slide under the status bar. To do this, create a new dimension named `status_bar_height` in your `dimens.xml` file and set it to 25dp.

Linking the List View to the Edit View

So you have a fancy new activity. Good for you. Now the question is, how do you get to it?

Because this activity will be used to edit tasks, you want to reach it from the list view you created in Chapter 9. To do that, you need to create an `OnClickListener` to listen to clicks on the list view (the `RecyclerView`), which then starts up the `TaskEditActivity`.

To do so, first open up `TaskListAdapter.java` and add code in bold to the end of `onBindViewHolder`:

```
@Override
public void onBindViewHolder(ViewHolder viewHolder, final int i) {          →2
    final Context context = viewHolder.titleView.getContext();

    viewHolder.titleView.setText(fakeData[i]);

    // set the thumbnail image
    Picasso.with(context)
        .load(getImageUrlForTask(i))
        .into(viewHolder.imageView);

    // Set the click action
    viewHolder.cardView.setOnClickListener(                                 →13
        new View.OnClickListener() {
            @Override
            public void onClick(View view) {
                ((OnEditTask) context).editTask(i);                         →17
            }
        });
}
```

Here's what this code does:

→ 2   The `i` parameter is used inside an inner class on line 17, so Java requires that you declare it final. Same thing for the context parameter on the next line.

→ 13   Here you set the `OnClickListener` on the `cardView` by calling `cardView.setOnClickListener`.

→ 17   The `OnClickListener` is going to ask the context (also the activity) to edit the task by calling `editTask` on the activity. The `editTask` method does not exist yet, but you will create it and the `OnEditTask` interface in the next section. Technically, you don't need an interface to use an `OnClickListener`, but using one here will be handy in Chapter 16 when you begin adapting your app for tablets.

Now that you have the `OnClickListener` set up, you need to create the `OnEditTask` interface so that it can be implemented by the `TaskListActivity`.

Create a new package named `com.dummies.tasks.interfaces` and add a new interface to it called `OnEditTask`. Edit the file to contain the following code:

```
public interface OnEditTask {
    /**
     * Called when the user asks to edit or insert a task.
     */
    public void editTask(long id);
}
```

Now if you go back to `TaskListAdapter.java`, it should compile fine. However, it won't run yet because you cast context to the `OnEditTask` interface, but your context does not yet implement `OnEditTask`. So modify `TaskListActivity.java` with the following changes:

```
public class TaskListActivity extends Activity implements OnEditTask {

    ...

    /**
     * Called when the user asks to edit or insert a task.
     */
    @Override
    public void editTask(long id) {
        // When we are asked to edit a reminder, start the
        // TaskEditActivity with the id of the task to edit.
        startActivity(new Intent(this, TaskEditActivity.class)
                .putExtra(TaskEditActivity.EXTRA_TASKID, id));
    }
}
```

Now run your app and try clicking on one of the items in your list view. You should then see a blank activity on your screen. You can press the Back button to go back to the list and try again with another item in the list.

Creating the TaskEditFragment

The edit fragment is going to do all the heavy lifting for editing tasks. It is the part of the app that knows how to display a detailed view of the current task and allow the user to edit it.

To create the edit fragment, first create the layout.

Creating the layout

Create a new file named `res/layout/fragment_task_edit.xml` and put the following in it:

```
<?xml version="1.0" encoding="utf-8"?>
<ScrollView xmlns:android="http://schemas.android.com/apk/res/android"    →2
        android:layout_width="match_parent"
        android:layout_height="match_parent" >

    <RelativeLayout                                                          →6
        android:layout_width="match_parent"
        android:layout_height="wrap_content" >

        <ImageView                                                           →10
            android:id="@+id/image"
            android:layout_width="match_parent"
            android:layout_height="wrap_content"
            android:minHeight="?android:actionBarSize"
            android:adjustViewBounds="true"
            android:layout_alignParentTop="true"
            />

        <EditText                                                            →19
            android:id="@+id/title"
            android:layout_width="match_parent"
            android:layout_height="wrap_content"
            android:layout_marginStart="@dimen/gutter"                       →23
            android:layout_marginEnd="@dimen/gutter"
            android:layout_below="@id/image"                                 →25
            android:hint="@string/title"/>                                   →26

        <TextView                                                            →28
            style="@android:style/TextAppearance.Medium"                     →29
            android:id="@+id/task_time"
            android:layout_width="wrap_content"
            android:layout_height="wrap_content"
            android:layout_below="@id/title"                                 →33
            android:layout_alignEnd="@id/title"                              →34
            android:layout_marginEnd="3dp"/>                                 →35

        <TextView                                                            →37
            style="@android:style/TextAppearance.Medium"
            android:id="@+id/task_date"
            android:layout_width="wrap_content"
            android:layout_height="wrap_content"
            android:layout_toStartOf="@id/task_time"                         →42
            android:layout_alignBottom="@id/task_time"                       →43
            android:layout_marginEnd="10dp"/>                                →44
```

```
        <EditText                                              →46
            android:id="@+id/notes"
            android:layout_width="match_parent"
            android:layout_height="wrap_content"
            android:layout_alignStart="@id/title"
            android:layout_marginEnd="@dimen/gutter"
            android:layout_below="@id/task_time"
            android:gravity="top"                              →53
            android:hint="@string/notes"
            android:minLines="5"/>                             →55
    </RelativeLayout>
</ScrollView>
```

Some additional information about the listing above:

→ 2   You place the entire edit fragment inside a scroll view. If you don't do this, the user can't see the bottom of the screen on small devices or when she is in landscape mode. Most screens should be wrapped inside a scroll view, except views like `RecyclerView` that have their own built-in scrolling.

→ 6   A `RelativeLayout` lets you position things directly relative to each other. It gives more control than something like a `LinearLayout`, which only allows you to position things in a line, one after another. To use a `RelativeLayout`, you utilize positioning commands such as `layout_below`, `layout_alignStart`, and `layout_parentStart`. You'll see examples of these commands in the child views of this layout. For more information about `RelativeLayout`, visit `http://d.android.com/guide/topics/ui/layout/relative.html`.

→ 10   This is the same image used on the list view, but here you show the full image instead of cropping it. When you downloaded the image, you made sure it was a size that fully filled the screen horizontally. You enable `adjustViewBounds` so that the `ImageView` shrinks or expands itself to properly fit the image after it's loaded. You set the `minHeight` to the height of the action bar, so that if the image isn't available yet, the action bar won't cover up the title field.

→ 19   Allows the user to edit the task's title. I provide hint text ("Title") which indicates what field the user is editing.

→ 23   Every well-designed page should have some margin on its left and right sides. This is called the *gutter*. This line tells Android to place a gutter of 10dp (defined in `dimens.xml`) on the left of the `EditText`. The next line adds the same gutter on the right.

TECHNICAL STUFF

You could also use `marginLeft` and `marginRight` rather than `marginStart` and `marginEnd`. However, it's better practice to use `marginStart` and `marginEnd`, because layouts that use start and end automagically work in locales where text is laid out right-to-left rather than left-to-right. Examples of right-to-left languages are Hebrew and Arabic. You might think you'll never translate your app to one of these languages, but it's better to follow the best practice just in case you ever find your app wildly popular in Israel or Saudi Arabia! See Chapter 17 for more information about using right-to-left languages.

→ 25   Positions the title directly below the image in the layout. All the layout parameters relate to the `Layout` view that this `TextView` is a child of, in this case a `RelativeLayout`.

→ 26   The hint text for the `EditText` displays a hint to users concerning what kind of information they can input into this field. For example, a hint might say "Phone number" or "(xxx) xxx-xxxx" for a field expecting a phone number in the U.S. The hint text appears in the `EditText` when the field is empty.

→ 28   The time button.

→ 29   The default text size is relatively small. Because the date and time `TextViews` are going to be clickable, you want them a little larger than normal. To do this, you change the style of the `textview` to use `android:style/TextAppearance.Medium`, which is a standard Android style for `TextViews`. The default is `android:style/TextAppearance.DeviceDefault`, but there is also `Large`, `Small`, and many others. See `http://d.android.com/reference/android/R.style.html#TextAppearance` for an exhaustive list.

→ 33-34   Positions the time button directly below the title, and aligns it to the right-hand side of the title as well. This puts the time on the far right side of the screen.

→ 35   Adds a little bit of extra padding to the right of this view to make the text line up with the horizontal line above it.

→ 37   The date button. You'll place this to the left of the time button.

→ 42-43   Positions the date button to the left of the time button, and aligns the bottom of the date and time so they line up.

→ 44   Adds a little padding to the right of this `EditText` to put a little space between the date and the time text. Without this space, the two sets of text look very crowded.

→ **46**   Allows the user to edit the task's notes. You'll place this below the title. You'll also give it a minimum of 5 lines of height to accommodate longer notes. You set the gravity to `"top"` to make the text align with the top of the text field because it looks better.

→ **53**   The default gravity for a `TextView` (as well as an `EditText`) is center. This looks a little funny for a multiline `TextView`, so change the gravity to `"top"`. You may recall using the `layout_gravity` parameter in Chapter 4. `layout_gravity` tells Android how to position the current view inside its parent, whereas the `gravity` parameter tells Android how to position the content inside the current view.

→ **55**   Make sure this `EditText` is at least 5 lines high. It expands to more lines for extra-long notes.

You used a couple of new strings in the layout, so open up `strings.xml` and add them there:

```
<string name="title">Title</string>
<string name="notes">Notes</string>
```

Creating the fragment

Now that you've created the layout, it's time to create the fragment. Create a new Java file in `com/dummies/tasks/fragment` named `TaskEditFragment.java`, and add the following to it:

```
public class TaskEditFragment extends Fragment {

    public static final String DEFAULT_FRAGMENT_TAG = "taskEditFragment";    →3

    // Views
    View rootView;
    EditText titleText;
    EditText notesText;
    ImageView imageView;

    long taskId;                                                              →11

    @Override
    public void onCreate(Bundle savedInstanceState) {
        super.onCreate(savedInstanceState);

        Bundle arguments = getArguments();                                    →17
        if (arguments != null) {
```

```
            taskId = arguments.getLong(TaskEditActivity.EXTRA_TASKID, 0L);
        }
    }

    @Override
    public View onCreateView(LayoutInflater inflater, ViewGroup container,
                        Bundle savedInstanceState) {
        View v = inflater.inflate(R.layout.fragment_task_edit,          →27
            container, false);

        rootView = v.getRootView();                                     →30
        titleText = (EditText) v.findViewById(R.id.title);
        notesText = (EditText) v.findViewById(R.id.notes);
        imageView = (ImageView) v.findViewById(R.id.image);

        return v;
    }
}
```

The class in the previous code does essentially two things. It knows how to

✔ Inflate the layout and find the views in the layout.

✔ Read the task ID from the fragment arguments.

Here are more details on the previous code:

→ 3   The "name" that you'll usually use to identify this fragment.
        You need this constant later in the chapter when you use the
        FragmentManager to add the fragment to the activity.

→ 11   The ID of the task being edited. When editing existing tasks, the ID
        is the ID of the task. When creating a new task, the ID is initially 0,
        but it is set to the new ID of the task after the task is saved.

→ 17   Sets the task ID from the intent arguments, if available. Fragments
        do not get their arguments from their constructors like normal
        Java objects. Instead, you must get and set their arguments using
        the getArguments and setArguments methods.

→ 27   Inflates the layout and sets the container. The layout is the view
        that you will return.

→ 30   From the layout, gets a few views that you're going to work with.

Those are the basics of creating a fragment that can show the details of a task.
However, there's one more very important step that you must not leave out.
You must remember to persist your in-memory state whenever the fragment
is destroyed, and use that persisted state (if it exists) when your fragment
starts up.

Saving your state

Android activities can be killed at any time to save memory when they're in the background. If the user returns to the activity, it may be re-created again. When it's destroyed, the Android OS automatically saves the current state of any views (such as `EditTexts`) that the user may have changed into the `outState` bundle. When it's re-created, those values are automatically set for you in `onCreate` from the `savedInstanceState` bundle.

However, although Android can save the state of views for you automatically, it cannot do that for non-views. So any time you have any state that you or the user may modify in your fragments or activities, it's UP TO YOU to make sure you save them properly! To do this, just save the value to the `outState` bundle, and then read it back in again from the `savedInstanceState` bundle in `onCreate`.

DO NOT FORGET TO DO THIS!

If you forget, your app will appear to work fine. You won't immediately notice anything wrong. But any time you rotate your phone, or leave an app running for awhile in the background and then later return to it, you may experience random crashes and unexpected behavior. It won't happen every time, and it will be very difficult to track down.

To make these situations easier to discover, you can enable the "Don't keep activities" option in the developer options for your phone. This tells Android to destroy each activity as soon as it goes to the background, as happens when your phone runs low on memory. If you hit the Back button to return to the activity, it is re-created from its `outState` bundle. See Chapter 5 to refresh your memory on how to access the developer options for your phone.

Saving your fragment's state involves two things:

- Overriding `onSaveInstanceState` to save any of your fields that may have changed while the fragment was running.

- Checking for any saved instance state when the activity is created in `onCreate`.

Go back to your `TaskEditFragment.java` and add the lines in bold:

```
public class TaskEditFragment extends Fragment {

    static final String TASK_ID = "taskId";                          →3

    ...
    long taskId;

    @Override
    public void onCreate(Bundle savedInstanceState) {
        super.onCreate(savedInstanceState);

        ...
```

```
        if (savedInstanceState != null) {                          →13
            taskId = savedInstanceState.getLong(TASK_ID);
        }
    }

    @Override                                                        →18
    public void onSaveInstanceState(Bundle outState) {
        super.onSaveInstanceState(outState);

        // This field may have changed while our activity was
        // running, so make sure we save it to our outState bundle so
        // we can restore it later in onCreate.
        outState.putLong(TASK_ID, taskId);
    }
}
```

→ 3   The name of the entry that you'll use to store the `taskId` when
        the fragment needs to save its state.

→ 13   Restores the `taskId` from `savedInstanceState`, if available.

→ 18   `onSaveInstanceState` is called whenever Android needs to
        destroy your fragment, most likely to free up memory. However, it
        may need to resurrect your fragment again later. You are respon-
        sible for saving any fields that may have changed into the bundle
        so that they can be used later when the activity is resurrected.
        See the "Saving your state" sidebar for more information.

Finally, there's one more thing you need to do in this fragment. Because the
fragment needs the ID of the task that it is going to edit, you need to create a
method that can create a new fragment for a given ID. To do this, add the following static factory method to the `TaskEditFragment` class:

```
public static TaskEditFragment newInstance(long id) {
    TaskEditFragment fragment = new TaskEditFragment();
    Bundle args = new Bundle();
    args.putLong(TaskEditActivity.EXTRA_TASKID, id);
    fragment.setArguments(args);
    return fragment;
}
```

You'll use this method in the next section.

But first, your page needs an image. Add the following to `onCreateView`:

```
// Set the thumbnail image
Picasso.with(getActivity())
    .load(TaskListAdapter.getImageUrlForTask(taskId))
    .into(imageView);
```

You Put the Fragment in the Activity and Shake It All Up

Now, you have an activity that you can reach by clicking on an item in the list, and you have a fragment that displays the details of an item, but you do not yet have any way to see the fragment from the activity. What you need to do is put the fragment in the activity.

You may recall from Chapter 9 that this was super-easy to do. All you needed to do was put a `<fragment>` tag in your activity's layout, and everything worked magically.

Things are a little more complicated this time around.

In Chapter 9, the fragment did not take any parameters, so it was easy to instantiate. The fragment in this chapter, on the other hand, does need a parameter. Specifically, it needs to know the ID of the task that's being edited. Because of this difference, you cannot just inflate the fragment in the layout. You must create the fragment programmatically using the `FragmentManager`.

Open up `TaskEditActivity` and add the lines in bold:

```
public class TaskEditActivity extends Activity {

    ...

    @Override
    protected void onCreate(Bundle savedInstanceState) {
        super.onCreate(savedInstanceState);
        setContentView(R.layout.activity_task_edit);
        setActionBar((Toolbar) findViewById(R.id.toolbar));

        long id = getIntent().getLongExtra(TaskEditActivity.EXTRA_TASKID,0L);
                                                                          →11
        Fragment fragment = TaskEditFragment.newInstance(id);

        String fragmentTag = TaskEditFragment.DEFAULT_FRAGMENT_TAG;       →14

        if (savedInstanceState == null)                                  →16
            getFragmentManager().beginTransaction().add(
                R.id.container,
                fragment,
                fragmentTag).commit();
    }

}
```

In brief, you are getting the ID of the task from the activity's intent extras, using that ID to create a new `TaskEditFragment`, and then using the `FragmentManager` to add the fragment to your activity in a fragment transaction. Some comments about the code are

→ 11   Creates a new edit fragment for the specified task ID.

→ 14   The tag that you'll use to add the fragment to the activity. This allows you to reference this fragment from other fragments, such as the Date and Time picker dialog fragments, which you will create in Chapter 12.

→ 16   Adds the fragment if it has not already been added to the `FragmentManager`. If you don't do this, a new fragment will be added every time this method is called (such as on orientation change). The `FragmentManager` saves previously added fragments to the `savedInstanceState`. So if `savedInstanceState` is `null`, you know there were no previous fragments. The fragment is attached as a child of the `container` view.

Updating the Styles

You're close to being able to view your handiwork. You can run it now, but there will be some bugs because there are a couple of changes you need to make to your activity's style.

This activity is a bit different from the list activity, so it should have a different style. Because the page is a detail view, you should remove as much of the app's distracting "chrome" from the page as possible, so that users can focus on their beautiful content. Things like the action bar, the status bar, and the navigation bar are all going to be reduced in prominence. You wouldn't want to do this on every page of your app because that chrome can give users a visual indication of where they are in the app and what app they're using, but it can be a powerful technique if used judiciously.

Open `styles.xml` and add the following to the bottom of the file:

```
<!-- A variation of the AppTheme, but with a transparent (clear)
     ActionBar. Also has a translucent (grey) status and navigation
     bar. -->
<style name="AppTheme.TransparentActionBar" parent="AppTheme">          →4
    <item name="android:windowTranslucentStatus">true</item>
```

```
            <item name="android:windowActionBarOverlay">true</item>            →6
            <item name="android:windowTranslucentNavigation">true</item>
            <item name="android:actionBarStyle">@style/TransparentActionBar</item>
                                                                                →8
     </style>

     <!-- The TransparentActionBar style used by
          AppTheme.TransparentActionBar -->
     <style name="TransparentActionBar" parent="android:Theme.Material">
         <item name="android:background">@android:color/transparent</item>      →14

     </style>
```

About the previous code:

→ **4**   This style definition is for activities that want a transparent action
           bar. It also uses a translucent (slightly opaque) status and naviga-
           tion bar. Notice that it inherits from the `AppTheme` you created in
           Chapter 9.

→ **6**   Normally the action bar is at the top of the page, and all the
           other content (such as the image) is arranged below it. However,
           because the action bar is transparent, you want to move the image
           all the way up to the top of the screen so that it is under the action
           bar. Setting the action bar to `windowActionBarOverlay=true`
           is the way to do that.

→ **8**   The way to make the action bar transparent is to set its style,
           so set the action bar style to a style that you will create on
           line 14.

→ **14**   Sets the background color of the action bar style to
           `transparent`.

Next, update the following lines in your `AndroidManifest.xml`:

```
    <activity
        android:theme="@style/AppTheme.TransparentActionBar"
        android:name="com.dummies.tasks.activity.TaskEditActivity"
        android:label=""
        android:parentActivityName=
            "com.dummies.tasks.activity.TaskListActivity">
    ...
```

Now run your app! You should be able to click on any item in the list and have it open a blank edit fragment like Figure 10-1:

Figure 10-1:
The blank
Edit activity
and frag-
ment.

A Special Bonus

There's a fun library called Palette that scans an image and picks out a few key colors. Try using this library to add some dynamic color to your fragment.

First, add the library to your dependencies in `build.gradle`:

```
compile 'com.android.support:palette-v7:21.0.3'
```

Then, update your call to Picasso in `TaskEditFragment.java` to be like the following:

```
        Picasso.with(getActivity())
            .load(TaskListAdapter.getImageUrlForTask(taskId))
            .into(
                imageView, new Callback() {                      →4
                    @Override
                    public void onSuccess() {                     →6
```

```
        Activity activity = getActivity();

        if (activity == null)                          →9
            return;

        // Set the colors of the activity based on the
        // colors of the image, if available
        Bitmap bitmap = ((BitmapDrawable) imageView
            .getDrawable())
            .getBitmap();                              →16
        Palette palette                                →17
            = Palette.generate(bitmap, 32);
        int bgColor = palette.getLightMutedColor(0);

        if (bgColor != 0) {
            rootView.setBackgroundColor(bgColor);      →22
        }
    }

    @Override
    public void onError() {
        // do nothing, we'll use the default colors
    }
});
```

What is this code doing?

→ **4**   Like before, you're still telling Picasso to load the image "into" the `imageView`. However, this time you're also adding a callback, which is invoked when the image is done loading. This callback is where you do the magic if you are inspecting the image for colors.

→ **6**   The callback has two methods: `onSuccess` and `onError`. If the image successfully loaded, `onSuccess` is called so that you can inspect the image. If there was an error, you do nothing.

→ **9**   Because Picasso downloads images in the background, you can't be sure that the user didn't close the activity while the images were loading. If he did, you will bomb out, so do a sanity check to be sure.

→ **16**   You'll get the image from the `imageView` because it's not passed into the callback for you directly.

→ **17**   Uses the Palette library to generate a color palette for the image. From that palette, you'll pick out the "light muted color" to use as the background for your activity.

→ **22**   If Palette can find a color for you, then use it to set your background. Palette is usually but not always successful at finding colors.

For more information about the Palette library, visit `https://d.android.com/reference/android/support/v7/graphics/Palette.html`.

Chapter 11

Going a la Carte with Your Menu

In This Chapter

▶ Building an Options menu

▶ Creating a long-press action

*E*very good Android application includes menus. If you have an Android device and you've downloaded a few applications from the Google Play Store, you've probably encountered plenty of menu implementations. You'll recognize them by their icons or text in the action bar, or their text in the drop-down overflow menu on the far right of the action bar.

Activities and fragments can both have menus, in which case they'll both be combined into one. In this chapter, you add option and context menus to the fragments in the Tasks app, but you could just as easily add them to an activity, too.

Understanding Options and Context Menus

Android provides a simple mechanism for you to add menus to your applications. This is the Options menu (also known as the action bar menu). This is, most likely, the most common type of menu that you'll work with. It's the primary menu for an activity or fragment.

The Options menu is in the action bar at the top of the screen (read more about the action bar in Chapter 1). Figure 11-1 shows the Options menu with the overflow menu collapsed and expanded.

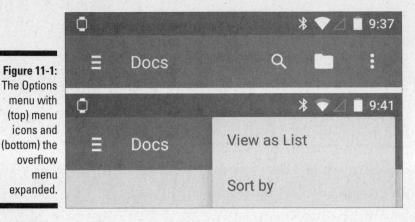

Figure 11-1:
The Options
menu with
(top) menu
icons and
(bottom) the
overflow
menu
expanded.

Android 2.x and earlier didn't have an action bar, so menus on those devices showed up behind a dedicated hardware menu button and were shown at the bottom of the screen in a grid of icons. Most apps won't need to worry about Android 2.x at this point. If you want to learn more about supporting older versions of Android, see Chapter 17.

You have two choices when making Options menus:

✔ **Show in action bar or put in the overflow menu:** Options menu items can either be shown in the action bar, as is the case with the magnifying glass and folder icons in Figure 11-1, or displayed in the overflow menu. Use the action bar for the one or two most important actions that can be taken in your activity. For anything less important, use the overflow menu. It's important to not overload your action bar with a ton of menu options, both because you have limited real estate, but also because too many options can be overwhelming to the user.

✔ **Icon or Text:** For option menus that are shown in the action bar, you have a choice between using an icon or using text. Icons are generally preferable, but in the case where you have only a single action in the action bar, it often makes sense to use text. For example, an app might have a single action called "Save" in the action bar, but you wouldn't want to have multiple text actions such as "Save" and "Share" because the text can start to get crowded.

Creating Your First Menu

You can create a menu through code or through an XML file that's provided in the res/menu directory. The preferred method of creating a menu is to define it through XML and then inflate it into a Java object that you can interact with. This helps separate the menu definition from the application code.

Defining the XML file

To define an XML menu, follow these steps:

1. **Create a menu folder in the res directory.**

2. **Add a file by the name of menu_list.xml to the menu directory.**

3. **Type the following code into the menu_list.xml file:**

```xml
<?xml version="1.0" encoding="utf-8"?>
<!-- Our default menu, which we'll load into the action bar of our main
     app activity -->
<menu xmlns:android="http://schemas.android.com/apk/res/android">

    <!-- The Insert button, used to create a new task. This button
         is important and small, so we'll force it to always be
         in the action bar. In general, you should try to have as
         few items as possible configured with showAsAction=always.
         We'll use the default Add button icon that ships with
         Android. If you want to see what other drawables Android
         ships with, you can look in
         $ANDROID_SDK/platforms/android-*/res/drawable-*
         -->
    <item
        android:id="@+id/menu_insert"
        android:icon="@android:drawable/ic_menu_add"
        android:showAsAction="always"
        android:title="@string/menu_insert"/>

</menu>
```

Notice that a new string resource is included (shown in bold). You'll create that in Step 4. The android:icon value is a built-in Android icon. The ldpi, mdpi, hdpi, xhdi, and so on, versions of this icon are all built into the Android platform, so you don't have to provide this bitmap in your drawable resources. To view other available resources, view the android.R.drawable documentation at

`http://d.android.com/reference/android/R.drawable.html`

All resources in the android.R class (as opposed to your own app's R class) give your application a common user interface and user experience with the Android platform.

4. **Create a new string resource with the name menu_insert with the value of Add Task in the strings.xml resource file.**

5. **Open the `TaskListFragment` class and add the following method:**

```
@Override
public void onActivityCreated(Bundle savedInstanceState) {
    super.onActivityCreated(savedInstanceState);
    setHasOptionsMenu(true);
}
```

`setHasOptionsMenu()` tells the activity that this fragment has an Options menu to show in the action bar. You place this call in `onActivityCreated` to be sure that the activity has finished calling its own `onCreate` before you call `setHasOptionsMenu`.

6. **Add the `onCreateOptionsMenu()` method to your class:**

```
@Override
public void onCreateOptionsMenu(Menu menu, MenuInflater inflater) {
    super.onCreateOptionsMenu(menu,inflater);
    inflater.inflate(R.menu.menu_list, menu);
}
```

The `MenuInflater` inflates the XML menu created earlier and adds it to the menu that was passed as an argument to the method call.

7. **Install the application in the emulator, and click the Menu button.**

Figure 11-2 shows the Add Task menu icon that you just created. If you long-press on the icon, you can see the text "Add Task".

Figure 11-2:
The Add
Task menu
icon.

Handling user actions

After you've created the menu, you then have to add what happens when a user clicks it. To do this, type the following code at the end of the `TaskListFragment` Java file:

```
@Override
public boolean onOptionsItemSelected(MenuItem item) {          →2
    switch (item.getItemId()) {                                →3
        case R.id.menu_insert:
```

```
            ((OnEditTask) getActivity()).editTask(0);              →5
            return true;                                           →6
    }

        return super.onOptionsItemSelected(item);                  →9
    }
```

The lines of code are explained in detail here:

→ 2   This is the method that's called when a menu item is selected. The item parameter identifies which menu item the user tapped.

→ 3   To determine which item you're working with, compare the ID of the menu items with the known menu items you have. Therefore, a switch statement is used to check each possible valid case. You obtain the menu's ID through the MenuItem method getItemId().

→ 5   If the user selected the Add Task menu item, the application is instructed to create a task through the editTask() method (defined in Chapter 10). By convention, calling editTask() with an ID of 0 means the app should create a new task.

→ 6   This line returns true to inform the onMenuItemSelected() method that a menu selection was handled.

→ 9   If the menu selection and return isn't handled earlier, the parent class tries to handle the menu item.

If you run your app, you will now be able to access the edit screen of the app by pressing the Add Task button in the action bar. You won't actually be able to create a new task, of course, because the app is using hardcoded dummy data for now, but you will be able to after you create your database in Chapter 13.

Creating your second menu

One good thing deserves another. Why stop at one menu when you could have two? In particular, your edit page needs an option to allow users to save their changes.

In this section, you will create a menu programmatically instead of using XML.

Open `TaskEditFragment.java` and add the following methods and constant:

```
private static final int MENU_SAVE = 1;                                          →1

@Override
public void onActivityCreated(Bundle savedInstanceState) {                       →4
    super.onActivityCreated(savedInstanceState);
    setHasOptionsMenu(true);
}

@Override
public void onCreateOptionsMenu(Menu menu, MenuInflater inflater) {
    super.onCreateOptionsMenu(menu, inflater);

    menu.add(0, MENU_SAVE, 0, R.string.confirm)                                  →13
            .setShowAsAction(MenuItem.SHOW_AS_ACTION_ALWAYS);                     →14
}
```

There are some differences from the previous menu:

→ **1**   Creates a constant `int` that will represent the Save menu. Each menu item within an activity should have a unique integer.

→ **4**   The `onActivityCreated` method is identical to the one you added to `TaskListFragment` in the previous section.

→ **13**   Creates a menu item named "Save" and gives it an id of 1. If you have multiple menu items, it's a good practice to create `static final ints` to name them.

→ **14**   `setShowAsAction` has several possible values that determine the way that the menu item appears in the action bar:

- `ifRoom`: Only place this item in the action bar if there is room for it.

- `withText`: Also include the title text (defined by `android:title`) with the action item. You can include this value along with one of the others as a flag set, by separating them with a pipe (|).

- `never`: Never place this item in the action bar.

- `always`: Always place this item in the action bar. Avoid using this unless it's critical that the item always appear in the action bar. Setting multiple items to always appear as action items can result in them overlapping with other UI in the action bar. In this case, because the Save option is a critical piece of UI functionality that we never want hidden, it's okay to use `always`.

- collapseActionView: The action view associated with this action item (as declared by android:actionLayout or android:actionViewClass) is collapsible. This is a more advanced option used for custom menu items.

You added a new string, so add it to strings.xml:

```
<string name="confirm">Save</string>
```

Now, add the following method to handle the menu option when it is selected:

```
@Override
public boolean onOptionsItemSelected(MenuItem item) {
    switch(item.getItemId()) {
        // The Save button was pressed
        case MENU_SAVE:                                          →5
            //save();                                            →6

            ((OnEditFinished) getActivity()).finishEditingTask();   →8

            return true;
    }

    return super.onOptionsItemSelected(item);                    →13
}
```

The onOptionsItemSelected method for TaskEditFragment is similar to the one you added to TaskListFragment, but it has some differences:

→ 5   Was onOptionItemsSelected called with a menu ID of MENU_SAVE? If so, then . . .

→ 6   . . . call the save method. But really, the save method is commented out for now because the Tasks app is using dummy data and does not yet have a way to save items. That will be added in Chapter 13.

→ 8   Tells the enclosing activity that you are done so that it can clean up whatever it needs to clean up. You will implement this method later in this section.

→ 13 If you can't handle this menu item, see if your parent can return super.onOptionsItemSelected(item);.

The previous code handles most of the things necessary to implement a Save menu item for the fragment. The one thing that remains is to figure out what to do after the Save button has been clicked. In this case, the activity should close and return the user to the previous activity. Much like you did when you created the `OnEditTask` interface in Chapter 10, you will create an interface named `OnEditFinished` that has a method called `finishEditingTask()` that handles this behavior. In Chapter 16, you will make `finishEditingTask` do something different for tablets, but for now it just needs to close the activity.

Create a new interface named `OnEditFinished` in `com/dummies/tasks/interfaces`. Put the following code in it:

```
public interface OnEditFinished {
    /**
     * Called when the user finishes editing a task.
     */
    public void finishEditingTask();
}
```

And then implement the interface in `TaskEditActivity.java`:

```
public class TaskEditActivity extends Activity
    implements OnEditFinished
{
    /**
     * Called when the user finishes editing a task.
     */
    @Override
    public void finishEditingTask() {
        // When the user dismisses the editor, call finish to destroy
        // this activity.
        finish();
    }

    ...
}
```

Now run the app; you should see a Save menu overlaying the task image, as in Figure 11-3. If you tap it, the activity should dismiss.

Figure 11-3:
The Save
menu
action.

Try setting `setAsActionBar` to `MenuItem.SHOW_AS_ACTION_NEVER` to see what the Add Task item would look like in the overflow menu.

Creating a Long-Press Action

The Tasks application needs a mechanism in which to delete a task when it's no longer needed. Users can long-press the task in the list, and a dialog appears that allows them to delete the task by selecting an item from the menu. For this section, you're going to implement a dialog.

Open `TaskListAdapter.java` and add the following code below your call to `setOnClickListener` in `onBindViewHolder`:

```
// Set the long-press action
viewHolder.cardView.setOnLongClickListener(
    new View.OnLongClickListener()
    {
        @Override
        public boolean onLongClick(View view) {
```

```
                        new AlertDialog.Builder(context)                    →7
                            .setTitle(R.string.delete_q)                    →8
                            .setMessage(viewHolder.titleView.getText())     →9
                            .setCancelable(true)                            →10
                            .setNegativeButton(android.R.string.cancel, null) →11
                            .setPositiveButton(                             →12
                                R.string.delete,
                                new DialogInterface.OnClickListener() {
                                    @Override
                                    public void onClick(
                                        DialogInterface dialogInterface,
                                        int i)
                                    {
                                        deleteTask(context, i);             →20
                                    }
                                })
                            .show();                                        →23
                    return true;
                }
            });
```

→ 7   Uses the `AlertDialog.Builder` class to construct a new `AlertDialog`. The Builder has several methods such as `setTitle`, `setMessage`, `setPositiveButton`, and so on, that will construct an alert to your specifications. When you're all done, you will call `show` on line 23 to show the dialog.

→ 8   Sets the top-line title of the dialog. Add the following line to your `strings.xml`:

```
<string name="delete_q">Delete?</string>
```

→ 9   Sets the message body of the dialog to the title of the task, so that the user can confirm exactly which item she is deleting.

→ 10   Makes the dialog cancelable. This means that if the user hits the Back button, the dialog behaves as if the user hit the Cancel button. You can set this to `false` to disable the Back button in dialogs.

→ 11   Sets the text and action for the negative button in the dialog. In this case, the text is `Cancel`. You don't need to add this string to your app because the `android.R` file has it built-in. Also, you can set the click action to `null`, because by default the negative button dismisses the dialog, and that's the only behavior you need for this dialog.

→ 12   Sets the text and action for the positive button in the dialog. The text is `Delete`, which you should add now to your `strings.xml`:

```
<string name="delete">Delete</string>
```

Unlike the negative button, the positive button has to do some specific stuff to the Tasks app, so you need to implement a `DialogInterface.OnClickListener` to handle the behavior of a positive button click.

→ 20   When the positive button is clicked, call the method `deleteTask`. For now, this method does not need to do anything, so add a `deleteTask` method to your `TaskListAdapter` like so:

```
void deleteTask(Context context, long id ) {
    Log.d("TaskListAdapter", "Called deleteTask" );
}
```

→ 23   You must call `show()` to display your dialog.

Because your `viewHolder` is being accessed from within an inner class, you also need to change the signature of your method:

```
public void onBindViewHolder(final ViewHolder viewHolder,  final int i)
```

Now run your app. When you long-press on a task, you should see a dialog like the one in Figure 11-4:

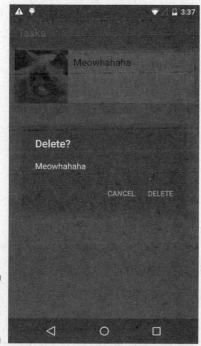

Figure 11-4:
The Delete dialog.

And when you press the Delete button, a message should appear in your logcat output that says `Called deleteTask`. See Chapter 3 for more information about how to use logcat.

In Chapter 10, you used `DialogFragments` to create dialogs, but here you are using an `AlertDialog` (which is not a `DialogFragment`). What is the difference?

`DialogFragments` are more complicated to set up, but they interact properly with the Android activity and fragment lifecycle (see Chapter 5 and 9 for more information about Android activities and fragments). In particular, if a fragment is asked to save itself in `onSaveInstanceState` and then re-create itself later in `onCreate` (see Chapter 10 for more information about `onSaveInstanceState`), a `DialogFragment` will behave properly but an `AlertDialog` will not.

You can see this in action by going to the edit page of your app, dismissing the keyboard, and then clicking on the date to open the date picker. If you rotate your device, the date picker remains on the screen and retains whatever date you clicked on.

However, if you long-press on an item in the list view to open the Delete dialog and then rotate your device, the Delete dialog disappears! This is because you did not use a `DialogFragment` to create it.

In general, it's best to always use `DialogFragments` because they result in the best user experience. As an exercise, try re-implementing the Delete dialog as a `DialogFragment` using the lessons described in Chapter 10.

Chapter 12

Handling User Input

In This Chapter
▶ Working with `EditText` views
▶ Creating date pickers and time pickers
▶ Setting up alert dialogs
▶ Validating user input

Rarely does an application not allow users to interact with it. Whether they use text, a date or time picker, a radio button, a check box, or any other input mechanism, users need to interact with your application in one way or another. This chapter focuses solely on user input in the form of alert confirmation, free-form text, and dates and times.

Creating the User Input Interface

The most common input type is the `EditText` view, used for free-form text entry. With an `EditText` view, you can provide an onscreen keyboard or let the user choose the physical keyboard (if the device provides one) to enter input.

Creating an EditText view

In Chapter 10, you created a view layout XML file, named `fragment_task_edit.xml`, that contained these lines of code:

```
<EditText
    android:id="@+id/title"
    android:layout_width="match_parent"
    android:layout_height="wrap_content"
    ...
    android:hint="@string/title"/>
```

The snippet creates an input mechanism on the screen where the user can type a task title. The EditText view spans the width of the screen and occupies only as much height as it needs. When the view is selected, Android automatically opens the onscreen keyboard to allow user input. And when the EditText is empty, it displays a hint to the user describing what it's for; in this case, the hint text is "Title".

The previous example takes a minimalistic approach, compared to the following EditText example, which is also present in the fragment_task_edit. xml layout file:

```
<EditText
    android:id="@+id/notes"
    android:layout_width="match_parent"
    android:layout_height="wrap_content"
    ...
    android:gravity="top"
    android:hint="@string/notes"
    android:minLines="5"/>
```

This code creates the body description text of the task. The layout width and height are the same as in the EditText view in the previous example. These three properties outline the differences in this EditText definition:

✔ minLines: Specifies the height of the EditText view. Because the EditText view is a subclass of the TextView object, they share this property. This code specifies a minimum of five lines for the EditText object onscreen so that the view resembles a text input mechanism for long messages.

Compare this view to the body portion of any email client, and you can see that they're much the same — the body is much larger than the subject. In this case, the body is much larger than the title.

✔ gravity: The default gravity of an EditText aligns text to the middle of the view when the user places focus into the field, though it isn't what users would expect when they work with a multiline input mechanism. To position the cursor at the top of the EditText view, as users might expect, you must set the gravity of the EditText view to top, to force the text to gravitate to the top of the EditText input as shown on the right in Figure 12-1.

Displaying an onscreen keyboard

The EditText view is responsible for the onscreen keyboard display. Because most devices have no physical keyboard, an onscreen keyboard

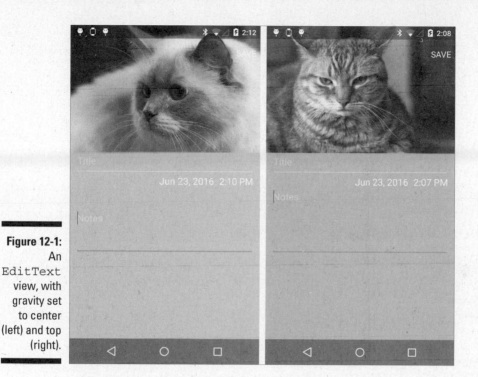

Figure 12-1:
An
`EditText`
view, with
gravity set
to center
(left) and top
(right).

must be present for interaction with the input mechanisms. One property
that the `EditText` view provides is a way to manipulate the visual aspect of
the onscreen keyboard.

You adjust the onscreen keyboard because different `EditText` input types
might need different keys. For example, if the `EditText` is a phone number,
the onscreen keyboard should display only numbers. If the `EditText` value
is an email address, however, the onscreen keyboard should display common
email style attributes — such as the at (@) symbol.

Configuring the onscreen keyboard properly can significantly increase the
usability of your application.

You can configure the way the onscreen keyboard looks by using the
`inputType` property on the `EditText` view. For example, if you set
`android:inputType="number"` on the body `EditText`, the keyboard
displays number keys rather than letter keys, as shown in Figure 12-2.

The `inputType` attribute has too many options to cover in this book, but
you can examine the full list at `http://d.android.com/reference/`
`android/widget/TextView.html#attr_android:inputType`.

Figure 12-2:
Keyboard
customized
for number
entry.

Getting Choosy with Dates and Times

A Task Reminder application without a way to set the date and time is a poor Task Reminder application — it would be only a simple task list application.

If you've programmed dates and times in another programming language, you realize that building a mechanism for a user to enter the date and time can be a painstaking process. The Android platform comes to your rescue by providing two classes to assist you: `DatePicker` and `TimePicker`. These pickers also provide built-in classes for opening a dialog where the user selects a date and time. Therefore, you can either embed the `DatePicker` or `TimePicker` into your application's views or use the `DialogFragment` classes.

Creating picker buttons

The `fragment_task_edit.xml` file contains two `TextViews` to help show the `DatePicker` and `TimePicker` (under the `EditText` definitions described earlier). You can see these two buttons in Listing 12-1.

Listing 12-1:   The Date and Time TextViews

```
<!-- The time button. -->
<TextView
    style="@android:style/TextAppearance.Medium"
    android:id="@+id/task_time"
    android:layout_width="wrap_content"
    android:layout_height="wrap_content"
    android:layout_below="@id/title"
    android:layout_alignEnd="@id/title"
    android:layout_marginEnd="3dp"/>

<!-- The date button. -->
<TextView
    style="@android:style/TextAppearance.Medium"
    android:id="@+id/task_date"
    android:layout_width="wrap_content"
    android:layout_height="wrap_content"
    android:layout_toStartOf="@id/task_time"
    android:layout_alignBottom="@id/task_time"
    android:layout_marginEnd="10dp"/>
```

You already added these buttons to your layout in Chapter 10. See that chapter for a description of what this code does.

Date and time pickers

Every task in your app should have an associated date and time, which can be used to set reminders for the user at a future date. As noted in the previous section, you already have two TextViews that represent the task's date and time. All that remains is to

✔ Show the task's date and time.

✔ Create picker dialogs that display the date and time.

✔ Hook up the dialogs to the TaskEditFragment to let the user change the date and time.

Showing the task's date and time

Open TaskEditFragment and add the lines in bold:

```
public class TaskEditFragment extends Fragment {
    ...
    // Constants for saving instance state
    static final String TASK_ID = "taskId";
    static final String TASK_DATE_AND_TIME = "taskDateAndTime";      →6
```

```
// Views
View rootView;
EditText titleText;
EditText notesText;
ImageView imageView;
TextView dateButton;                                          →13
TextView timeButton;

// Some information about this task that we'll store here until we
// save it to the database
long taskId;
Calendar taskDateAndTime;                                     →19

@Override
public void onCreate(Bundle savedInstanceState) {
    super.onCreate(savedInstanceState);

    // If we're restoring state from a previous activity, restore the
    // previous date as well
    if (savedInstanceState != null) {
        taskId = savedInstanceState.getLong(TASK_ID);
        taskDateAndTime =                                     →29
            (Calendar) savedInstanceState.getSerializable
                (TASK_DATE_AND_TIME);
    }

    // If we didn't have a previous date, use "now"
    if (taskDateAndTime == null) {                            →35
        taskDateAndTime = Calendar.getInstance();
    }

    ...
}

@Override
public View onCreateView(LayoutInflater inflater, ViewGroup container,
                         Bundle savedInstanceState) {

    ...

    // From the layout, get a few views that we're going to work with
    rootView = v.getRootView();
    titleText = (EditText) v.findViewById(R.id.title);
    notesText = (EditText) v.findViewById(R.id.notes);
    imageView = (ImageView) v.findViewById(R.id.image);
    dateButton = (TextView) v.findViewById(R.id.task_date);   →53
    timeButton = (TextView) v.findViewById(R.id.task_time);

    ...
```

```
        updateDateAndTimeButtons();                                →58

        return v;
    }


    @Override
    public void onSaveInstanceState(Bundle outState) {
        super.onSaveInstanceState(outState);

        // These two fields may have changed while our activity was
        // running, so make sure we save them to our outState bundle so
        // we can restore them later in onCreate.
        outState.putLong(TASK_ID, taskId);
        outState.putSerializable(TASK_DATE_AND_TIME, taskDateAndTime);  →71
    }


    /**
     * Call this method whenever the task's date/time has changed and
     * we need to update our date and time buttons.
     */
    private void updateDateAndTimeButtons() {
        // Set the time button text
        DateFormat timeFormat =                                     →80
            DateFormat.getTimeInstance(DateFormat.SHORT);
        String timeForButton = timeFormat.format(
            taskDateAndTime.getTime());
        timeButton.setText(timeForButton);

        // Set the date button text
        DateFormat dateFormat = DateFormat.getDateInstance();       →87
        String dateForButton = dateFormat.format(
            taskDateAndTime.getTime());
        dateButton.setText(dateForButton);
    }
}
```

Now if you run the app, you will see that each edit page has a date and time appear underneath the title. Here's an explanation of what the additions in the previous code do:

→ 6   Much like you needed to create a constant string to name the `taskId` data when it's saved in `onSaveInstanceState`, you do the same here for the date and time information.

→ 13   Creates two `TextView`s, one for the date of the task and one for the time. You will make each one individually clickable later in the chapter so that the user can set them.

→ 19   The `taskDateAndTime` field stores both the date and the time for the task. Remember: Because this is a new field that may be changed, you must remember to save it in `onSaveInstanceState` and restore it in `onCreate`!

→ 29   When the activity is created, check and see if there was already a date and time saved for it. If there was, then read it out of the `savedInstanceState` bundle and save it to `taskDateAndTime`.

→ 35   If there wasn't a previous value set for the date and time, then just use the current time.

→ 53   Finds the date and time `TextViews` from the layout.

→ 58   At the end of `onCreate`, call `updateDateAndTimeButtons` to . . . you guessed it, update the date and time buttons. You will end up calling this method a few times later, whenever the user changes the values of the date and time.

→ 71   If Android is shutting down this activity and asking you to save your instance state, then make sure to save the `taskDateAndTime` to the `outState` bundle. Calendar objects can be serialized (stored as data), so this line uses the `putSerializable()` method to save them.

Find out more information about Java serialization at `http://java.sun.com/developer/technicalArticles/Programming/serialization`.

Saving field names in Android

Android activities and fragments aren't like standard Java objects, where you can store information in a field in the object and expect it always to be there. Normally in Java, if a `person` object is set to the name `"Michael"`, you can expect that name to always be `"Michael"`, but surprisingly this isn't always the case in Android.

Unlike in Java, Android can destroy activities and fragments at any time. These elements can also be re-created later — and a re-created activity needs to look indistinguishable from one that was never destroyed and re-created. Android reserves the right to destroy objects when memory is running low, but it retains the ability to re-create them later, to offer the user a seamless experience.

If you store the string `"Michael"` in a field named `name`, that field isn't saved automatically if the activity or fragment is destroyed and re-created. You have to save the field manually, by storing it in a bundle in `onSaveInstanceState()` and restoring it from the `savedInstanceState` bundle in `onCreate()`.

**Remember:** Anytime you add a field to an activity or a fragment, you must add the appropriate code to the `onSavedInstanceState()` and `onCreate()` methods to save it and restore it — otherwise, your app will behave strangely in some circumstances but not in others.

> You can save all kinds of other types into bundles, such as ints, longs, strings, parcelables, and other exotic elements, so check `http://d.android.com/reference/android/os/Bundle.html` to see the full list.

→ 80　Updates the time button text. First, get a Time formatter by calling `DateFormat.getTimeInstance(DateFormat.SHORT)`, which will return times such as `"5:45 PM"` in the United States (but different formats in other locales). Then call format on this formatter to format the `taskDateAndTime`. Finally, update the `timeButton` with the string returned by the formatter.

→ 87　Updates the date button text. This is the same as the code for the time formatter, but it uses `getDateInstance` rather than `getTimeInstance`. Because we didn't specify a type of format to the `getDateInstance` call, it will use the default, which evaluates to strings like `"Jan 19, 2038"` in the United States.

Creating date and time pickers

Android has built-in date picker and time picker dialogs that you may use to let users pick dates and times. They require a little bit of massaging to work in recent versions of Android, so here is how you use them.

First, create a file in the `com/dummies/tasks/fragment` directory named `DatePickerDialogFragment.java`. The `DatePickerDialogFragment` will be a reusable dialog fragment that "wraps" a standard Android `DatePickerDialog`.

In the file, put the following code:

```
/**
 * A lightweight wrapper for a DatePickerDialog that wraps the dialog
 * in a fragment.
 */
public class DatePickerDialogFragment extends DialogFragment {          →5
    static final String YEAR = "year";                                 →6
    static final String MONTH = "month";
    static final String DAY = "day";

    public static DatePickerDialogFragment newInstance(                 →10
            Calendar date) {
        DatePickerDialogFragment fragment =
                new DatePickerDialogFragment();

        Bundle args = new Bundle();
        args.putInt(YEAR, date.get(Calendar.YEAR));
        args.putInt(MONTH, date.get(Calendar.MONTH));
        args.putInt(DAY, date.get(Calendar.DAY_OF_MONTH));
```

```
        fragment.setArguments(args);

        return fragment;
    }

    @Override
    public Dialog onCreateDialog(Bundle savedInstanceState) {

        OnDateSetListener callback = (OnDateSetListener)          →27
                getFragmentManager()
                        .findFragmentByTag
                                (TaskEditFragment
                                        .DEFAULT_FRAGMENT_TAG);

        Bundle args = getArguments();                             →33
        return new DatePickerDialog(getActivity(), callback,
                args.getInt(YEAR),
                args.getInt(MONTH),
                args.getInt(DAY));
    }
}
```

Here's what the code does:

→ 5   Every dialog that you use in your app should extend
       `DialogFragment`. For more information about
       `DialogFragment`, visit `http://d.android.com/reference/`
       `android/app/DialogFragment.html`.

→ 6   The constant strings that will be used in this class to read and
       write the year, month, and day in bundles.

→ 10   Creates a `newInstance` method like you created for
       the `TaskEditFragment` earlier in this chapter. The
       `newInstance` method knows how to construct an instance
       of the date picker for a given date. First, it constructs a new
       `DatePickerDialogFragment`. Then, it constructs the bundle
       of parameters containing the year, month, and day, which the
       `DatePickerDialogFragment` will use to create a dialog
       showing that date.

→ 27   Finds the `TaskEditFragment` that created this dialog by name.
       You'll use that fragment as the edit callback, so that when the
       user chooses a new date in the `DatePicker` dialog, the dialog
       calls back into the edit fragment to set the new date.

→ 33   Constructs a new `DatePicker` dialog that is hosted by this frag-
       ment. It sets its Year, Month, and Day to the values specified in
       the `args` bundle.

Next, you do the same thing but for the `TimePickerDialogFragment`. Create `TimePickerDialogFragment.java` in `com/dummies/tasks/fragment`, and add the following code:

```java
/**
 * A lightweight wrapper for a TimePickerDialog that wraps the dialog
 * in a fragment.
 */
public class TimePickerDialogFragment extends DialogFragment {
    static final String HOUR = "hour";
    static final String MINS = "mins";

    public static TimePickerDialogFragment newInstance(
            Calendar time) {

        TimePickerDialogFragment fragment =
                new TimePickerDialogFragment();

        Bundle args = new Bundle();
        args.putInt(HOUR, time.get(Calendar.HOUR_OF_DAY));
        args.putInt(MINS, time.get(Calendar.MINUTE));
        fragment.setArguments(args);
        return fragment;
    }

    @Override
    public Dialog onCreateDialog(Bundle savedInstanceState) {
        OnTimeSetListener listener = (OnTimeSetListener)
                getFragmentManager()
                        .findFragmentByTag(
                                TaskEditFragment
                                        .DEFAULT_FRAGMENT_TAG);

        Bundle args = getArguments();
        return new TimePickerDialog(getActivity(), listener,
                args.getInt(HOUR),
                args.getInt(MINS), false);
    }
}
```

This code is basically identical to the `DatePickerDialogFragment` in the previous listing, but this one is for time rather than for dates.

Sometimes you may need to use `savedInstanceState` to restore the state from previous instances. However, in this case, the dialog already does it for you, so you can safely ignore `savedInstanceState` in this method.

Hooking up the date and time pickers to the fragment

Now modify the `TaskEditFragment` to open the date and time pickers when the date or time is clicked.

Edit `TaskEditFragment.java` and add the code in bold:

```
public class TaskEditFragment extends Fragment {

    ...

    @Override
    public View onCreateView(LayoutInflater inflater, ViewGroup container,
                             Bundle savedInstanceState) {

        ...

        updateDateAndTimeButtons();

        // Tell the date and time buttons what to do when we click on
        // them.
        dateButton.setOnClickListener(                                    →15
            new View.OnClickListener() {
                @Override
                public void onClick(View v) {
                    showDatePicker();
                }
            });
        timeButton.setOnClickListener(
            new View.OnClickListener() {
                @Override
                public void onClick(View v) {
                    showTimePicker();
                }
            });

        return v;
    }

    /**
     * A helper method to show our Date picker
     */
    private void showDatePicker() {
        // Create a fragment transaction
```

```
        FragmentTransaction ft = getFragmentManager().beginTransaction()    →40

        DatePickerDialogFragment newFragment =                              →42
            DatePickerDialogFragment.newInstance( taskDateAndTime );

        newFragment.show(ft, "datePicker");                                 →45
    }

    private void showTimePicker() {                                         →48
        // Create a fragment transaction
        FragmentTransaction ft = getFragmentManager().beginTransaction();

        TimePickerDialogFragment fragment =                                 →52
            TimePickerDialogFragment.newInstance(taskDateAndTime);

        fragment.show(ft, "timePicker");                                    →55
    }
}
```

This code adds two methods: showDatePicker and showTimePicker.
It also calls those two methods from inside OnClickListeners that are
attached to the date and time text views. Here are some more details:

→ 15   Creates an OnClickListener and attaches it to the dateButton.
        When clicked, the OnClickListener will call showDatePicker,
        which is defined on line 40. The same thing is next done for the
        timeButton.

→ 40   The showDatePicker method does three things. First, it begins
        a fragment transaction using the FragmentManager, just like you
        did earlier in the chapter inside TaskEditActivity. Then . . .

→ 42   . . . it creates the DatePickerDialogFragment and initializes it
        with the appropriate values.

→ 45   Show the dialog, and name it datePicker. By naming it, Android
        can automatically manage its state for you if it needs to be killed
        and re-created.

→ 48   The showTimePicker method does the same thing that show-
        DatePicker did, except for times rather than dates.

→ 52   Creates the TimePickerDialogFragment and initializes it with
        the appropriate values.

→ 55   Shows the dialog, and names it timePicker. By naming it,
        Android can automatically manage its state for you if the dialog
        needs to be killed and re-created.

In theory, you should now be able to run the app and click on a date or time
to see the picker dialogs. However, there's a bug in the code. The app will

crash because the pickers have no way to return the value that the user picks to the `TaskEditFragment`. If the user selects a new date or time, how does the `TaskEditFragment` know?

The answer is to have `TaskEditFragment` implement `OnDateSetListener` and `OnTimeSetListener`.

Edit `TaskEditFragment` and make the following changes:

```java
public class TaskEditFragment extends Fragment
    implements DatePickerDialog.OnDateSetListener,
    TimePickerDialog.OnTimeSetListener
{

    ...

    /**
     * This is the method that our DatePicker dialog will call when
     * the user picks a date in the dialog.
     */
    @Override
    public void onDateSet(DatePicker view, int year, int monthOfYear,
                          int dayOfMonth) {
        taskDateAndTime.set(Calendar.YEAR, year);
        taskDateAndTime.set(Calendar.MONTH, monthOfYear);
        taskDateAndTime.set(Calendar.DAY_OF_MONTH, dayOfMonth);
        updateDateAndTimeButtons();
    }

    /**
     * This is the method that our TimePicker dialog will call when
     * the user picks a time in the dialog.
     */
    @Override
    public void onTimeSet(TimePicker view, int hour, int minute) {
        taskDateAndTime.set(Calendar.HOUR_OF_DAY, hour);
        taskDateAndTime.set(Calendar.MINUTE, minute);
        updateDateAndTimeButtons();
    }
}
```

These two methods are callbacks. When the user chooses a new date or time in the picker dialogs, the dialogs call back to the fragment named DEFAULT_ FRAGMENT_TAG (see line 27 of `DatePickerDialogFragment`), in this case the `TaskEditFragment`, and call `onDateSet` or `onTimeSet` as appropriate.

The `onDateSet` method then sets the year, month, and day of `taskDateAndTime`, and calls `updateDateAndTimeButtons`. The `onTimeSet` method does the same, except for the time.

Try running your app! You should now be able to click any date or time, choose a new date or time, and watch that date and time update when you return to the `TaskEditFragment`. You should see something like Figure 12-3.

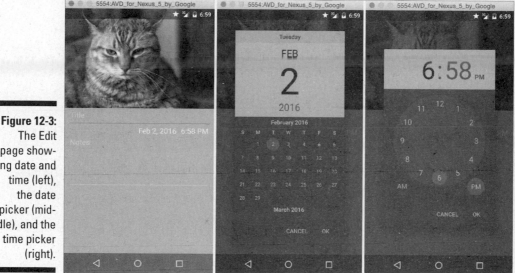

Figure 12-3:
The Edit page showing date and time (left), the date picker (middle), and the time picker (right).

If you leave the `TaskEditActivity` and return to it later, you may wonder why the date and time don't remember the values you set. This is because you have not yet implemented the database to store all these values. You will do that in Chapter 13.

Creating an Alert Dialog

From time to time it may be necessary to alert the user to something that has happened. In the Tasks app, perhaps you want to display a welcome message and offer instructions on how to create a task. The Android system has a framework built around dialogs that provide you with the implementation you may need.

Various types of dialogs are available:

✔ **Alert:** Notifies the user of an important occurrence. Also allows you to set the text value of a button and the action to be performed when it's clicked. As a developer, you can provide the `AlertDialog` with a list of items to display, from which the user can make a selection. You used an `AlertDialog` in Chapter 11 to confirm whether the user wanted to delete a task or not.

✔ **Custom:** A custom dialog created and programmed by you, the master Android developer. You create a custom dialog class by extending the `Dialog` base class or using custom layout XML files.

Seeing why you should work with dialogs

If you've never worked with an application that failed to alert you, or warn you appropriately, consider the example of an email client not notifying you that you have new email. How annoying would that be? Alerting users to important issues or choices that need to be made is an integral part of any user experience.

This list gives a few examples of using a dialog to inform the user of a message or a necessary action:

✔ The user is trying to input some data that is invalid.

✔ The network has become unavailable.

✔ The user needs to select a date or time (as in the Tasks app).

✔ The state of the phone is incompatible with the application. (It might need to have GPS enabled or an SD card added, for example.)

✔ The user needs to choose from a list of items.

Though this list isn't comprehensive, it gives you an idea into what is possible with dialogs.

Choosing the appropriate dialog for a task

Though you determine which dialog to use for a given scenario, you can ask a logical series of questions to choose the appropriate one:

1. **Does the user need to be able to perform an advanced action in the dialog?**

   An *advanced action* isn't supported by the `AlertDialog` class.

   • *Yes:* Create a custom `Dialog` class by extending the `Dialog` base class or creating one from a custom layout XML file. You can find more information about custom dialogs at `http://`

```
developer.android.com/guide/topics/ui/dialogs.
html#CustomLayout.
```

- *No:* Continue to Step 2.

2. **Does the user need to answer a question such as "Are you sure?" with a Yes or No value?**

   - *Yes:* Create an AlertDialog and react to the buttons on the AlertDialog by using onClickListener() calls.

   - *No:* Continue to Step 3.

3. **Does the user need to make a selection from a simple list of items?**

   - *Yes:* Create an AlertDialog.

   - *No:* Continue to Step 4.

4. **Does the user simply need to be alerted?**

   - *Yes:* Create a simple AlertDialog.

   - *No:* You may not need a dialog if you can notify the user another way.

Creating your own alert dialog

At times, you need to notify the user of important information by presenting a dialog. Android makes it quite simple with its introduction of the AlertDialog.Builder class, which lets you easily create an AlertDialog with various options and buttons. Your app can react to these button clicks via the onClickListener() of each button.

You used the AlertDialog.Builder in Chapter 11. Listing 12-2 shows another example of how to create one, this time using a DialogFragment.

Dialogs should always use DialogFragment in Android apps. Refer to Chapter 11 for more details.

Suppose that the user has tapped the Save button in the Tasks application, and you want to open a window (similar to the one in Figure 12-4) so that the user can confirm.

In Listing 12-2, you create an AlertDialog object using the AlertDialog.Builder class and then add an AlertDialogFragment (which works similarly to DatePickerDialogFragment and TimePickerDialogFragment).

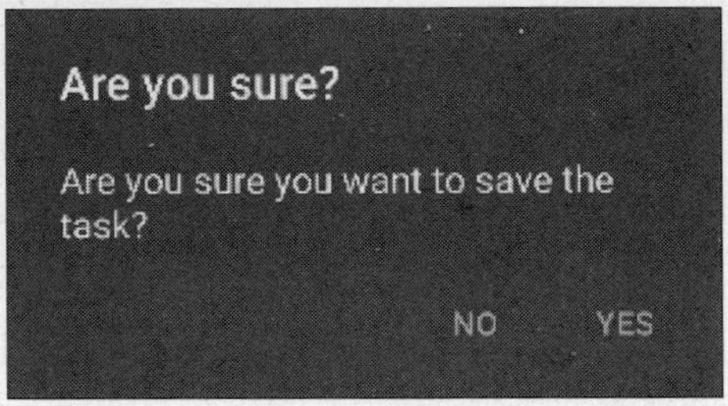

Figure 12-4:
A hypo-
thetical
confirmation
`Alert`
`Dialog.`

Listing 12-2:   Creating an AlertDialogFragment with the AlertDialog.
               Builder Class

```
public class AlertDialogFragment extends DialogFragment {
    @Override
    public Dialog onCreateDialog(Bundle savedInstanceState) {
        AlertDialog.Builder builder
            = new AlertDialog.Builder(getActivity());                    →5
        builder.setMessage("Are you sure you want to save the task?")    →6
            .setTitle("Are you sure?")                                   →7
            .setCancelable(false)                                        →8
            .setPositiveButton("Yes",                                    →9
            new DialogInterface.OnClickListener() {                      →10
                public void onClick(DialogInterface dialog, int id) {
                        // Perform some action such as saving the item   →12
                }
            })
            .setNegativeButton("No", new DialogInterface.OnClickListener() →15
                public void onClick(DialogInterface dialog, int id) {
                        dialog.cancel();                                 →17
                }
        });
        return builder.create();                                         →20
    }
}
```

The code is explained in this list:

→ 5   Sets up the `AlertDialog.Builder` class with the context of the
       `AlertDialog.Builder` as the current running activity.

→ 6   Specifies the message to show in the middle of the `AlertDialog`
       (as shown in Figure 12-4). The value can be a string or a string
       resource.

→ **7**   Sets the title of the `AlertDialog`. The value can be a string or a string resource.

→ **8**   Sets the cancelable attribute to `false`, requiring the user to select a button in the `AlertDialog`. If this flag is set to `false`, the user cannot tap the Back button on the device to exit the `AlertDialog`. Set it to `true` and the user can tap the Back button.

→ **9**   Specifies the text on the positive button. The user clicks the Yes button to perform the action indicated on line 10. This value can be a string or a string resource.

→ **10**   A block of code (ending on line 12) that defines the `onClickListener()` for the Yes button. The code on line 12 executes when the button is tapped.

→ **15**   Specifies the text on the negative button. This button indicates that the user doesn't want to perform the action being requested via `AlertDialog`. The text value of this button is set to No. It can be a string or a string resource.

→ **17**   Sets the `onClickListener()` for the negative button. The listener provides a reference to the dialog that's being shown. It's called the `cancel()` method on the `Dialog` object to close the dialog when the user clicks No on the `AlertDialog`.

→ **20**   Notifies Android to create the `AlertDialog` via the `create()` method.

To show the dialog, you start a fragment transaction in the usual manner:

```
FragmentTransaction ft = getFragmentManager().beginTransaction();
DialogFragment newFragment = new AlertDialogFragment();
newFragment.show(ft, "alertDialog");
```

 Creating a dialog with the `AlertDialog.Builder` class is easier than having to derive your own `Dialog` class. If possible, create your dialog with the `AlertDialog.Builder` class because it gives your application a consistent user experience that's familiar to most Android users.

When the user taps the Save button (or whatever button the code is attached to), an `AlertDialog` opens so that the user can confirm saving the task. This data most likely is stored in a database, as covered in Chapter 13.

You can find helpful examples of using other options on the `Dialog` class at http://d.android.com/guide/topics/ui/dialogs.html.

Validating Input

What happens when the user enters invalid text or no text? Input validation now enters the picture.

Input validation verifies the input before the save takes place. If a user enters no text for the title or the message and attempts to save, should she be allowed to? Of course not.

The method in which you provide validation to the user is up to you. Here are some common methods:

- ✔ `EditText.setError()`: If you detect that the user has tried to enter invalid text in a field, simply call `setError()` and pass the error message. Android then decorates `EditText` with an error icon and displays an error message. The message stays onscreen until the user changes the value of the field or until you call `setError(null)`.

- ✔ `TextWatcher`: Implement a `TextWatcher` on the `EditText` view. This class provides callbacks to you every time the text changes in the `EditText` view. Therefore, you can inspect the text on each keystroke.

- ✔ `On Save`: When the user attempts to save a form, inspect all the form fields at that time and inform the user of any issues that were found.

- ✔ `onFocusChanged()`: Inspect the values of the form when the `onFocus-Changed()` event is called — which is called when the view has focus and when it loses focus. This is usually a good place to set up validation.

The Task application provides no input validation. However, you can add validation via one or more of the methods described.

Toasting the user

The most common way to inform the user of a potential problem, such as an error in input value, is to display a `Toast` message. This type of message appears onscreen for only a few seconds by default.

Providing a `Toast` message is as simple as implementing the following code, where you inform the user of the input error:

```
Toast.makeText(getActivity(), "Title must be filled in", Toast.LENGTH_SHORT).
            show();
```

You might show this message when the user fails to enter a title in the title field and then clicks the Save button.

The only problem with a `Toast` message is that it's short-lived by default. A user who happens to glance away at the wrong time will likely miss seeing it. You can configure your `Toast` messages to appear longer by using `Toast.LENGTH_LONG` rather than `Toast.LENGTH_SHORT`, but remember that it still disappears after a slightly longer time. Use a dialog rather than a `Toast` for critical messages that you need to be sure a user sees.

Using other validation techniques

A `Toast` message isn't the only way to inform users of a problem with their input. A few other popular validation techniques are described in this list:

- ✔ `AlertDialog`: Create an instance of an `AlertDialog` that informs the user of errors. This method ensures that the user sees the error message because the alert must be either canceled or accepted.

- ✔ **Input-field highlighting:** If the field is invalid, the background color of the input field (the `EditText` view) can change to indicate that the value is incorrect.

- ✔ **Custom validation:** If you're feeling adventurous, you can create a custom validation library to handle validations of all sorts. It might highlight the field and draw small views with arrows pointing to the error, for example, similar to the Google validation of its sign-in window when you log on to a device for the first time.

You can use these common methods to display input validation information, or you can dream up new ways to inform users of errors. For example, Chapter 9 mentions the `NotificationManager`, which you can use to inform users of a problem with a background service in the status bar.

Chapter 13

Getting Persistent with Data Storage

In certain types of applications, Android requires application developers to use data persistence, where information about a user's preferences, such as favorite background colors or radio stations, is saved on the device for reuse later, after the device is turned off and then on again. For example, the Tasks application wouldn't be useful if it didn't save tasks, would it? Thankfully, the Android platform provides a robust set of tools that you can use to store user data.

This chapter delves deeply into creating and updating an SQLite database and producing a `ContentProvider` to access it. You need to be familiar with a certain level of database theory to tackle the data storage tasks in this chapter.

TIP

If you're unfamiliar with SQL (Structured Query Language) or the SQL database, see the SQLite website at `www.sqlite.org` for more information.

This chapter is code intensive — if you start feeling lost, you can download the completed application source code from this book's website.

Finding Places to Put Data

Depending on the requirements of your application, you may need to store data in a variety of places. For example, if an application interacts with music files and a user wants to play them in more than one music program, you have to store them in a location where all applications can access them. An application that needs to store sensitive data, such as encrypted usernames and password details, shouldn't share data — placing it in a secure, local storage environment is the best strategy. Regardless of your situation, Android provides various options for storing data.

Viewing your storage options

The Android ecosystem provides various locations where data can be persisted:

- ✔ **Shared preferences:** Private data stored in key-value pairs. (See Chapter 15 to find out how to handle shared preferences.)

- ✔ **Internal storage:** A location for saving files on the device. Files stored in internal storage are private to your application by default, and other applications cannot access them. (Neither can the user, except by using your application.) When the application is uninstalled, the private files are deleted as well.

- ✔ **Local cache:** The internal data directory for caching data rather than storing it persistently. Cached files may be deleted at any time. You use the getCacheDir() method, available on the Activity or Context objects in Android.

If you store data in an internal data directory and the internal storage space begins to run low, Android may delete files to reclaim space. Don't rely on Android to delete your files for you though! You should delete your cache files yourself to stay within a reasonable limit (for example, around 1MB) of space consumed in the cache directory.

- ✔ **External storage:** Every Android device supports shared external storage for files — either removable storage, such as a Secure Digital card (SD card) or non-removable storage. Files saved to external storage are *public* (any person or application can alter them), and no level of security is enforced. Users can modify files by either using a file manager application or connecting the device to a computer via a USB cable and mounting the device as external storage. Before you work with external storage, check the current state of the external storage with the Environment object, using a call to getExternalStorageState() to check whether the media is available.

The main method is a call on the `Context` object — `getExternal FilesDir()`. This call takes a string parameter as a key to help define the type of media you're saving, such as ringtones, music, or photos. For more information, view the external data storage examples and documents at `http://d.android.com/guide/topics/data/ data-storage.html#filesExternal`.

✔ **SQLite database:** A lightweight SQL database implementation that's available across various platforms (including Android, iPhone, Windows, Linux, and Mac) and fully supported by Android. You can create tables and perform SQL queries against the tables accordingly. You implement an SQLite database in this chapter to handle the persistence of the tasks in the Tasks application.

✔ **Content provider:** A "wrapper" around another storage mechanism. A content provider is used by an app to read and write application data that can be stored in preferences, files, or SQLite databases, for example. `ContentProviders` are smart in that they also keep track of when your data is modified, and automatically notify any listeners to changes. In this chapter, you will implement a `ContentProvider` to wrap your database access.

✔ **Network connection:** (Also known as remote storage.) Any remote data source that you have access to. For example, because Flickr exposes an API that allows you to store images on its servers, your application might work with Flickr to store images. If your application works with a popular tool on the Internet (such as Twitter, Facebook, or Basecamp), your app might send information via HTTP — or any other protocol you deem necessary — to third-party APIs to store the data.

✔ **Storage Access Framework:** The SAF makes it simple for users to browse and open documents, images, and other files across all their preferred document storage providers. A standard, easy-to-use UI lets users browse files and access recents in a consistent way across apps and providers. For example, you can use the SAF to provide access to a remote cloud storage provider for documents.

Choosing a storage option

The various data storage locations offer quite the palette of options. However, you have to figure out which one to use, and you may even want to use *multiple* storage mechanisms.

Suppose that your application communicates with a third-party remote API such as Twitter, and network communication is slow and less than 100 percent reliable. You may want to retain a local copy of all data since the last update from the server, to allow the application to remain usable (in some fashion) until the next update. When you store the data in a local copy of an SQLite database and the user initiates an update, the new updates refresh the SQLite database with the new data.

If your application relies solely on network communication for information retrieval and storage, use the SQLite database (or any other storage mechanism) to make the application remain usable when the user cannot connect to a network and must work offline — a common occurrence. If your application doesn't function when a network connection is unavailable, you'll likely receive negative reviews in the Google Play Store — as well as feature requests to make your app work offline. This strategy introduces quite a bit of extra work into the application development process, but it's worth your time tenfold in user experience.

Understanding How the SQLite ContentProvider Works

The two fragments in the Tasks application need to perform various duties to operate. `TaskEditFragment` needs to complete these steps:

1. **Create a new record.**
2. **Read a record so that it can display the details for editing.**
3. **Update the existing record.**

The `TaskListFragment` needs to perform these duties:

1. **Read all tasks to show them onscreen.**
2. **Delete a task by responding to the click event from the context menu after a user has long-pressed an item.**

To work with an SQLite database, you communicate with the database via a `ContentProvider`. Programmers commonly remove as much of the database communication as possible from the `Activity` and `Fragment` objects. The database mechanisms are placed into a `ContentProvider` to help separate the application into layers of functionality. Therefore, if you need to alter code that affects the database, you know that you need to change the code in only one location to do so.

Creating Your Application's SQLite Database

The first step to creating a new SQLite database `ContentProvider` is to create the SQLite database that it will use.

Visualizing the SQL table

The *table* in SQL is what holds the data you manage. Visualizing a table in SQLite is similar to looking at a spreadsheet: Each row consists of data, and each column represents the data inside the row. Listing 13-1 defines column names for the database. These column names equate to the header values in a spreadsheet, as shown in Figure 13-1. Each row contains a value for each column, which is how data is stored in SQLite.

Figure 13-1: Visualizing data in the Tasks application.

	Tasks		
_id	title	notes	date_time
1	Collect underpants	Obviously.	1/23/16 10:00AM
2	?	Details TBD, check with Cartman	1/30/16 12:30PM
3	PROFIT!		1/30/16 12:31PM

The SQL script to create a table like the one in the previous figure is shown in Listing 13-1:

Listing 13-1:   Creating an SQL Database Table

```
create table tasks (                                  →1
    _id integer primary key autoincrement,            →2
    title text not null,                              →3
    notes text not null,                              →4
    task_date_time integer not null );                →5
```

Getting into the details about SQL is beyond the scope of the book, but here's a brief synopsis about what this SQL script does:

→ 1   Creates a table named `tasks`.

→ 2   Adds a primary key to that table named `_id`. Android assumes that the id field for every table begins with an underscore.

→ 3   Adds a non-null field named `title` to the table. This field can be any length.

→ 4   Adds a non-null `notes` field.

→ 5   Adds a `date/time` field to the table. In this table, the date/time is stored as an integer.

For more information on dates and times in SQLite, visit `www.sqlite.org/datatype3.html`.

Creating the database table

Android apps create SQLite databases using an `SQLiteOpenHelper`. Because this database is going to be used exclusively from a `ContentProvider`, you're going to create an `SQLiteOpenHelper` class nested inside a `ContentProvider`.

Create a new class named `TaskProvider` in the directory `com/dummies/tasks/provider`. Add the following code to it:

```
public class TaskProvider extends ContentProvider {            →1

    // Database Columns                                        →3
    public static final String COLUMN_TASKID = "_id";
    public static final String COLUMN_DATE_TIME = "task_date_time";
    public static final String COLUMN_NOTES = "notes";
    public static final String COLUMN_TITLE = "title";

    // Database Related Constants                              →9
    private static final int DATABASE_VERSION = 1;            →10
    private static final String DATABASE_NAME = "data";       →11
    private static final String DATABASE_TABLE = "tasks";     →12

    // The database itself
    SQLiteDatabase db;                                        →15

    @Override                                                 →18
    public boolean onCreate() {
        // Grab a connection to our database
        db = new DatabaseHelper(getContext()).getWritableDatabase();  →21
        return true;
    }

    /**
     * A helper class which knows how to create and update our database.
     */
    protected static class DatabaseHelper extends SQLiteOpenHelper {
```

```
        static final String DATABASE_CREATE =                      →30
            "create table " + DATABASE_TABLE + " (" +
                COLUMN_TASKID + " integer primary key autoincrement, " +
                COLUMN_TITLE + " text not null, " +
                COLUMN_NOTES + " text not null, " +
                COLUMN_DATE_TIME + " integer not null);";

        DatabaseHelper(Context context) {
            super(context, DATABASE_NAME, null, DATABASE_VERSION);    →39
        }

        @Override                                                   →42
        public void onCreate(SQLiteDatabase db) {
            db.execSQL(DATABASE_CREATE);
        }

        @Override                                                   →48
        public void onUpgrade(SQLiteDatabase db, int oldVersion,
                             int newVersion) {
            throw new UnsupportedOperationException();               →51
        }
    }
}
```

The numbered lines are described in this list:

→ 1   A `ContentProvider` that knows how to read and write tasks from your tasks database. For now, it's practically empty. The only thing it does is create a database using a `SQLiteOpenHelper`.

→ 3   The names of the various columns in the Task table. These correspond to the columns in Listing 13-1 and Figure 13-1. These column names are going to be needed outside of this class, so make them public.

→ 9   Various database-related constants. These constants will not be needed outside this class, so they are private.

→ 10   The version number for this database. Because it's the first version, give it a version of `1`. Whenever you change the database, increment this number by one so that Android knows that the database has changed. This allows you to know whether you need to upgrade the database schema in `onUpgrade` on line 48 (an advanced topic outside of the scope of this book).

→ 11   The database name. This is the name of the file on the file system.

→ 12   The name of the database table. This table is named `"tasks"`.

→ 15   The database object that will be created in `onCreate` using your `SQLiteOpenHelper` below. This is the object that your `ContentProvider` will use to read and write from your database.

→ 18   This method is called when the `ContentProvider` is created. This is usually done once on app startup.

→ 21   Creates the database object by using a `DatabaseHelper`. First you create a new `DatabaseHelper`, passing in the current context. Then, you call `getWritableDatabase()`. Some apps might want to use `getReadableDatabase()` instead, but because this app is reading and writing, it needs a writable database.

→ 30   The database creation script from Listing 13-1.

→ 39   The constructor for the database helper. It must call the super's constructor, and pass in the current context, the database name, an optional `CursorFactory` for advanced usages, and the version of the database.

→ 42   This method is called when the app is first installed and no database has yet been created. This is where the magic happens and your database creation SQL script is executed.

→ 48   This method will be called in the future when version 2.0 of the Tasks app is released. At that point, you'll need to upgrade the database from version 1.0 to version 2.0. For now, there's nothing you need to do here.

→ 51   Because this method will never be called (because there was no version 0 of the database before version 1), just throw an `UnsupportedOperationException` here. You will need to change this code before you release version 2 of the database.

TIP

Upgrading your database

Suppose that you release your application and 10,000 users install it and are using it — and they love it! Some even send you feature requests, so you implement one that requires a change in the database schema. You then perform SQL `ALTER` statements inside the `onUpgrade()` call to update your database. If you were lazy, you could upgrade the database by "dropping" the existing one and then creating a new one. But you don't want to do this — dropping a database *deletes all the user's data*. Imagine updating your favorite Tasks application, only to see that the upgrade has erased all preexisting tasks (a *major* bug).

Using ContentProvider URIs

Now that you've created the basic SQLite table, you need to start providing all the methods you'll need to read and write from that table using your `ContentProvider`. But first, you need to understand how `ContentProviders` use URIs.

An Android `ContentProvider` uses URIs to identify data. Typically, you can use a URI to identify a specific piece of data, such as a single task, or all the tasks in your database. If you store other types of data there, you can use URIs for them, too.

In your application, you use two kinds of URIs — `content://com.dummies.tasks.provider.TaskProvider/task` to retrieve a list of all tasks in your database, or `content://com.dummies.tasks.provider.TaskProvider/task/9` to retrieve a specific task from the database (in this case the task with the ID of 9).

These `ContentProvider` URIs are undoubtedly similar to the URIs you're already familiar with. Their main differences are described in this list:

- `content://`: A `ContentProvider` begins with `content://` rather than with `http://`.

- `com.dummies.tasks.provider.TaskProvider`: The second part of the URI identifies the authority (the `TaskProvider`) of the content. Though this string can be virtually anything, convention dictates using the fully qualified class name of your `ContentProvider`.

- `task`: The third part of the URI identifies the path — in this case, the type of data you're looking up. This string identifies which table in the database to read. If the application stores multiple types in the database (say, a list of users in addition to a list of tasks), a second type of path might be named `user`, for example.

- `9`: In the first URI, the path ends with `task`. However, in the second URI, the path continues to include the specific ID of the task being requested.

Now you have to add the code to support these URIs in your `ContentProvider`. Open `TaskProvider` and add the following lines to the class:

```
// Content Provider Uri and Authority
public static final String AUTHORITY
    = "com.dummies.tasks.provider.TaskProvider";      →3
public static final Uri CONTENT_URI
    = Uri.parse("content://" + AUTHORITY + "/task");   →5
```

```
    // MIME types used for listing tasks or looking up a single
    // task
    private static final String TASKS_MIME_TYPE
        = ContentResolver.CURSOR_DIR_BASE_TYPE
            + "/vnd.com.dummies.tasks.tasks";                          →11
    private static final String TASK_MIME_TYPE
        = ContentResolver.CURSOR_ITEM_BASE_TYPE
            + "/vnd.com.dummies.tasks.task";
    // UriMatcher stuff
    private static final int LIST_TASK = 0;                            →17
    private static final int ITEM_TASK = 1;
    private static final UriMatcher URI_MATCHER = buildUriMatcher();    →19

    /**
     * Builds up a UriMatcher for search suggestion and shortcut refresh
     * queries.
     */
    private static UriMatcher buildUriMatcher() {
        UriMatcher matcher = new UriMatcher(UriMatcher.NO_MATCH);       →26
        matcher.addURI(AUTHORITY, "task", LIST_TASK);                  →27
        matcher.addURI(AUTHORITY, "task/#", ITEM_TASK);                →28
        return matcher;
    }

    /**
     * This method is required in order to query the supported types.
     */
    @Override
    public String getType(Uri uri) {
        switch (URI_MATCHER.match(uri)) {                              →37
            case LIST_TASK:
                return TASKS_MIME_TYPE;
            case ITEM_TASK:
                return TASK_MIME_TYPE;
            default:
                throw new IllegalArgumentException("Unknown Uri: " + uri);
        }
    }
```

This chunk of code may seem intimidating, but it consists mostly of constants with one useful method (getType()). Here's how the numbered lines work:

→ 3   The authority for the ContentProvider — by convention, the same as the fully qualified class name. This value must match the value you will add to your AndroidManifest.xml file for the provider authorities.

→ 5   The base URI for the ContentProvider. Every time your application asks for data for this URI, Android routes the request to this ContentProvider.

The `ContentProvider` supports two types of URIs: one for listing all tasks and one for listing a specific task.

The first type of URI is the `CONTENT_URI`, and the second one is the `CONTENT_URI` with the task ID appended to the end.

→ 11 Because the `ContentProvider` supports two types of data, it defines two types (or MIME types) for this data. *MIME types* are simply strings commonly used on the web to identify data types. For example, web HTML content typically has a MIME type of `text/html`, and audio MP3 files have `audio/mpeg3`. Because the tasks are of no known standard type, you can make up MIME type strings as long as you follow Android and MIME conventions.

The list MIME type begins with `ContentResolver.CURSOR_DIR_BASE_TYPE`, and the individual task MIME type begins with `ContentResolver.CURSOR_ITEM_BASE_TYPE`. `DIR` represents the list, and `ITEM` represents the item — simple enough.

The subtype (which follows the /) must begin with `vnd`. The subtype is followed by the fully qualified class name and the type of data — in this case, `com.dummies.tasks` and `task`. Visit `http://developer.android.com/reference/android/content/ContentResolver.html` for more information about the Android conventions for MIME types.

You use `"task"` singular almost everywhere in the `ContentProvider`. The only places where it is plural is in the MIME type for lists, in the name of the database file, and when referring to the name of the app. Everywhere else it is singular.

→ 17 Uses another constant to identify list types versus item types, which are `ints`.

→ 19 The `UriMatcher` is used to determine the URI type: list or item. You build a `UriMatcher` using the method named `buildUriMatcher()` on line 25.

→ 26 Creates the `UriMatcher`, which can indicate whether a given URI is the list type or item type. The `UriMatcher.NO_MATCH` parameter tells the application which default value to return for a match.

→ 27 Defines the list type. Any URI that uses the `com.dummies.tasks.provider.TaskProvider` authority and has a path named `"task"` returns the value `LIST_TASK`.

→ 28 Defines the item type. Any URI that uses the `com.dummies.tasks.TaskProvider` authority and has a path that looks like `task/#` (where # is a number) returns the value `ITEM_TASK`.

→ 37   Uses the `UriMatcher` on line 19 to determine which MIME type to return. If the URI is a list URI, it returns `TASKS_MIME_TYPE`. If it's an item URI, it returns `TASK_MIME_TYPE`.

Before you can use the `TaskProvider`, make sure that it's listed in the `AndroidManifest.xml` file, by adding this code before the `</application>` tag:

```
<provider
    android:name=".provider.TaskProvider"
    android:authorities="com.dummies.tasks.provider.TaskProvider"
    android:exported="false" />
```

It tells Android that a `ContentProvider` named `TaskProvider` will handle URIs that use the specific authority of `com.dummies.tasks.TaskProvider`. It also indicates that the data in the provider is not exported to other apps on the user's phone. In general, you should set `exported="false"` unless you want to make your provider available to other apps.

There are two main times when you need a `ContentProvider` instead of just using a database directly. The first is when you want to export your content to other apps. The Android Calendar app allows you to browse your calendar from other apps using this mechanism. The second case is when you need to use a `CursorLoader`, which you will use later in this chapter.

Dealing with CRUD

Your `ContentProvider` needs to be able to deal with CRUD. Specifically, it needs to handle the following operations:

- ✔ Create
- ✔ Read
- ✔ Update
- ✔ Delete

To do this, you must add the necessary methods to support these four operations to the `TaskProvider`. I'll tackle these slightly out of order.

Create

Adding a new item to the database is easy. Add the following method to your `TaskProvider`:

```
/**
 * This method is called when someone wants to insert something
 * into our content provider.
 */
@Override
public Uri insert(Uri uri, ContentValues values) {          →6
    // you can't choose your own task id
    if( values.containsKey(COLUMN_TASKID))
        throw new UnsupportedOperationException();          →9

    long id = db.insertOrThrow(DATABASE_TABLE, null,
        values);                                            →12
    getContext().getContentResolver().notifyChange(uri, null);  →13
    return ContentUris.withAppendedId(uri, id);             →14
}
```

Here's what the `insert` method is doing:

→ 6   The `insert` method takes two parameters. The first is the URI that identifies which table to insert into, which will always be `CONTENT_URI` for this `ContentProvider`. The second parameter is a hashmap with keys and values that represent the data being inserted into the database. Typically, this would include the task's title and notes.

→ 9   When you insert something into the database, the database creates a new row and returns the ID to you. Because of this, it doesn't make sense to allow you to specify a row `id` when you insert into the `db`. Doing so is an error, so throw an exception.

→ 12   Calls `insertOrThrow` on the database object to insert the value. As the name implies, this method throws an exception if there's any problem inserting into the database. Typically, this would only happen if the user is running out of space on his or her phone. Because this is fairly rare, you do not need to add any explicit exception handling to catch this case. The `insertOrThrow` method returns the ID of the task that was added to the `db`.

→ 13 As mentioned before, one of the main responsibilities of a `ContentProvider` is to notify listeners of changes to their data. If a list page in your app is watching the tasks table, and the edit page adds a new item to the table, the list page needs to be notified of the change so that it can be refreshed. This is done on this line by calling `notifyChange()` on the context's `ContentResolver`. The `notifyChange()` method takes the `uri` of the content that has changed. The second parameter of `notifyChange()` can be ignored.

→ 14 Returns the `URI` for the newly added task. To do this, take the URI and append the new ID using `ContentUris.withAppendedId()`.

Update

Editing (also known as updating) a task in the database is very similar to creating a new one. Add the following method to your `TaskProvider`:

```
/**
 * This method is called when someone wants to update something
 * in our content provider.
 */
@Override
public int update(Uri uri, ContentValues values, String ignored1,
                  String[] ignored2) {                              →7
    // you can't change a task id
    if( values.containsKey(COLUMN_TASKID))
        throw new UnsupportedOperationException();                  →10

    int count = db.update(                                          →12
        DATABASE_TABLE,
        values,
        COLUMN_TASKID + "=?",                                       →15
        new String[]{Long.toString(ContentUris.parseId(uri))});     →16

    if (count > 0)
        getContext().getContentResolver().notifyChange(uri, null);  →19

    return count;                                                   →21
}
```

Here's a description of what this listing is doing:

→ **7**   The `update` method takes four parameters. The first is the URI, which is the same URI as the `insert` method, except this URI will also have the ID of the task to be edited appended to the end. For example, the URI might be `content://com.dummies.tasks.provider.TaskProvider/task/8` to edit the eighth task in the db. The second parameter is the values to be set for that task. Typically this would include the title and/or the notes. The third and fourth parameters are SQL selection arguments for advanced usages and can be ignored.

→ **10**   Just like in the `insert` method, it is illegal to try to change the ID of a given task, so throw an exception if anyone tries.

→ **12**   Calls the `update()` method on the `db` object. Much like in the call to `insertOrThrow()` in the previous section, the first two parameters to the update call are the table to be edited and the values to be set. The next parameters, however, are different.

→ **15**   Specifies the `WHERE` clause to the SQL query. In this case, the `WHERE` clause will be `"_id=?"`, indicating that you want to update the row that has an `_id` of `"?"`. The `"?"` will be replaced by the value on line 16.

→ **16**   Computes the `id` of the task to be edited. This is done by parsing it from the URI using `ContentUris.parseId()`, converting the resulting long into a `String`, and then putting that `String` into an array of `Strings` to be passed as the `whereArgs` for the update call. Each `"?"` in the `where` clause will be replaced by the respective entry from the `String` array, so there should always be exactly as many question marks in the `where` clause as there are items in the `String` array.

The lazy or enterprising among you might wonder, why do I need to use a bunch of question marks and `String` arrays? Can't I just make a `WHERE` clause that says `"_id=10"` and skip the whole question mark business entirely? Don't do it! Using a question mark is a security practice that can prevent you from getting hit from SQL injection attacks. To learn more about SQL injection, visit `http://en.wikipedia.org/wiki/SQL_injection`.

→ **19**   If anything in the table was changed, notify any listeners.

→ **21**   Returns the count of items update. It should only ever be zero or one.

Delete

The `delete` method is even easier to implement than the `update` method.

```
/**
 * This method is called when someone wants to delete something
 * from our content provider.
 */
@Override
public int delete(Uri uri, String ignored1, String[] ignored2) {        →6
    int count = db.delete(                                              →7
        DATABASE_TABLE,
        COLUMN_TASKID + "=?",
        new String[]{Long.toString(ContentUris.parseId(uri))});

    if (count > 0)
        getContext().getContentResolver().notifyChange(uri, null);      →13

    return count;
}
```

By now, most of this should be familiar to you. However, there are some differences:

→ 6   As was the case with the `update` method, the last two arguments (the `selection` and the `selectionArgs`) can be ignored for `delete`.

→ 7   Calls the `delete` method, and passes in the table name, the `where` clause for the `_id`, and the `_id`.

→ 13   If anything was deleted, notify any listeners. Then return the count of rows that were deleted (should be zero or one).

Read

Were `insert`, `update`, and `delete` too easy for you? Are you ready for a challenge? Well, let's give you something a little trickier. Here's how you implement the `query` (also known as `Read`) method:

```
/**
 * This method is called when someone wants to read something from
 * our content provider. We'll turn around and ask our database
 * for the information, and then return it in a Cursor.
 */
@Override
public Cursor query(Uri uri, String[] ignored1, String selection,      →7
                String[] selectionArgs, String sortOrder) {
```

```
    String[] projection = new String[]{                    →10
        COLUMN_TASKID,
        COLUMN_TITLE,
        COLUMN_NOTES,
        COLUMN_DATE_TIME};

    Cursor c;
    switch (URI_MATCHER.match(uri)) {                       →17

        case LIST_TASK:                                     →19
            c = db.query(DATABASE_TABLE,                    →20
                    projection, selection,
                    selectionArgs, null, null, sortOrder);
            break;

        case ITEM_TASK:                                     →25
            c = db.query(DATABASE_TABLE, projection,        →26
                    COLUMN_TASKID + "=?",
                    new String[]{Long.toString(ContentUris.parseId
                        (uri))},
                    null, null, null, null);
            if (c.getCount() > 0) {
                c.moveToFirst();                            →32
            }
            break;
        default:
            throw new IllegalArgumentException("Unknown Uri: " + uri); →36
    }

    c.setNotificationUri(getContext().getContentResolver(), uri);     →39
    return c;
}
```

Okay, that wasn't so bad, but it still warrants some explanation:

→7   The `query` method takes a URI that represents the content to be
      queried. The selection parameter specifies an optional `where`
      clause (such as `title=?`), and the `selectionArgs` parameter is
      an array of strings that fill in any question marks in that selection
      parameter. The `sortOrder` parameter indicates how the results
      should be sorted.

→10   Creates a list of column names to represent the data and the order
      of the data that will be returned. This is called a *projection* to
      people who hold their pinkies up when they drink tea.

→17   Uses the `UriMatcher` to see what kind of query you have and
      formats the database query accordingly.

→19   You are asked to return a list of tasks.

→20 Queries the database table named `"tasks"` with the projection specified on line 10. The selection parameter indicates which tasks will be selected. If no selection is specified, this returns `ALL` of the rows in this table. The result is an SQL cursor that contains each of the columns specified in the projection.

→ 25 You are asked to return a specific task.

→ 26 Unlike line 20, line 26 is about querying a single specific task. To do that, you construct a `where` clause with an `_id` specified in the `where` args, exactly like you did for the `update` and `delete` methods. The other parameters of the `db.query` method can be ignored.

→ 32 If the query returned any results (for example, `getCount()` is larger than zero), then move the cursor to the first item in the list.

→ 36 If the URI wasn't a list URI and it wasn't an item URI, then something went wrong, so throw an error.

→ 39 Sets the notification URI for this cursor. This URI must agree with the URIs you used in `insert`, `update`, and `delete`. The loader (explained later in this chapter) uses this URI to watch for any changes to the data; and if the data changes, the loader automatically refreshes the UI.

Your `ContentProvider` is now complete! The next step is to use it in your app.

Implementing the Save Button

There are two fundamental things your `ContentProvider` is used for. The first is reading from your database, and the second is writing to your database. Let's look at the simpler of the two first, which is writing to your database.

Open `TaskEditFragment.java` and add the following method:

```
private void save() {
    // Put all the values the user entered into a
    // ContentValues object
    String title = titleText.getText().toString();              →4
    ContentValues values = new ContentValues();
    values.put(TaskProvider.COLUMN_TITLE, title);
    values.put(TaskProvider.COLUMN_NOTES,
            notesText.getText().toString());
```

```
        values.put(TaskProvider.COLUMN_DATE_TIME,
            taskDateAndTime.getTimeInMillis());

        // taskId==0 when we create a new task,
        // otherwise it's the id of the task being edited.
        if (taskId == 0) {

            // Create the new task and set taskId to the id of
            // the new task.
            Uri itemUri = getActivity().getContentResolver()
                .insert(TaskProvider.CONTENT_URI, values);                →19
            taskId = ContentUris.parseId(itemUri);                       ↦20

        } else {

            // Update the existing task
            Uri uri = ContentUris.withAppendedId(TaskProvider.CONTENT_URI,
                taskId);                                                  →26
            int count = getActivity().getContentResolver().update(
                uri, values, null, null);                                →28

            // If somehow we didn't edit exactly one task,
            // throw an error
            if (count != 1)                                              →32
                throw new IllegalStateException(
                    "Unable to update " + taskId);

        }

        Toast.makeText(                                                  →38
            getActivity(),
            getString(R.string.task_saved_message),
            Toast.LENGTH_SHORT).show();

    }
```

At a high level, the save method is doing three things:

✔ It's putting all the values that the user entered into a ContentValues key-value map.

✔ It's using a ContentResolver to insert or update those values, depending on whether the taskId is zero (to insert a new task) or non-zero (to edit an existing task). Most of the time, you don't access a ContentProvider directly. Instead, you use a ContentResolver to resolve an operation on a ContentProvider by using a URI.

✔ It's messaging the user that the save was successful using a Toast.

Here is the code in more detail:

→ **4**   Creates a new `ContentValues` map, then takes all the values that the user entered into the fragment (such as title, notes, date, and time), and puts them into the `ContentValues` instance. Note that you do not put the task ID into the `ContentValues` because it's illegal to try to change it.

→ **19**   This line gets a `ContentResolver` from the activity. It then calls `insert()` on that `ContentResolver` and specifies the URI of the task table and all the values that you want to insert. The `ContentResolver` will inspect that URI, figure out which `ContentProvider` is responsible for that URI, and ultimately call into your `TaskProvider.insert` method to insert the data for you.

→ **20**   The call to `insert()` returns the URI of the data that was inserted, so parse out the ID of the newly inserted task and update the `taskId` field with the new value. That way, if the fragment does anything else later, the `taskId` will be set correctly and everything will work as it should. (In this case, it's not strictly necessary because the fragment finishes itself as soon as the save is complete, but it's usually better to leave yourself in a clean state than to open yourself up to future bugs.)

→ **26**   In this section, you are updating an existing task rather than inserting a new one, so figure out what the URI is for that task by appending it to the `CONTENT_URI` using `ContentUris.withAppendedId`.

→ **28**   Edit the task by giving the task's URI and new values to the `ContentResolver`, like you did on line 19.

→ **32**   If everything went well, then exactly one task should have been edited. If somehow more or less than one task was edited, throw an error.

→ **38**   Notifies the user of the change using a `Toast`.

You added a new string, so add it to `strings.xml`:

```
<string name="task_saved_message">Task has been saved</string>
```

Now that you have a `save()` method, you need to call it. Uncomment the line you added in Chapter 11 in `TaskEditFragment.onOptionsItemSelected` that called `save`:

```
@Override
public boolean onOptionsItemSelected(MenuItem item) {
    switch(item.getItemId()) {
```

```
        case MENU_SAVE:
            save();

            ((OnEditFinished) getActivity()).finishEditingTask();
            return true;
    }

    // If we can't handle this menu item, see if our parent can
    return super.onOptionsItemSelected(item);
}
```

Now run your app! Click the Add button in the action bar and create a new task with whatever title you want, then click Save. A `Toast` message will pop up and indicate the task was saved. But how do you know for sure it was saved? The app has no way to show you the saved task yet.

You may not be able to view the data in the app, but if you are using an emulator or a rooted phone, you should be able to examine the SQLite database directly from the command line.

If you would like to consider rooting your phone (not all phones allow this), visit `http://www.androidcentral.com/root`.

To view the database directly:

1. **Open a terminal on your computer and type** adb shell **to get a login shell on your device.**

2. **Type** cd /data/data/com.dummies.tasks/databases**.**

3. **If your device has the sqlite3 command installed (most do), you can run** sqlite3 data **to examine and manipulate your database directly.**

    "data" is the DATABASE_NAME of the database you created in the SQLiteOpenHelper.

4. **Try running** select * from tasks; **to get a list of your tasks.**

    You should now see the task you just created.

If your device does not have sqlite3 installed, you can search the App Store to find an sqlite3 binary that you can install on rooted phones.

Implementing the List View

You might think that reading from a database should be simpler than writing to a database. After all, you don't have to change anything when you do a read. However, reading from a database is actually more complicated than writing for this example.

The reason is that when you're doing any kind of I/O operation, such as reading from a network or from disk (reading a database, for example), you must do this work from a background thread. If you work from the main thread of the user interface, you run the risk of locking it up for an unknown period, which can cause it to feel jerky and unresponsive. Under particularly bad circumstances, it can even lead to displaying the dreaded Application Not Responsive dialog box, which can leave many users believing that your application has crashed.

Because the read operation is reading a bunch of items in a list, it may take a little time. It might take a few hundred milliseconds or so, for example. That may not seem like a long time, but it's long enough to make your app stutter, and in rare circumstances it's possible you might see an ANR.

Technically, both reading and writing from a database should be done on a background thread. So if we're following best practices, the previous section on implementing the Save button should have used a background thread to write to the database. However, because the save operation is writing such a small amount of data to just a single task at a time, and because the UI isn't doing anything fancy during that time, we took a shortcut and skipped the background thread. It's reasonably safe to do so in this case, but you may want to consider going back after reading this chapter and reimplementing save using a loader.

Android provides a system based on loaders and adapters to read a list of data from a datastore (such as a database or file system) on a background thread.

- ✔ *Loaders* are objects that read data from somewhere, often a database. Loaders have two responsibilities:

  - They must be able to load data into memory. This is usually accomplished by using an SQLite cursor to read data from the database into memory a few records at a time.

  - They must watch your database table for changes, and if they are notified of a change, they will reload the data as necessary.

- ✔ *Adapters* are objects that know how to create views for each item in a list. You created a simple adapter named `TaskListAdapter` in Chapter 9 to read data from a dummy list of strings and create `CardViews` for each item.

In the next sections, you are going to create a loader to load data from your database, and an adapter to create views for that data.

Using loaders

The loader provides a mechanism by which you can launch background operations (such as reading from your database) and then get a callback when those operations finish so that you can update the user interface.

A typical example of a loader is a `CursorLoader`. You use a `CursorLoader` to load data from an SQLite database using a cursor. To add a `CursorLoader` to one of your list fragments, you implement the `LoaderCallback` interface in your callback and implement the three `LoaderCallback` methods:

✔ `onCreateLoader()`: This method is called in a background thread when you create a loader using `initLoader()`. In this method, you're responsible for creating a `CursorLoader` object and returning it. The `CursorLoader` uses a URI to ask a `ContentProvider` for data.

✔ `onLoadFinished()`: This method is called when the `CursorLoader` object finishes loading its data from the database. In this method, you're responsible for updating the UI to show the new data to the user.

✔ `onLoaderReset()`: This method is called when the loader is being reset or shut down. When this happens you're responsible for making sure your fragment no longer uses the loader or its cursor.

To kick off a loader, you first obtain a `LoaderManager` from your activity by calling `getLoaderManager()` and then `initLoader()`. `initLoader()` starts loading data in the background by calling `onCreateLoader()`, and when it finishes it executes `onLoaderFinished()` in your `LoaderCallback` object.

You can use loaders for things other than loading data from a database, but all loaders must implement the same three methods regardless of whether they're loading their data from a database, a network, or somewhere else entirely.

Visit `http://developer.android.com/guide/components/loaders.html` for more information about loaders.

Open `TaskListFragment.java` and add the following code in bold:

```
public class TaskListFragment extends Fragment
      implements LoaderManager.LoaderCallbacks<Cursor>            →2
{
    @Override
    public void onCreate(Bundle savedInstanceState) {
        ...

        getLoaderManager().initLoader(0, null, this);             →8
    }
```

```
@Override
public Loader<Cursor> onCreateLoader(int ignored, Bundle args) {
    return new CursorLoader(getActivity(),                              →13
            TaskProvider.CONTENT_URI, null, null, null, null);
}

@Override
public void onLoadFinished(Loader<Cursor> loader, Cursor cursor) {
    adapter.swapCursor(cursor);                                          →19
}

@Override
public void onLoaderReset(Loader<Cursor> loader) {
    adapter.swapCursor(null);                                            →24
}
}
```

You will get a couple of errors when you add this code, but skip those for now. What this code is doing:

→ 2   Adds the `LoaderManager.LoaderCallbacks` interface to this fragment, which is needed when we call `initLoader` on line 8.

→ 8   This is where you tell Android to start up a loader for you. Get a `LoaderManager` by calling `getLoaderManager()`, then initialize a loader by calling `initLoader`. `initLoader` takes three parameters:

  • An ID for the loader. If you have multiple loaders, it's handy to give them each different IDs.

  • A `Bundle` of `args` that can be used to initialize the loader. In this case, there's nothing special we need to initialize, so we'll pass in `null` for the `args`.

  • A `LoaderManager.LoaderCallbacks` implementation. Oh hey, that's us!

→ 13   `initLoader` on line 8 will call `onCreateLoader` to create a new loader. Because you are going to be reading data from an SQL database, you will use Android's built-in `CursorLoader` to do the heavy lifting. Create a new `CursorLoader` and initialize it with the URI of the `ContentProvider` you want to use. The other parameters are for advanced usage; see `http://d.android.com/reference/android/content/CursorLoader.html` for more information.

→ 19   When the loader is finished loading data into memory, it needs to do something with that data. You can do whatever you want with the data, but the traditional thing is to give the data to an adapter so that the adapter can display it to the user. The adapter has a method called `swapCursor`, which replaces whatever cursor it was using with a new cursor, so call `swapCursor` with the new cursor you just received.

→ **24**   `onLoaderReset` is called when the last cursor provided to `onLoadFinished()` above is about to be closed. You need to make sure the adapter is no longer using it, so set it to `null`.

That is essentially all you need to do to use a loader. The next step is to implement the adapter that can take the data and create a view for it.

Using adapters

Adapters are objects that know how to create views for each item in a list. You created a simple adapter in Chapter 9, and now you are going to update it to read data from an SQL `Cursor`.

Open `TaskListAdapter` and add the bold lines to it:

```
public class TaskListAdapter
    extends RecyclerView.Adapter<TaskListAdapter.ViewHolder>
{
    static String[] fakeData = new String[] {                              →4
        "One",
        "Two",
        "Three",
        "Four",
        "Five",
        "Ah... ah... ah!"
    };

    Cursor cursor;                                                         →13
    int titleColumnIndex;                                                  →14
    int notesColumnIndex;
    int idColumnIndex;

    public void swapCursor(Cursor c) {                                     →18
        cursor = c;                                                        →19
        if(cursor!=null) {
            cursor.moveToFirst();                                          →21
            titleColumnIndex = cursor.getColumnIndex(TaskProvider.COLUMN_TITLE);
                                                                           →22
            notesColumnIndex = cursor.getColumnIndex(TaskProvider.COLUMN_NOTES);
            idColumnIndex = cursor.getColumnIndex(TaskProvider.COLUMN_TASKID);
        }
        notifyDataSetChanged();                                            →26
    }
```

```java
@Override
public void onBindViewHolder(final ViewHolder viewHolder,
                             final int i) {
    final Context context = viewHolder.titleView.getContext();
    final long id = getItemId(i);                                          →33

    // set the text
    cursor.moveToPosition(i);                                              →36
    viewHolder.titleView.setText(cursor.getString(titleColumnIndex));      →37
    viewHolder.notesView.setText(cursor.getString(notesColumnIndex));      →38

    // set the thumbnail image
    Picasso.with(context)
        .load(getImageUrlForTask(id))                                      →42
        .into(viewHolder.imageView);

    // Set the click action
    viewHolder.cardView.setOnClickListener(
        ...
                ((OnEditTask) context).editTask(id);                       →48
        });

    viewHolder.cardView.setOnLongClickListener(
        new View.OnLongClickListener()
        {
            ...
                            deleteTask(context, id);                       →55
        });

}

@Override
public long getItemId(int position) {                                      →61
    cursor.moveToPosition(position);
    return cursor.getLong(idColumnIndex);                                  →63
}

@Override
public int getItemCount() {
    return cursor!=null ? cursor.getCount() : 0;                           →68
}

static class ViewHolder extends RecyclerView.ViewHolder {
    CardView cardView;
    TextView titleView;
    TextView notesView;                                                    →74
    ImageView imageView;

    public ViewHolder(CardView card) {
        super(card);
        cardView = card;
```

```
        titleView = (TextView)card.findViewById(R.id.text1);
        notesView = (TextView) itemView.findViewById(R.id.text2);        →81
        imageView = (ImageView)card.findViewById(R.id.image);
    }
}
}
```

These changes to `TaskListAdapter` make it possible to read the list of tasks from a cursor rather than from a hardcoded `fakeData` array. In more detail:

→ 4   Remove the `fakeData` array; it is no longer necessary. You also need to remove the call to `titleView.setText(fakeData[position])` in `onBindViewHolder`.

→ 13   The `TaskListAdapter` is going to read data from a cursor, so add a field for the cursor here.

→ 14   When reading through the cursor, each column of data is referred to by an index. For example, the index of the title column might be 1, the index of notes might be 2, and so on. You don't need the index for the date/time column because the list view does not display the date/time of each task. Store the indices of each column here for quick reference; you will determine their values on line 22.

→ 18   Creates a method named `swapCursor`. This method is called whenever the data in your database has changed. This might occur because someone added or deleted an item from the database, or because the app just started up and is reading all the previously created tasks for the first time. `swapCursor` is responsible for

• Replacing the previous cursor (if there was one) with the new cursor

• Figuring out the indices of the various columns of data

• Notifying any listeners that the data has changed

→ 19   Replaces the previous cursor with the new cursor.

→ 21   Whenever you use a cursor, you must first move the cursor to its first location before you may attempt to read data from it. This line moves to the first position so that we can read the various column indices in the next few lines.

→ 22   Determines the column index for the title column in the cursor. This is done by asking the cursor for the index of the column named `"title"`. Technically, you can skip this step entirely and just ask for columns by their name rather than by their index, but it's more efficient to ask by index. On the next two lines, do the same thing for the `notes` and `id` columns.

→ 26   When the cursor has been swapped, that means that the data likely has changed. Notify any listeners (in particular, the `RecyclerView` from Chapter 9) that the data has changed so that they can refresh their displays.

→ 33   Each task in the database has an ID associated with it. You will need the `id` later, so find the ID for this task by calling `getItemId` and passing in the position of the item in the list.

→ 36   You are about to update the view with the data from the cursor, so make sure you move your cursor to the proper position before you begin to read.

→ 37   Reads the title string from the cursor using the `getString` method, and then uses that string to set the `titleView` `TextView`.

→ 38   Does the same for the `notesView`.

→ 42–55 In the old `TaskListAdapter`, items in the `fakeData` array didn't have an ID, so we just used the position in the index as a sort of fake ID. In the new version of `TaskListAdapter`, every task has an ID that is stored in the database, so make sure to use that ID when calling `getImageUrlForTask`, `editTask`, and `deleteTask`.

→ 61   The implementation for `getItemId` which was called from line 33.

→ 63   After moving the cursor to the appropriate row in the database, this line asks the cursor what the ID is for that row.

→ 68   Updates `getItemCount` to return the count of items in the cursor, assuming that the cursor is not `null`. If the cursor is `null`, this line just returns `0`.

→ 74   Adds the `notesView` `TextView` to your `ViewHolder`. Return to Chapter 9 for a reminder of what a `ViewHolder` does.

→ 81   Sets the `notesView` field by looking for the `TextView` named `text2` in the `card_task.xml` layout.

If you run your app now, you should be able to add tasks! Give it a try.

Deleting a task

There is one more thing to do. You need to add the ability to delete tasks from your database.

This is pretty straightforward. Update `TaskListAdapter` to implement the `deleteTask` method as shown:

```
private void deleteTask(Context context, long id) {
    context.getContentResolver()
            .delete(
                    ContentUris.withAppendedId(
                            TaskProvider.CONTENT_URI,
                            id),
                    null, null);
}
```

This code gets the `ContentResolver` from the context, calls `delete` on it, and passes in the URI of the task to be deleted.

Run the app and long-press on an item in the list to try deleting it. You should see it automatically disappear from the list after the delete is confirmed.

Reading Data into the Edit Page

The Edit page can now save data into the database, but it cannot yet read data from the database. This makes it impossible for users to edit existing tasks, so let's wrap up this final bit of functionality now.

Now that you know how loaders work, let's use a loader to read the task data from the database into the edit page. As you recall, loaders are the best way to perform I/O on a background thread without blocking the main UI thread.

Open `TaskEditFragment` and make the following changes:

```
public class TaskEditFragment extends Fragment
    implements DatePickerDialog.OnDateSetListener,
    TimePickerDialog.OnTimeSetListener,
    LoaderManager.LoaderCallbacks<Cursor>                           →4
{
    ...

    @Override
    public View onCreateView(LayoutInflater inflater, ViewGroup container,
                        Bundle savedInstanceState) {

        // Inflate the layout and set the container. The layout is the
        // view that we will return.
        View v = inflater.inflate(R.layout.fragment_task_edit,
            container, false);
```

```
        // From the layout, get a few views that we're going to work with
        rootView = v.getRootView();
        titleText = (EditText) v.findViewById(R.id.title);
        notesText = (EditText) v.findViewById(R.id.notes);
        imageView = (ImageView) v.findViewById(R.id.image);
        dateButton = (TextView) v.findViewById(R.id.task_date);
        timeButton = (TextView) v.findViewById(R.id.task_time);

        // Set the thumbnail image                                           →25
        Picasso.with(getActivity())
            .load(TaskListAdapter.getImageUrlForTask(taskId))
            .into(. . .);

        updateDateAndTimeButtons();                                          →30

        // Tell the date and time buttons what to do when we click on
        // them.
        dateButton.setOnClickListener(new View.OnClickListener() {
                                  @Override
                                  public void onClick(View v) {
                                      showDatePicker();
                                  }
                              });
        timeButton.setOnClickListener(new View.OnClickListener() {
                                  @Override
                                  public void onClick(View v) {
                                      showTimePicker();
                                  }
                              });

        if (taskId == 0) {                                                   →47

            updateDateAndTimeButtons();

        } else {

            // Fire off a background loader to retrieve the data from the
            // database
            getLoaderManager().initLoader(0, null, this);                    →55

        }

        return v;
    }

    @Override
    public Loader<Cursor> onCreateLoader(int id, Bundle args) {              →63
        Uri taskUri = ContentUris.withAppendedId(                           →64
            TaskProvider.CONTENT_URI, taskId);
```

```
        return new CursorLoader(                                      →67
            getActivity(),
            taskUri, null, null, null, null);
    }
    /**
     * This method is called when the loader has finished loading its
     * data
     */
    @Override
    public void onLoadFinished(Loader<Cursor> loader, Cursor task) {
        if (task.getCount() == 0) {                                   →78
            getActivity().runOnUiThread(                              →79
                new Runnable() {
                    @Override
                    public void run() {
                        ((OnEditFinished) getActivity())
                            .finishEditingTask();                     →84
                    }
                });
            return;
        }

        titleText.setText(                                            →90
            task.getString(
                task.getColumnIndexOrThrow(TaskProvider.COLUMN_TITLE)));
        notesText.setText(
            task.getString(
                task.getColumnIndexOrThrow(TaskProvider.COLUMN_NOTES)));

        Long dateInMillis = task.getLong(                             →97
            task.getColumnIndexOrThrow(TaskProvider.COLUMN_DATE_TIME));
        Date date = new Date(dateInMillis);
        taskDateAndTime.setTime(date);


        Picasso.with(getActivity())                                   →103
            .load(TaskListAdapter.getImageUrlForTask(taskId))
            .into(...);

        updateDateAndTimeButtons();                                   →107
    }

    @Override
    public void onLoaderReset(Loader<Cursor> arg0) {                  →111
        // nothing to reset for this fragment.
    }
}
```

This code reads the task information from the database rather than from the `fakeData` list. It does it using a loader to avoid blocking the main UI thread. Here's what the code does in more detail:

→ 4   Similar to what you did when you put a loader into the list view, you must implement `LoaderManager.LoaderCallbacks` in your fragment to use a loader here.

→ 25-30   It doesn't make sense to try to download the image or update the date and time buttons yet if you don't know what data has been loaded from the task, so move these lines from here to lines 103–107 when the loader has finished.

→ 47   If the task ID is 0, then you know you're inserting a new item into the database. This means that there's no data to load, so skip the loader and just update the time and date buttons instead.

→ 55   If the task ID was non-zero, then the loader needs to read data out of the database. Start it up by calling `initLoader`, and pass in yourself as the `LoaderManager.LoaderCallbacks` object.

→ 63   `onCreateLoader` is called by `initLoader` when it is time to create the loader.

→ 54   Computes the URI for the task you want to load.

→ 67   Creates a cursor loader to load the specified task.

→ 78   Sanity check. If you weren't able to load anything, just close this activity.

→ 79   `onLoadFinished` is called from a background thread. Many operations that affect the UI aren't allowed from background threads. So make sure that you call `finishEditingTask` from the UI thread instead of from a background thread.

→ 84   Calls `finishEditingTask` from the main UI thread. You implemented `finishEditingTask` in Chapter 11.

→ 90   Sets the title and notes from the DB.

→ 97   Sets the task date/time from the DB.

→ 103-107   The code that you moved from lines 25–30.

→ 111   `onLoaderReset` is called when a previously created loader is being reset, thus making its data unavailable. In the list view, you needed to tell the adapter to stop using the old cursor. But in this fragment, there is nothing using the old cursor, so there is nothing to be done in this method.

Now you should have a fully working Tasks app that can create, read, update, and delete tasks from its database. Congratulations! Try running the app now and test it out.

Chapter 14

Reminding the User

*M*any tasks need to happen daily, right? Wake up, take a shower, eat breakfast — we do all these things every day. These tasks make up the standard Monday-through-Friday morning routine for many people. You may have an internal clock and awaken every day on time, but most people have to set alarms to wake up on time. At work, employees have calendars that remind them of upcoming events they need to attend, such as meetings and important server upgrades. Reminders and alarms are part of most everyday routines, and people rely on them in one way or another.

Building your own scheduled task system from scratch would be a pain. Thankfully, Windows has scheduled tasks, Linux has `cron`, and Android has the `AlarmManager` class. Though Android is based on Linux, it doesn't have access to `cron`; therefore, you have to set up scheduled actions via the Android `AlarmManager`.

These are the steps to reminding the user of something when the app isn't running:

✔ Asking for permissions to wake up the device

✔ Registering a new alarm

✔ Creating a class to handle the alarm

✔ Re-registering alarms when the phone reboots

✔ Creating a notification

Seeing Why You Need AlarmManager

A user adds a couple of tasks in the Tasks application (all due later today), puts his device away, and goes about his business. If he isn't reminded about the tasks, he might forget about them; therefore, he needs a way to be reminded of what should happen — which is where the `AlarmManager` class comes into play.

The `AlarmManager` class allows users to schedule a time when the Tasks application should be run. When an alarm goes off, an intent is broadcast by the system. Your application then responds to that broadcast intent and performs an action, such as opening the application, notifying the user via a status bar notification (which you will write later in this chapter), or performing another type of action.

Asking the User for Permission

You wouldn't let your next-door neighbor store holiday decorations in your shed without permission, would you? Probably not. Android is no different. Performing some actions on a user's Android device requires permission, as explained in the following sections.

You added the `INTERNET` permission to the Tasks app in Chapter 9. In this section, you'll learn more about how Android permissions work.

Seeing how permissions affect the user experience

When a user installs an application from the Google Play Store, the application's manifest file is inspected for required permissions. Anytime your application needs access to sensitive components (such as external storage, the Internet, or device information), the user is notified at install time and decides whether to continue the installation.

Don't request unnecessary permissions for your app — security-savvy users are likely to reject it. For example, the Silent Mode Toggle application (described in Part II) doesn't need GPS locations, Internet access, or hardware-related information. (But if you'd like to learn how to incorporate GPS location into your apps, visit the book's online web extras at `www.dummies.com/extras/androidappdevelopment`.)

If your application doesn't need a permission, yank it. The fewer permissions your application requests, the more likely the user is to install it.

Setting requested permissions in the AndroidManifest.xml file

When you need to request permissions, add them to the `AndroidManifest.xml` file in your project. You need to add the `android.permission.RECEIVE_BOOT_COMPLETED` permission to the Tasks application. It allows the application to know when the device reboots so that it can re-register its alarms with the `AlarmManager`.

You edit the `AndroidManifest.xml` file to add the `uses-permission` element to the manifest `element`. The XML permission request looks like this:

```
<uses-permission
    android:name="android.permission.RECEIVE_BOOT_COMPLETED"/>
```

To view a full list of available permissions, view the Android permission documentation at `http://d.android.com/reference/android/Manifest.permission.html`.

If you don't declare the permissions that your application needs, it won't function as expected on either a device or an emulator, and any runtime exceptions that are thrown may crash your application. Always ensure that your permissions are present.

Waking Up a Process with AlarmManager

To wake up a process with `AlarmManager`, you have to set the alarm first. In the Tasks application, the best place to do it is right after you save a task in the Save button's `save()` call.

Creating the ReminderManager helper

Creating an alarm isn't hard, but it does take a few lines of code. You will use this code in a couple of places, so it makes sense to have a method to do it for you. Put this method into a new class named `ReminderManager.java` in a new package named `com/dummies/tasks/util`:

```
/**
 * A helper class that knows how to set reminders using the AlarmManager
 */
public class ReminderManager {

    private ReminderManager() {}                                        →6

    public static void setReminder(Context context, long taskId,       →8
                             String title, Calendar when) {

        AlarmManager alarmManager = (AlarmManager) context
            .getSystemService(Context.ALARM_SERVICE);                  →12

        Intent i = new Intent(context, OnAlarmReceiver.class);         →14
        i.putExtra(TaskProvider.COLUMN_TASKID, taskId);
        i.putExtra(TaskProvider.COLUMN_TITLE, title);

        PendingIntent pi = PendingIntent.getBroadcast(context, 0, i,   →18
            PendingIntent.FLAG_ONE_SHOT);

        alarmManager.setExact(AlarmManager.RTC_WAKEUP,                 →21
            when.getTimeInMillis(), pi);
    }
}
```

Here's an explanation of what the previous code does:

→ 6 The `ReminderManager` class should not be instantiated, so make the constructor private.

→ 8 The `setReminder` method takes the task ID, the task's title, and the date/time of the reminder and creates an alarm to wake up your `OnAlarmReceiver` (not yet written) at the specified time.

→ 12 Asks the context for an `AlarmManager` by calling `getSystemService(ALARM_SERVICE)`.

→ 14 Creates an intent for the `AlarmReceiver` class, which you haven't written yet. The intent tells the `AlarmReceiver` the ID and the title of the task that the `AlarmReceiver` needs to create a notification for.

→ 18 Creates the `PendingIntent` that will wrap the intent from line 14. All intents used in the `AlarmManager` must be wrapped in a `PendingIntent` to "give permission" to the `AlarmManager` to call back into our application.

A *pending intent* is a wrapper around an intent and target action to perform with it. A pending intent can be handed to other applications so that they can perform the action you described on your behalf at a later time.

By giving a `PendingIntent` to another application (in this case, the Android OS which runs the `AlarmManager`), you are granting it the right to perform the operation you have specified as if the other application was yourself (with the same permissions and identity). As such, you should be careful about how you build the `PendingIntent`: Almost always, for example, the base intent you supply should have the component name explicitly set to one of your own components, to ensure it is ultimately sent there and nowhere else.

→ **21** Sets the alarm using the pending intent and the date/time for the task. The `AlarmManager` can use one of the following:

- `RTC` (Real Time Clock): Specifies the exact time to wake up

- `ELAPSED_REALTIME`: Specifies the exact time to wake up relative to when the device booted

- `INTERVAL`: Specifies a periodic wake up

Additionally, most of the settings just described have `WAKEUP` and non-`WAKEUP` options:

✔ `WAKEUP`: Specifying this means that the phone will wake up at exactly the time you specified and do whatever you say.

✔ non-`WAKEUP`: Specifying this means that the device will wake up sometime around the time you specified.

Whenever possible you should choose non-`WAKEUP` so that the device can group wakeup alarms together and minimize draining your battery. In this app, a `WAKEUP` is necessary because we don't want to remind the user later than expected.

The next step is to call `setReminder` when a task is created or edited. To do this, open up `TaskEditFragment` and add the following to the bottom of your `save()` method:

```
// Create a reminder for this task
ReminderManager.setReminder( getActivity(),
        taskId, title, taskDateAndTime);
```

This line of code instructs `ReminderManager` to set a new reminder for the task with a row ID of `taskId` at the particular date and time as defined by the `taskDateAndTime` variable.

If an alarm is already scheduled with a pending intent that contains the same signature, the previous alarm is canceled and the new one is set up.

Creating the notification in OnAlarmReceiver

Now that you have created an alarm, you need to specify what happens when the alarm fires.

The `OnAlarmReceiver` class, shown in Listing 14-1, is responsible for handling the intent that's fired when an alarm is raised. It's a simple `BroadcastReceiver` called whenever an intent is broadcast that is addressed to it, like the one that was registered in `TaskEditFragment` in the previous section.

Create a new package named `com.dummies.tasks.receiver`, and add the `OnAlarmReceiver` class as follows:

Listing 14-1:   The OnAlarmReceiver Class

```
/**
 * This class is called when our reminder alarm fires,
 * at which point we'll create a notification and show it to the user.
 */
public class OnAlarmReceiver extends BroadcastReceiver {            →5
    @Override
    public void onReceive(Context context, Intent intent) {        →7

        // Important: Do not do any asynchronous operations in
        // BroadcastReceive.onReceive! See the sidebar

        NotificationManager mgr = (NotificationManager) context
                .getSystemService(Context.NOTIFICATION_SERVICE);   →13

        Intent taskEditIntent =                                    →15
                new Intent(context, TaskEditActivity.class);
        long taskId = intent.getLongExtra(TaskProvider.COLUMN_TASKID, -1);  →17
        String title = intent.getStringExtra(TaskProvider.COLUMN_TITLE);    →18
        taskEditIntent.putExtra(TaskProvider.COLUMN_TASKID, taskId);        →19

        PendingIntent pi = PendingIntent.getActivity(context, 0,   →21
                taskEditIntent, PendingIntent.FLAG_ONE_SHOT);

        // Build the Notification object using a Notification.Builder
        Notification note = new Notification.Builder(context)      →25
                .setContentTitle(
```

```
                    context.getString(R.string.notify_new_task_title))    →27
            .setContentText(title)                                          →28
            .setSmallIcon(android.R.drawable.stat_sys_warning)              →29
            .setContentIntent(pi)                                           →30
            .setAutoCancel(true)                                            →31
            .build();                                                       →32
    // Send the notification.
    mgr.notify((int) taskId, note);                                         →35
    }
}
```

The numbered lines are explained in this list:

→ **5**   The `OnAlarmReceiver` is a `BroadcastReceiver`. This means that when the `AlarmManager` broadcasts the intent you created previously, the `OnAlarmReceiver` will wake up and receive the intent.

→ **7**   `onReceive` is called when the intent is received. The intent passed in will be the intent inside of your pending intent (not the pending intent itself).

→ **13**   Gets a `NotificationManager` from the context, which you'll use to create a notification.

→ **15**   Creates the intent that opens the `TaskEditActivity` for the specified task id. You get the ID of the task from the `OnAlarmReceiver`'s broadcast intent. This intent is invoked when the user clicks on your notification. When that happens, the `TaskEditActivity` starts and users can view and edit their task.

→ **17–18** Gets the task's ID and title from the intent that you created in `TaskEditFragment`.

→ **19**   Adds the task's ID to the edit intent because the receiver of the intent needs to know which task to edit.

→ **21**   Creates the `PendingIntent` that wraps the `taskEditIntent`. See the previous section to find out more about pending intents.

→ **25–32** Now that you have the task's ID, title, and an intent that starts the `TaskEditActivity` when invoked, it's time to create the actual notification itself. Create a notification using the `Notification.Builder`.

→ **27**   Sets the title of the notification. Add the following string to your `strings.xml`:

```
<string name="notify_new_task_title">Task Reminder!</string>
```

→ **28**   Sets the content of the notification (displayed below the title) to the text of the task itself.

→ **29**   Gives the notification a simple icon. The `stat_sys_warning` is built into Android and works as a reasonable default.

→ **30**   Sets the intent for the notification to the pending intent that you created on line 21. This is the intent fired when the user clicks a notification.

→ **31**   Turns on "auto cancel." This means that when a user clicks the notification, it is automatically dismissed. If you turn this off, the user must manually dismiss his notifications, or you must programmatically dismiss them for the user.

→ **32**   Builds the notification object and returns it.

→ **35**   Takes the notification object created on the previous line, and asks the `NotificationManager` to display it to the user.

Do not do any asynchronous operations (for example, using background threads) in `BroadcastReceiver.onReceive`!

The OS may kill your process immediately after `onReceive` returns, so if you attempt to do asynchronous operations in `onReceive`, they may get killed before they ever finish! The result is that sometimes things will appear to work, and sometimes they won't.

Similarly, do not do any long-running operations (such as network requests, disk or database reads or writes, and so on) in `BroadcastReceiver.onReceive`! `onReceive` is called from the UI thread, so if you do anything that may take more than a few hundred milliseconds, you can cause your app to appear to hang.

If you need to do asynchronous or long-running operations, update `OnAlarmReceiver` to subclass `android.support.v4.content.WakefulBroadcastReceiver` and create a new service to do all your heavy lifting. Remember to call `startWakefulService` to start your service, and remember to call `WakefulBroadcastReceiver.completeWakefulIntent` from your service when you are done.

See `http://d.android.com/reference/android/content/BroadcastReceiver.html` and `https://developer.android.com/reference/android/support/v4/content/WakefulBroadcastReceiver.html` for more information.

Now, register the `OnAlarmReceiver` in your `AndroidManifest.xml` by adding the following line inside your `application` element:

```
<receiver android:name=".receiver.OnAlarmReceiver"
          android:exported="false"/>
```

At this point, you should be able to run your app, create a new task, and watch it immediately pop up a reminder notification in your status bar, as in Figure 14-1.

Figure 14-1:
An important reminder.

The `NotificationManager` has a lot of other options for getting the user's attention. You can augment a notification using one — or more — of these options:

- ✔ **Vibration:** The device vibrates briefly when a notification is received — useful when the device is in the user's pocket.

- ✔ **Sound:** An alarm sounds when the notification is received. A ringtone or a prerecorded tone that you install along with your application is useful when the user has cranked up the notification sound level.

- ✔ **Light:** The LED light on the device flashes at a given interval in the color you specify. (Many devices contain an LED that you can program.) If the LED supports only a single color, such as white, it flashes in that color and ignores your color specification. If the user has set the volume level to silent, the light provides an excellent cue that something needs attention.

✔ **Expandable preview:** The user can expand a notification by using the pinch-and-zoom gesture. The expandable notification is a helpful way to show users an expanded preview of the notification content, such as a message preview for an email application.

✔ **Action buttons:** A user has always been able to tap a notification to launch the app that created it. However, you can add as many as three additional buttons to a Jelly Bean app to make it perform whatever operations you want. One outstanding example in the Tasks app is having the Snooze button temporarily dismiss the notification and bring it back later.

Go to `http://d.android.com/guide/topics/ui/notifiers/notifications.html` for more information about creating more advanced notifications.

Updating a Notification

At some point, you might need to update the view of your notification, such as when your code runs in the background, to see whether tasks have been reviewed. This code checks to see whether any notifications are overdue. Suppose that after the two-hour mark passes, you want to change the icon of the notification to a red exclamation point and quickly flash the LED in red. Thankfully, updating the notification is a fairly simple process.

If you call the `notify()` method again with an ID that's already active on the status bar, the notification is updated on the status bar. Therefore, to update the notification, you simply create a new `Notification` object with the same ID and text (but with a different red icon) and then call `notify()` again to update the notification.

Clearing a Notification

Users constitute an unpredictable group — whether they're first-time users or advanced power users, they can be located anywhere in the world and use their devices in their own, special ways. At some point, a user may see a notification and decide to open the app using the app launcher instead. If this happens while a notification is active, the notification persists. Even if the user looks at the task at hand, the notification still persists on the status bar. Your application should be able to simply recognize the state of the application and take the appropriate measures to cancel any existing notifications for the task. However, if the user opens your app and reviews a different task that has no active notification, your app shouldn't clear the notification.

Clear only the notification that the user is reviewing.

The `NotificationManager` makes it simple to cancel an existing notification by using the `cancel()` method. This method accepts one parameter — the ID of the notification. You may recall using the ID of the task as the ID of the note. The ID of the task is unique to the Tasks application. By doing this, you can easily open a task and cancel any existing notification by calling the `cancel()` method with the ID of the task.

At some point, you might also need to clear all previously shown notifications. To do this, simply call the `cancelAll()` method on the `NotificationManager`.

Rebooting Devices

You probably forget things from time to time. It's only human. The Android `AlarmManager` is no different. The `AlarmManager` doesn't persist alarms; therefore, when the device reboots, you must set up the alarms again.

If you don't set up your alarms again, they simply don't fire because, to Android, they don't exist.

Creating a boot receiver

The `RECEIVE_BOOT_COMPLETED` permission allows your application to receive a broadcast notification from Android when the device is done booting and is eligible to be interactive with the user. Because the Android system can broadcast a message when this event is complete, you need to add another `BroadcastReceiver` to your project. This `BroadcastReceiver` is responsible for handling the boot notification from Android. When the broadcast is received, the receiver needs to retrieve the tasks from the `TaskProvider` and loop through each task and schedule an alarm for it, to ensure that your alarms don't get lost in the reboot.

Add a new `BroadcastReceiver` to your application. For the Tasks application, the `BroadcastReceiver` has the name `OnBootReceiver`. You also need to add the following lines of code to the application element in the `AndroidManifest.xml` file:

```
<receiver android:name=".receiver.OnBootReceiver" android:exported="false">
    <intent-filter>
        <action android:name="android.intent.action.BOOT_COMPLETED"/>
    </intent-filter>
</receiver>
```

This snippet informs Android that OnBootReceiver should receive boot notifications for the BOOT_COMPLETED action. In layman's terms, it lets OnBootReceiver know when the device is done booting up.

The full implementation of OnBootReceiver is shown in Listing 14-2. Add this class to your com/dummies/tasks/receiver directory:

Listing 14-2: The OnBootReceiver Class

```
public class OnBootReceiver extends BroadcastReceiver {                      →1

    @Override
    public void onReceive(Context context, Intent intent) {                 →4

        Cursor cursor = context.getContentResolver().query(
            TaskProvider.CONTENT_URI, null, null, null, null);              →7

        // If our db is empty, don't do anything
        if (cursor == null)
            return;

        try {
            cursor.moveToFirst();                                           →14

            int taskIdColumnIndex = cursor
                .getColumnIndex(TaskProvider.COLUMN_TASKID);                →17
            int dateTimeColumnIndex = cursor
                .getColumnIndex(TaskProvider.COLUMN_DATE_TIME);
            int titleColumnIndex = cursor
                .getColumnIndex(TaskProvider.COLUMN_TITLE);                 →21

            while (!cursor.isAfterLast()) {                                 →23

                long taskId = cursor.getLong(taskIdColumnIndex);            →25
                long dateTime = cursor.getLong(dateTimeColumnIndex);        →26
                String title = cursor.getString(titleColumnIndex);         →27

                Calendar cal = Calendar.getInstance();
                cal.setTime(new Date(dateTime));                           →30

                ReminderManager.setReminder(context, taskId,               →32
                        title, cal);

                cursor.moveToNext();                                       →35
            }

        } finally {
            cursor.close();                                                →39
        }
    }
}
```

The numbered lines are detailed in this list:

→ **1**　　The definition of the `OnBootReceiver`.

→ **4**　　The `onReceive()` method that's called when the receiver receives an intent to perform an action.

→ **7**　　Obtains a cursor with all the reminders from the `TaskProvider` via the `ContentResolver`. It's similar to the calls used to update and delete reminders in the `TaskEditFragment` and `TaskListFragment`.

→ **14**　　Moves to the first record in the `Cursor`.

→ **17–21**　Each row in the cursor contains several columns of data. These lines get the index for the task, date/time, and title.

You want to find the ID of the row as well as the date and time so that you can schedule the reminder. You also need the title to display to the user. To get this information, you need to find the index of the columns that contain this information.

→ **23**　　Sets up a `while` loop that checks to see whether the cursor has moved past the last record. If it equals false, the app moves to line 25. If this value is true, no more records are available to use in the cursor.

→ **25–27**　The ID, title, and `dateTime` are retrieved from the cursor for this row using the column indices from lines 17–21.

→ **30**　　After the date is retrieved from the cursor, the `Calendar` variable needs to be updated with the correct time. This line sets the local `Calendar` object to the time of the task in the row.

→ **32**　　Schedules a new reminder with the row ID from the database at the time defined by the recently built `Calendar` variable.

→ **35**　　Moves to the next record in the cursor. If no more records exist in the cursor, the call to `isAfterLast()` on line 23 returns `true`, which means that the `while` loop exits. Otherwise, the next row is processed.

→ **39**　　Closes the cursor because it's no longer needed. `BroadcastReceivers` generally don't use loaders, so you need to close the cursor.

When you previously worked with the `Cursor` object in Chapter 13, you didn't have to close the cursor. This is because the `Loader` object was managing the cursor.

If you were to start the application, create a few reminders, and then reboot the device, you would see that the reminders persisted.

Checking the boot receiver

If you're unsure whether OnBootReceiver is working, you can place log statements into the while loop, like this:

```
Log.d("OnBootReceiver", "Adding alarm from boot.");
Log.d("OnBootReceiver", "Row Id - " + rowId);
```

This snippet prints messages to the system log. You can then shut down the emulator (or device) and start it again. Watch the messages stream in logcat, and look for OnBootReceiver messages. If you have two tasks in your database, you should see two sets of messages informing you of the system adding an alarm during boot.

Interested in adding even more features to your feature-rich app? Visit the book's online web extras at www.dummies.com/extras/androidapp development to learn how to incorporate GPS location information into your Tasks app.

Chapter 15

Working with Android Preferences

. . . .

In This Chapter

▶ Seeing how preferences work in Android

▶ Building a preferences screen

▶ Working with preferences programmatically

. . . .

Most programs need to be configured to suit a user's needs with individual settings or preferences. Allowing users to configure your Android application gives it a usability advantage. Thankfully, creating and providing a mechanism to edit preferences in Android is a fairly easy process.

Android provides, out of the box, a robust preferences framework that lets you define preferences for your application. Android stores preferences as persistent key-value pairs of primitive data types for you. The Android preferences framework commits the values you provide to internal storage on behalf of your application. You can use the preferences framework to store Boolean, float, int, long, and string elements. The data *persists* across user sessions — if the user closes the app and reopens it later, the preferences are saved and can be used, even if your application is killed or the phone restarts.

This chapter delves into the Android preferences framework and describes how to incorporate it into your applications. You find out how to use the built-in `PreferenceFragment` to create and edit preferences and how to read and write preferences from code within your application. At the end of this chapter, you'll have integrated preferences fully into the Tasks app.

Understanding the Android Preferences Framework

One outstanding quality of the Android preferences framework is the simplicity of developing a screen that allows users to modify their preferences. Most of the heavy lifting is done for you by Android because developing a preferences screen is as simple as defining it in the XML located in the `res/xml` folder of your project. Though these XML files aren't the same as layout files, there are specific XML definitions that define screens, categories, and actual preferences. Common preferences that are built into the framework include

- `EditTextPreference`: Stores plain text as a string
- `CheckBoxPreference`: Stores a Boolean value
- `RingtonePreference`: Allows the user to store a preferred ringtone from those available on the device
- `ListPreference`: Allows the user to select a preferred item from a list of items in the dialog box

If the built-in preferences don't suit your needs, you can create your own preference by deriving it from the base `Preference` class or `DialogPreference`. A `DialogPreference` is the base class for preferences that are dialog-box-based. Tapping one of these preferences opens a dialog box showing the preference controls. Examples of built-in `DialogPreferences` are `EditTextPreference` and `ListPreference`.

Android also provides a `PreferenceFragment` in which you can load a preferences screen similar to how you load a layout for a basic `Fragment` class. This base class allows you to tap into the `PreferenceFragment` events and perform advanced work, such as setting an `EditTextPreference` to accept only numbers.

Understanding the Preference Fragment Class

The responsibility of the `PreferenceFragment` class is to show a hierarchy of `Preference` objects as lists, possibly spanning multiple screens, as shown in Figure 15-1.

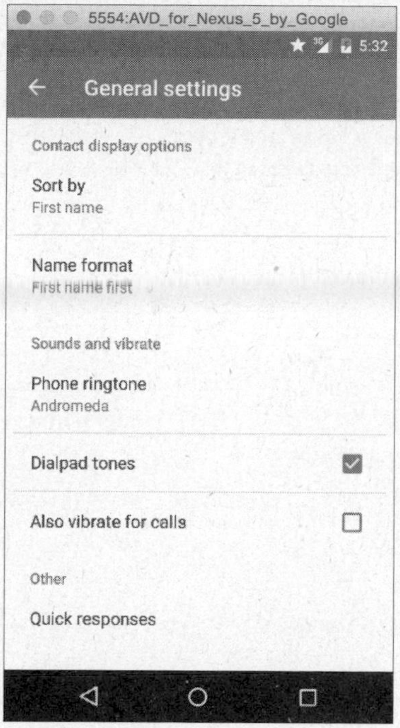

Figure 15-1:
The
preferences
screen for
the call
settings in
Android.

When preferences are edited, they're stored using an instance of
`SharedPreferences`. The `SharedPreferences` class is an interface
for accessing and modifying preference data returned by `getShared`
`Preferences()` from any `Context` object.

A `PreferenceFragment` is a base class that's similar to the `Fragment`
base class. However, the `PreferenceFragment` behaves a bit differently. One of the most important features that the `PreferenceFragment`
handles is the displaying of preferences in the visual style that resembles
the system preferences. This gives your application a consistent feel across
the board in regard to Android user interface components. You should use
the `PreferenceFragment` when dealing with preferences screens in your
Android applications.

Persisting preference values

Because the Android framework stores preferences in the
`SharedPreferences`, which automatically stores the preference data in
internal storage, you can easily create a preference. When a user edits a

preference, the value is automatically saved for you; you don't have to do any persisting yourself.

Figure 15-2 shows a preference being set in the Tasks app. After the user taps OK, Android persists the value to `SharedPreferences`. Android does all the heavy lifting in regard to persisting the preference values.

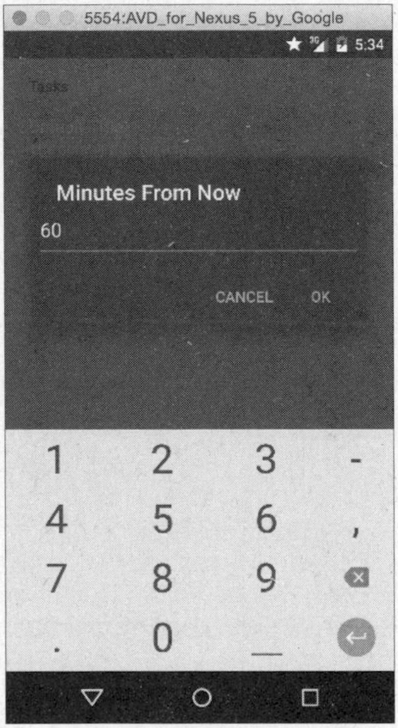

Figure 15-2:
Setting a
preference.

Laying out preferences

Working with layouts in Android can sometimes be a painstaking process of alignment, gravity, and other complicating factors. Building layouts is almost like building a website with various tables all over the place. Sometimes it's easy; sometimes it isn't. Thankfully, laying out Android preferences is much simpler than defining a layout for the application screen.

Android preference building blocks are broken into these types:

✔ `Preference`: A preference that's shown onscreen. This preference can be any common preference (such as a check box or text field), or a custom one that you define.

✔ `PreferenceCategory`: This building block is used to group preference objects and provide a title that describes the category. In Figure 15-1, the Contact display options item is a `PreferenceCategory`.

✔ `PreferenceScreen`: Represents a top-level preference that's the root of a preference hierarchy. All the categories and preferences in Figure 15-1 are rooted in a `PreferenceScreen` called "General settings." You can use a `PreferenceScreen` in these two places:

- *In a* `PreferenceFragment`: All the categories and preferences in the `PreferenceScreen` are shown in the `PreferenceFragment`.

- *In another preference hierarchy:* When present in another hierarchy, the `PreferenceScreen` serves as a gateway to another screen of preferences (similar to nesting `PreferenceScreen` declarations inside other `PreferenceScreen` declarations). Though this concept might seem confusing, you can think of it as XML, where you can declare an element and any element can contain the same parent element. At that point, you're nesting the elements. The same statement applies to the `PreferenceScreen`. By nesting `PreferenceScreens`, you're informing Android that it should show a new screen when selected.

By laying out a combination of the `PreferenceScreen`, `PreferenceCategory`, and `Preference` in XML, you can easily create a preferences screen that looks similar to Figure 15-1.

Creating Your Preferences Screen

Creating preferences using the `PreferenceFragment` and a preference XML file is a fairly straightforward process. The first thing you do is create the preference XML file, which defines the layout of the preferences and the string resource values that show up onscreen. These string resources are presented as `TextViews` onscreen to help the user determine what the preference does.

Your `PreferenceScreen` should give users the chance to set the default time for a reminder (in minutes) and a default title for a new task. As the application stands now, the default title is empty and the default reminder time is set to the current time. These preferences allow the user to save a couple of steps while building new tasks. For example, if the user normally builds tasks with a reminder time of 60 minutes from the current time, the user can now specify it in the preferences. This new value becomes the value of the reminder time when the user creates a new task.

Building the preferences file

To build your first preferences screen, create a res/xml folder in your project. Inside the res/xml folder, create an XML file and name it task_preferences.xml. Add the code in Listing 15-1 to the file.

Listing 15-1: The task_preferences.xml File

```
<?xml version="1.0" encoding="utf-8"?>
<PreferenceScreen xmlns:android="http://schemas.android.com/apk/res/android">  →2

    <PreferenceCategory                                                         →4
        android:title="@string/tasks">                                          →5

        <EditTextPreference                                                     →7
            android:key="@string/pref_task_title_key"                           →8
            android:summary="@string/default_title_description"                 →9
            android:title="@string/default_title"/>                             →10

        <EditTextPreference                                                     →12
            android:key="@string/pref_default_time_from_now_key"                →13
            android:summary="@string/minutes_from_now_description"              →14
            android:title="@string/minutes_from_now"/>                          →15

    </PreferenceCategory>
</PreferenceScreen>
```

Each numbered line of code is explained as follows:

→ 2   The root-level PreferenceScreen; it's the container for the screen itself. All other preferences live below this declaration.

→ 4   A PreferenceCategory that defines the category for task defaults, such as title or body.

→ 5   Defines the category title. You define the @string/tasks and other strings in the next section.

→ 7   Contains the definition of the EditTextPreference, which is responsible for storing the preference for the default title of a task.

→ 8   Contains the key for the default title text EditTextPreference. The key is the name of the preference, which you will use when you want to check the value of the preference.

→ 9   Defines the summary text that's present on the preferences screen. It's a helpful message that describes what the preference does in more detail.

→ 10   Defines the title of the preference on the preferences screen. It is also the title used in the dialog box that pops up when the user edits the preference.

→ 12   The start of the definition of the EditTextPreference, which stores the default time in minutes (digits) that the task reminder time defaults to from the current time.

→ 13   Defines the key for the default task time preference.

→ 14   Defines the summary of the preference that's present on the main preferences screen.

→ 15   Defines the title of the preference on the preferences screen.

Adding string resources

For your application to compile, you need the string resources for the preferences. In the res/values/strings.xml file, add these values:

```
<string name="default_title">Default Title</string>
<string name="tasks">Tasks</string>
<string name="default_title_description">
    The default title for a task.</string>
<string name="minutes_from_now">Minutes From Now</string>
<string name="minutes_from_now_description">
    The number of minutes into the future to set the reminder.</string>
<string name="pref_task_title_key">default_task_title</string>
<string name="pref_default_time_from_now_key">time_from_now_default</string>
```

You should now be able to compile your application.

Working with the Preference Fragment Class

Defining a preferences screen is fairly simple: You provide the values to the necessary attributes and you're done. Though the preferences screen may be defined in XML, simply defining it in XML doesn't mean that it will show up onscreen. To display your preferences screen, you create a PreferenceFragment.

To inflate and display the PreferenceScreen you may have just built, add a fragment that derives from PreferenceFragment to your application and name it PreferencesFragment. Add the code in Listing 15-2.

Listing 15-2: **The PreferencesFragment File**

```
public class PreferencesFragment extends PreferenceFragment {          →1

    @Override
    public void onCreate(Bundle savedInstanceState) {
        super.onCreate(savedInstanceState);

        // Construct the preferences screen from the XML config
        addPreferencesFromResource(R.xml.task_preferences);            →8

        // Use the number keyboard when editing the time preference
        EditTextPreference timeDefault = (EditTextPreference)          →11
                findPreference(getString(R.string
                        .pref_default_time_from_now_key));
        timeDefault.getEditText().setKeyListener(DigitsKeyListener     →14
                .getInstance());
    }
}
```

That's all the code needed to display, edit, and persist preferences in Android. The numbered lines of code are explained in this list:

→ **1**   The `PreferencesFragment` class file is defined by inheriting from the `PreferenceFragment` base class.

→ **8**   The call to the `addPreferencesFromResource()` method is provided with the resource ID of the `task_preferences.xml` file that's stored in the `res/xml` directory.

→ **11**   Retrieves the `EditTextPreference` for the default task reminder time by calling the `findPreference()` method and providing it with the key that was defined in the `task_preferences.xml` file.

→ **14**   Obtains the `EditText` object from the `EditTextPreference` using the `getEditText()` method. The `setKeyListener()` method is called to set the key listener on the `EditText` to an instance of `DigitsKeyListener`, which allows only digits to be typed into the `EditTextPreference`.

You don't want users to enter string values such as `foo` or `bar` into the field because it isn't a valid integer value. Using the `DigitsKeyListener` ensures that the only values passed into the preferences are digits.

Now that you have the `PreferencesFragment`, you need an activity to display it. Create a new file named `PreferencesActivity.java` in `com/dummies/tasks/activity` and add the following code:

```
/**
 * An activity for displaying and editing preferences.
 * Uses a PreferencesFragment to do all of the dirty work.
 */
public class PreferencesActivity extends Activity {

    @Override
    protected void onCreate(Bundle savedInstanceState) {
        super.onCreate(savedInstanceState);

        getFragmentManager().beginTransaction().replace(          →11
                android.R.id.content,
                new PreferencesFragment()).commit();
    }

}
```

This activity is very simple. All it does is create a new `PreferencesFragment` and replace the existing activity content with that fragment on line 11.

At this point, you can use your activity. This `PreferencesActivity` allows users to edit and save their preferences. As you can see, this implementation requires only a snippet of code.

Add your new `PreferencesActivity` to the `AndroidManifest.xml` file by using this line of code:

```
<activity android:name="com.dummies.tasks.activity.PreferencesActivity"/>
```

The next step is displaying the preferences screen by adding a menu item.

Starting the PreferencesActivity

To open this new activity, you add a menu item to the `TaskListFragment` by simply adding a new menu definition to the `menu_list.xml` file that's located in the `res/menu` directory. Updating this file updates the menu on the `TaskListFragment`. The updated `menu_list.xml` file is shown here with the new entry in bold:

```xml
<?xml version="1.0" encoding="utf-8"?>
<menu xmlns:android="http://schemas.android.com/apk/res/android">

    <item
        android:id="@+id/menu_insert"
        android:icon="@android:drawable/ic_menu_add"
        android:showAsAction="always"
        android:title="@string/menu_insert"/>

    <item
        android:id="@+id/menu_settings"
        android:showAsAction="never"
        android:title="@string/menu_settings"/>
</menu>
```

The last item adds a menu item for settings, which uses the `menu_settings` string resource. You add a new string resource named `menu_settings` with a value of `Settings` in your string resources. Because the Settings menu is significantly less important than the Insert menu item, you don't want to clutter the action bar with an icon for the Settings menu. Instead, use `showAsAction="never"` to ensure that the Settings menu is always displayed in the overflow menu rather than directly on the action bar.

See `http://d.android.com/design/patterns/settings.html` and `http://www.google.com/design/spec/patterns/settings.html` for more tips about how to create your settings menus.

Handling menu selections

After your menu is updated, the app needs to respond whenever the user taps a menu item. To make it do this, you add code to the `onOptions ItemSelected()` method in the `TaskListFragment`. The code to handle the Settings menu selection is bold in this snippet:

```java
@Override
public boolean onOptionsItemSelected(MenuItem item) {
    switch (item.getItemId()) {
        case R.id.menu_insert:
            ((OnEditTask) getActivity()).editTask(0);
            return true;
        case R.id.menu_settings:
            startActivity(new Intent(getActivity(),
                    PreferencesActivity.class));
            return true;
    }

    return super.onOptionsItemSelected(item);
}
```

This code creates a new `Intent` object with a destination class of `PreferencesActivity`. A user who selects the Settings menu item is shown the preferences screen to edit his preferences. If you start the app and select Settings, you should see a screen similar to the one shown in Figure 15-3.

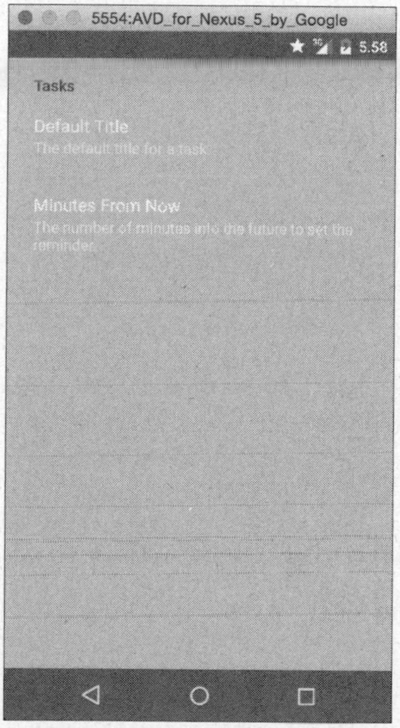

Figure 15-3: The preferences screen.

Working with Preferences in Your Activities at Runtime

Though setting preferences in a `PreferencesFragment` is useful, it provides no value in the end unless you can read the preferences from the `SharedPreferences` object at runtime and use them in your application. Thankfully, Android makes the process fairly simple.

In the Tasks app, you read these values in the `TaskEditFragment` to set the default values when a user creates a new task. Because the preferences are stored in `SharedPreferences`, you can access the preferences across various activities in your application.

Retrieving preference values

Open the `TaskEditFragment` and navigate to the `onCreateView()` method. It determines whether the task is an existing task or a new task. If the task is new, you pull the default values from `SharedPreferences` and load them into the activity for the user. If for some reason the user has never specified her preferences, they're empty strings and you ignore the defaults. You use the preferences only if the user has set them.

To retrieve preference values, you use the `SharedPreferences` object, as shown in Listing 15-3. Add the bold code to the very bottom of `onCreateView()`.

Listing 15-3:   Retrieving Values from SharedPreferences

```
        if (taskId == 0) {                                          →1
            SharedPreferences prefs = PreferenceManager             →2
                .getDefaultSharedPreferences(getActivity());
            String defaultTitleKey = getString(R.string             →4
                .pref_task_title_key);
            String defaultTimeKey = getString(R.string              →6
                .pref_default_time_from_now_key);

            String defaultTitle = prefs.getString(defaultTitleKey, null);   →9
            String defaultTime = prefs.getString(defaultTimeKey, null);     →10

            if (defaultTitle != null)
                titleText.setText(defaultTitle);                    →13

            if (defaultTime != null && defaultTime.length() > 0)
                taskDateAndTime.add(Calendar.MINUTE,                →16
                    Integer.parseInt(defaultTime));

            updateDateAndTimeButtons();                             →19

        } else {

            // Fire off a background loader to retrieve the data from the
            // database
            getLoaderManager().initLoader(0, null, this);

        }
```

Each new line of code is explained in this list:

→ **1**   If the `taskId` is 0, then you know the task's ID hasn't been set yet. This means it's a new task.

→ 2   Retrieves the `SharedPreferences` object from the static `getDefaultSharedPreferences()` call on the `PreferenceManager` object.

→ 4   Retrieves the key value for the default title preference from the string resources. This same key is used in Listing 15-1 to define the preference.

→ 6   Retrieves the key value for the default time offset, in minutes, from the preferences.

→ 9   Retrieves the default title value from the preferences with a call to `getString()` on the `SharedPreferences` object. The first parameter is the key for the preference, and the second parameter is the default value if the preference doesn't exist (or hasn't been set). In this instance, the default value is `null` if the preference doesn't exist.

→ 10   Retrieves the default time value from the preferences, using the same method as described on line 9 with a different key.

→ 13   Sets the text value of the `EditText` view — which is the title of the task. This value is set if the preference wasn't `null`.

→ 16   Increments time on the `taskDateAndTime Calendar` field by calling the `add()` method with the parameter of `Calendar.MINUTE` if the value from the preferences wasn't equal to an empty string. The `Calendar.MINUTE` constant informs the `Calendar` object that the next parameter should be treated as minutes and the value should be added to the calendar's Minute field. If the minutes force the calendar into a new hour or day, the `Calendar` object updates the other fields for you.

    For example, if the calendar was originally set to 2016-08-31 11:45 p.m. and you add 60 minutes to the calendar, the new value of the calendar is 2016-09-01 12:45 a.m. Because `EditTextPreference` stores all values as strings, the string parses the minute value to an integer with the `Integer.parseInt()` method. By adding time to the `taskDateAndTime Calendar` field, the time picker and button text associated with opening the time picker update as well.

→ 19   Updates the date and time buttons to reflect the time added to the existing `taskDateAndTime Calendar` field.

When you build, reinstall, and start the application, you can now set the preferences and see them reflected when you choose to add a new task to the list. Try clearing the preferences and then choosing to create a new task. Notice that the defaults no longer apply — easy!

Setting preference values

Though updating preference values via Java isn't done in the Tasks app, at times you might need to in your own apps. Suppose that you develop a help-desk ticket system application that requires users to enter their current departments. You have a `Preference` object for the default department, but the user never uses the preferences screen and therefore repeatedly enters the department into your application manually. Using logic that you define and write, you determine that the user is entering the same department for each help-desk ticket (assume that it's the Accounting department), so you prompt him to determine whether he wants to set the default department to Accounting. If he chooses Yes, you programmatically update the preferences for him.

To edit preferences programmatically, you need an instance of `Shared Preferences`. You can obtain it via `PreferenceManager`, as shown in Listing 15-4. After you obtain an instance of `SharedPreferences`, you can edit various preferences by obtaining an instance of the preference `Editor` object. After the preferences are edited, you need to apply the changes, also demonstrated in Listing 15-4.

Listing 15-4:   Programmatically Editing Preferences

```
SharedPreferences prefs =
    PreferenceManager.getDefaultSharedPreferences(this);      →2
Editor editor = prefs.edit();                                 →3
editor.putString("default_department", "Accounting");         →4
editor.apply();                                               →5
```

The numbered lines of code are explained in this list:

→ 2   An instance of `SharedPreferences` is retrieved from the `PreferenceManager`.

→ 3   An instance of the preferences `Editor` object is obtained by calling the `edit()` method on the `SharedPreferences` object.

→ 4   Edits a preference with the key value of `default_department` by calling the `putString()` method on the `Editor` object. The value is set to `"Accounting"`. Normally, the key value is retrieved from the string resources, and the value of the string is retrieved via your program or user input. The code snippet remains simple for brevity.

→ 5   After changes are made to any preferences, you must call the `apply()` method on the `Editor` object to persist them to `Shared Preferences`. The `apply` call automatically replaces any value stored in `SharedPreferences` with the key given in the `putString()` call.

If you don't call `apply()` on the `Editor` object, your changes don't persist and your application may not function as you expect.

Part IV
Android Is More than Phones

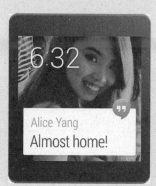

In this part . . .

Part IV introduces you to the world beyond Android phones. Android tablets, watches, and TVs are a different sort of beast than Android phones, and this part walks you through all the changes you need to make to your app so it can run on these other Android devices.

Should you want to go beyond the realm of standard Android, you will also find everything you need to add support for Android-based (but non-Google) devices, such as the Amazon Fire.

Chapter 16

Developing for Tablets

You need to master some tricks of the trade to make your apps work on tablets and on phones. In this chapter, you can get an overview of the differences betweeen phones and tablets, and then find out how to design the Tasks application to work on both types of devices.

Considering the Differences between Phones and Tablets

Android tablets and Android phones have some obvious differences, and size immediately comes to mind, but that is only one of the differences:

✔ Tablets are designed to be held in two hands, whereas phones are designed for only one.

✔ Android tablet screens tend not to extend past the 7-to-10-inch range, and the largest phones max out around 6 inches.

The line between tablet and phone can blur at the 5-inch mark. Some "tweener" devices are marketed as phones, and others with nearly the same specs are marketed as tablets.

✔ Tablet orientation varies depending on usage, whereas almost all Android phones have settled on portrait orientation for their screens.

Many Android tablets are designed for wide-screen media viewing, so they favor landscape orientation. Others, such as the Nexus 7 and Kindle Fire, are designed primarily for use in portrait mode. That's not to say that you can't run an app in portrait mode on a landscape tablet (or vice versa), but be aware that many users may run your app in an orientation other than the one in which you completed most of your testing.

Tablets and phones also have some differences in hardware design and operation that affect app design. This list describes them from the tablet perspective:

✔ Tablets often lack always-on 3G or 4G data connections.

✔ Tablets tend to be larger, use larger batteries, and benefit from much longer battery life than their phone counterparts.

✔ Tablets may have cheaper cameras — or no cameras — because tablet cameras typically get less use than phone cameras.

✔ Tablets often lack such common phone capabilities as GPS location service.

In addition, don't be surprised if you have to design your app (or tweak an existing one) to accommodate new tablet features.

Tweaking the Tasks App for Tablets

To help accommodate the differences, you use a few techniques to upgrade the Tasks app so that it can work on both tablets and phones.

Use these strategies every time you design an Android application because it's likely that most of your apps target users of both types of devices.

Anticipating screen size with a responsive layout

Go with the flow when you're designing your layout to fit multiple screen sizes. A flowing, or *responsive*, layout skips a lot of hassle and frustration for both the designer and the user.

If you're familiar with iOS development from a few years back, you know that back then you only had a few screen sizes to worry about: a couple of iPhone sizes, and a couple of iPad sizes. Each size required both low- and high-resolution images, but that was easy enough to handle: Design for iPhone first, and *then* for iPad, and then plug in the low- and high-resolution images in the respective versions and you were done.

Android has never been quite as simple to design for. Layouts in Android need to "flow" — that is, resize and rearrange themselves — so that they can accommodate minor (and sometimes major) differences in the width and height of users' devices. Android developers have dozens or hundreds of different sizes of devices to worry about.

It's similar to designing for websites — when you're building a website, you can't assume that all users will view it in browser windows that are exactly the same size (800 x 600 pixels). Users may view the site from bigger (or sometimes smaller) browser windows; your design must be flexible enough to give a good experience to the whole range of sizes. Designing for Android makes the same requirement. In fact, iOS is now moving in this same direction, and encouraging their developers to use flowing layouts as well.

So how do you perform this bit of magic? For openers, don't try to use fixed dimensions (such as 10px or 120dp) in your layouts. Instead, favor *relative* dimensions, such as "wrap_content" and "match_parent" as much as possible. The idea is to achieve a *responsive* layout that can resize to fit the device.

The following code shows a layout that makes too many assumptions about the device it's on:

```
<?xml version="1.0" encoding="utf-8"?>
<TextView xmlns:android="http://schemas.android.com/apk/res/android"
    android:layout_width="300px"
    android:layout_height="match_parent"
    android:lines="1"
    android:text="Occurrences of the word 'Internet' in the Gettysburg
            Address: 0 (unverified)"/>
```

The code has multiple problems:

- ✔ It uses a fixed-sized TextView rather than flexible dimensions, like wrap_content and match_parent.

- ✔ It uses pixels (px) to measure size, which doesn't scale automatically across different devices, as dp (device-independent pixels) would.

- ✔ It hard-codes the number of lines in TextView to 1 and doesn't tell Android what to do with any overflow.

✔ It doesn't use `ScrollView`, so if your layout is taller than the device screen, there's no way to see the offscreen views.

✔ Generally speaking, many of your layouts should be wrapped in a single `ScrollView` to handle unanticipated overflow off the bottom of the screen. Exceptions include layouts that already handle scrolling, such as `ListView`, which shouldn't be wrapped in a `ScrollView`. The example above uses only a single `TextView`, so it's unlikely to need a `ScrollView`, but more complicated layouts should consider them.

Figure 16-1 shows the `TextView` from the above code. It abruptly cuts off text midsentence because of the fixed size. If the developer had used a responsive layout, the text wouldn't have been cut off.

Figure 16-1:
A non-responsive layout that abruptly truncates after "Occurr-ences of …"

Fixing this particular example is easy by changing the width of the `TextView` and replacing `android:lines="1"` with `android:maxLines="3"`:

```xml
<?xml version="1.0" encoding="utf-8"?>
<TextView xmlns:android="http://schemas.android.com/apk/res/android"
    android:layout_width="match_parent"
    android:layout_height="match_parent"
    android:maxLines="3"
    android:text="Occurrences of the word 'Internet' in the Gettysburg Address:
            0 (unverified)"/>
```

When you're designing your layouts, always consider the maximum size of each item in your layout. The app content can take up more space than you expect, and it's important to anticipate these situations and plan for them rather than end up with an app that looks ugly.

Adding more fragments

Android uses fragments to help you deal with the additional real estate on tablets. The basic idea is that a typical phone activity centers on one, two, or three distinct groups of reusable onscreen items. Put each of these groups into its own fragment and it becomes easy to reuse across multiple activities.

You're going to do exactly this — you'll add the `TaskEditFragment` and the `TaskListFragment` from your two phone activities into a single new activity that tablet users will enjoy.

Figure 16-2 shows how Tasks fragments lay out on a phone and on a tablet.

Figure 16-2: Fragments can handle a single activity on a phone (left) or two activities on a tablet (right).

Without fragments, you'd have to reinvent the wheel every time you wanted to make an activity that shows a list of tasks. Using fragments, just write the code once and you can reuse it as many times as you want.

Creating different layouts for different devices

The fragment is a handy feature for the designer, but how do you slice and dice fragments to show the right experience for the right device? The tablet's relatively vast screen real estate (compared to a phone) can show one or two more fragments on a single activity.

You can use one layout containing a single activity for your phone and another layout containing multiple fragments for your tablet. For example, here's the `TaskListActivity` layout for the phone size in the Tasks app:

```xml
<?xml version="1.0" encoding="utf-8"?>
<fragment xmlns:android="http://schemas.android.com/apk/res/android"
          android:name="com.dummies.tasks.fragment.TaskListFragment"
          android:layout_width="match_parent"
          android:layout_height="match_parent"
/>
```

And Listing 16-1 shows how you might modify the code using two fragments to create a two-column layout on a tablet:

Listing 16-1: Two-Column Table Layout Example

```xml
<?xml version="1.0" encoding="utf-8?>"
<LinearLayout xmlns:android="http://schemas.android.com/apk/res/android"
      android:layout_width="match_parent"
      android:orientation="horizontal"
      android:layout_height="match_parent">

<fragment
          android:id="@+id/list_fragment"
          android:name="com.dummies.tasks.fragment.TaskListFragment"
          android:layout_width="0dp"
          android:layout_weight="1"
          android:layout_height="match_parent"
/>

<fragment
          android:id="@+id/edit_fragment"
          android:name="com.dummies.tasks.fragment.TaskEditFragment"
          android:layout_width="0dp"
          android:layout_weight="1"
          android:layout_height="match_parent"
/>

</LinearLayout>
```

This is very similar to what you'll do later in the chapter to put two fragments next to each other.

Three strategies for adding tablet support

There are three main strategies that you can use to make your phone app work on tablets. Each is perfectly reasonable and has its own set of advantages and disadvantages.

The first strategy is to make two different apps: one for phones and one for tablets. This sounds wasteful, but in fact it's quite easy to use *build variants* to create two different apps from nearly the same codebase.

The advantage of this strategy is that you can keep all your shared code in one place but keep any phone-specific or tablet-specific code in separate directories. That way, the tablet code won't need to be installed on phones where it won't be used, and vice versa. The disadvantage of this strategy is that you need to manage two APKs, one for phones and one for tablets, every time you make a new release of your app.

The second strategy is to use a single app for both types of devices, but use different activities and choose between them when you launch the app. For example, the phone app might have a `TaskListActivity` which shows a list of tasks, and the tablet might have a `TaskListAndEditActivity` which shows a list of tasks, but also shows the edit fragment next to the list (as described in the previous section). You would then add a special `LaunchActivity` which would be your app's main launcher activity in the `AndroidManifest`. At startup, the `LaunchActivity` would quickly detect if you were on a tablet or on a phone, and start the appropriate activity before finishing itself. It would happen so fast that users would never even see the `LaunchActivity` itself.

The advantage of this strategy is that your app will still appear as a single app in the Google Play Store. The disadvantage is that all the phone code will also be installed on all your tablets, and vice versa.

The third strategy is to use the exact same activities on both phones and tablets, but to change the layouts for each type of device. This can work great for simple apps. The advantage of this strategy is that you don't need to worry about writing additional activities to handle different device types. The disadvantage is that your phone and tablet code can start getting tangled in your activities, potentially making the activities complicated.

In this chapter, you will use the first strategy and build two separate apps for phones and tablets. However, you may want to experiment with the second strategy (or even the third) after you finish this chapter.

Configuring a Tablet Emulator

First things first — you need a tablet on which to test your application. If you already have a tablet, you're well on your way; if you don't, then you need an emulator to emulate an Android device on your computer. Google calls these Android Virtual Devices (AVDs). Follow these steps to get the Google Nexus 7 AVD:

1. **Choose Tools⇨Android⇨AVD Manager in Android Studio.**
2. **Click Create Virtual Device.**

> 3. **Choose Tablet, then Nexus 7, and click Next.**
>
> 4. **Choose Lollipop 21 x86 and click Next.**
>
> 5. **Click Finish.**
>
> 6. **Choose the AVD you just created from the list of AVDs, and click the Start button to launch it.**

See Chapter 3 for a reminder of how to configure an emulator.

Creating a New Product Flavor

As mentioned in the "Three strategies for adding tablet support" sidebar, you are going to create two product "flavors" for your app — one for phones and one for tablets. Each flavor will have its own APK file. For the most part, the flavors will share the same code, but they can have some slight differences in code and configuration.

Add the following to the `android` section of your Tasks `build.gradle`:

```
productFlavors {
    phone {}
    tablet {}
}
```

Both flavors will use all of the default settings, so there is no need to add any configuration to either of them. Later, you will set up each flavor to use a slightly different set of files, but for now they're identical. When you do this, the shared code and resources will go into `src/main` (shared by all flavors), and the code for phones and tablets will go into `src/phone` and `src/tablet`, respectively, as specified by the name of the flavors you defined in the previous code.

Now choose Build➪Rebuild Project and build your project again. If you then choose View➪Tool Windows➪Messages, you should see your project being built for both phones and tablets as in Figure 16-3.

Figure 16-3:
Build
Messages
showing
Tasks being
built for
phones and
tablets.

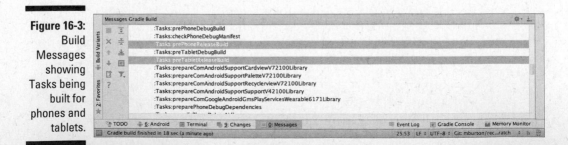

There's more to do, so go through the next sections before you try to install and run your two flavors.

Creating an AndroidManifest for Phones

There are going to be slight differences between your phone and tablet apps. Both require their own `AndroidManifest.xml` file. For the most part, the configuration will remain in your existing `AndroidManifest.xml`, but you'll need to make some specific changes for each flavor that goes into a phone and tablet `AndroidManifest.xml`. The information in the phone and tablet `AndroidManifest.xml` will override the information in the main `AndroidManifest.xml`.

Moving the TaskListAdapter

First, go to your `AndroidManifest.xml` file and remove the following code:

```
<activity
    android:name="com.dummies.tasks.activity.TaskListActivity"
    ...>
    <intent-filter>
        <action android:name="android.intent.action.MAIN" />
        <category android:name="android.intent.category.LAUNCHER" />
    <intent-filter>
</activity>
```

The `TaskListActivity` will be used only on your phone. You create a different activity for tablets. So for that reason, you just removed it from the shared `AndroidManifest.xml`.

The next step is to create the phone's `AndroidManifest.xml`. But before creating it, first create the phone directory by going to your `src` directory and creating a new directory named `phone`. The directory `phone` must match the name of the flavor you created in your `build.gradle` in the previous section.

Next, create a new `AndroidManifest.xml` file in the `src/phone` directory with the following contents:

```
<?xml version="1.0" encoding="utf-8"?>
<manifest xmlns:android="http://schemas.android.com/apk/res/android" >

    <application>
        <activity android:name="com.dummies.tasks.activity.TaskListActivity" >
            <intent-filter>
                <action android:name="android.intent.action.MAIN"/>
                <category android:name="android.intent.category.LAUNCHER"/>
            </intent-filter>
        </activity>
    </application>

</manifest>
```

You just moved the `TaskListActivity` from the shared `AndroidManifest.xml` to the phone-specific `AndroidManifest.xml`.

Now build and run your app to make sure you haven't broken anything. If everything worked properly, the app should run identically to how it did before you split the `AndroidManifest.xml`.

Informing the Google Play Store

There is one more thing you need to do: Tell the Google Play Store that the phone version of your app should only be visible and installable on phones, not tablets. If you do not do this, the Google Play Store will show the phone app to people on tablets!

Open the `src/phone/AndroidManifest.xml` file and add the code in bold:

```
<?xml version="1.0" encoding="utf-8"?>
<manifest xmlns:android="http://schemas.android.com/apk/res/android" >

    <compatible-screens>
        <!-- all small size screens -->
        <screen android:screenSize="small" android:screenDensity="ldpi" />      →6
        <screen android:screenSize="small" android:screenDensity="mdpi" />
        <screen android:screenSize="small" android:screenDensity="hdpi" />
        <screen android:screenSize="small" android:screenDensity="xhdpi"/>
        <screen android:screenSize="small" android:screenDensity="480" />       →10
        <!-- all normal size screens -->
        <screen android:screenSize="normal" android:screenDensity="ldpi" />     →12
        <screen android:screenSize="normal" android:screenDensity="mdpi" />
        <screen android:screenSize="normal" android:screenDensity="hdpi" />
```

```
      <screen android:screenSize="normal" android:screenDensity="xhdpi"/>
      <screen android:screenSize="normal" android:screenDensity="480" /> →16
   </compatible-screens>

   <application>
      <activity android:name="com.dummies.tasks.activity.TaskListActivity" >
         <intent-filter>
            <action android:name="android.intent.action.MAIN"/>
            <category android:name="android.intent.category.LAUNCHER"/>
         </intent-filter>
      </activity>
   </application>

</manifest>
```

The `compatible-screens` element is not used by Android or your app directly. It is used only by the Google Play Store to determine which devices this app is compatible with.

→ **10**   Declares that your app is compatible with all five resolutions of "`small`" screens (ldpi, mdpi, hdpi, xhdpi, and xxhdpi). You'll notice that instead of saying xxhdpi on line 10, we say 480. This is because, at the time of this writing, the `compatible-screens` element does not yet support xxhdpi directly, so we need to use the numerical value for xxhdpi, which is 480.

→ **12–16** Does the same, but for "`normal`" size devices.

These two sections declare that your app will run fine on small and normal devices, but will *not* run on large or extra-large devices (generally tablets).

The `compatible-screen` element is a little tricky. If you want to make changes to this section, make sure you read `http://d.android.com/guide/practices/screens-distribution.html`.

Creating an AndroidManifest for Tablets

Now that you have a fully functioning phone app again, it's time to start working on the tablet app.

Create a directory named `tablet` Inside the `src` directory. Inside the `tablet` directory, create an `AndroidManifest.xml` for tablets that looks like the following:

When creating new product flavors, the name of the directory under `src` must match the name of the flavor in the `build.gradle`. You can name them whatever you want, as long as they agree.

```
<?xml version="1.0" encoding="utf-8"?>
<manifest xmlns:android="http://schemas.android.com/apk/res/android" >

  <application>

      <!-- Declare our main activity, which will be different than the
           main activity for phones.
           -->
      <activity android:name=
           "com.dummies.tasks.tablet.activity.TaskListAndEditorActivity" >➡10
         <intent-filter>
             <action android:name="android.intent.action.MAIN"/>
             <category android:name="android.intent.category.LAUNCHER"/>
         </intent-filter>
      </activity>

  </application>

</manifest>
```

Just like the phone manifest in the previous section, this manifest declares a single activity that will be the main launcher activity for the app — except the activity for tablets is different from the one for phones.

You should receive an error on line 10. That's okay; you create the TaskListAndEditorActivity in the next section.

There is one more thing to do. You must tell the Google Play Store that this app is available only for tablets and not for phones. Add the following to your manifest:

```
<?xml version="1.0" encoding="utf-8"?>
<manifest xmlns:android="http://schemas.android.com/apk/res/android" >

  <compatible-screens>
      <!-- all large size screens -->
      <screen android:screenSize="large" android:screenDensity="ldpi" />
      <screen android:screenSize="large" android:screenDensity="mdpi" />
      <screen android:screenSize="large" android:screenDensity="hdpi" />
      <screen android:screenSize="large" android:screenDensity="xhdpi"/>
      <screen android:screenSize="large" android:screenDensity="480"  />
      <!-- all xlarge size screens -->
      <screen android:screenSize="xlarge" android:screenDensity="ldpi" />
      <screen android:screenSize="xlarge" android:screenDensity="mdpi" />
      <screen android:screenSize="xlarge" android:screenDensity="hdpi" />
      <screen android:screenSize="xlarge" android:screenDensity="xhdpi"/>
      <screen android:screenSize="xlarge" android:screenDensity="480"  />
  </compatible-screens>
```

```
<application>

    <!-- Declare our main activity, which will be different than the
        main activity for phones.
        -->
    <activity android:name=
        "com.dummies.tasks.tablet.activity.TaskListAndEditorActivity" >
        <intent-filter>
            <action android:name="android.intent.action.MAIN"/>
            <category android:name="android.intent.category.LAUNCHER"/>
        </intent-filter>
    </activity>

</application>

</manifest>
```

Notice the difference between the phone manifest and the tablet manifest. In the phone manifest, you said the flavor supported small and normal screens, but in the tablet manifest you say it supports large and xlarge screens.

Making the TaskListAndEditorActivity for Tablets

You've created and built the phone app. You've declared the manifest file for the tablet app. The next step is to create the TaskListAndEditorActivity which only tablets will use.

Creating the tablet activity class

The first step is to create the directories you need. Create the following directories inside the tablet directory:

- ✔ java
- ✔ java/com
- ✔ java/com/dummies
- ✔ java/com/dummies/tasks
- ✔ java/com/dummies/tasks/tablet
- ✔ java/com/dummies/tasks/tablet/activity

Then create a new file inside the `tablet/java/com/dummies/tasks/` `tablet/activity` directory named `TaskListAndEditorActivity.java` with the following code:

```
public class TaskListAndEditorActivity extends Activity
    implements OnEditTask, OnEditFinished                              →2
{

    @Override
    public void onCreate(Bundle savedInstanceState) {
        super.onCreate(savedInstanceState);
        setContentView(R.layout.activity_task_list_and_editor);
        setActionBar((Toolbar) findViewById(R.id.toolbar));
    }

    /**
     * Called when the user asks to edit or insert a task.
     */
    @Override
    public void editTask(long id) {                                    →16
    }

    /**
     * Called when the user finishes editing a task.
     */
    @Override
    public void finishEditingTask() {                                  →23
    }

}
```

The `onCreate` method creates a new activity, sets its content to the `activity_task_list_and_editor.xml` layout (which you will create), and sets its action bar to the `toolbar` element.

In addition, you'll see the following happen on these lines:

→ 2   You declare that this activity will implement the `OnEditTask` and `OnEditFinished` interfaces.

→ 16-23 The methods from the interfaces on line 2 are defined on these lines. Currently they are empty, but you will recall from Chapters 9 and 10 that these methods are used to figure out what the fragment will do when the user asks to edit a task and finishes editing a task. You will complete these methods in a later section.

Adding the tablet layout

Next, add the layout file. Create a new directory inside the `src/tablet` directory called `res`. Inside `res`, create a directory named `layout`, and inside the `layout` directory create the layout file named `activity_task_list_and_editor.xml`:

```xml
<?xml version="1.0" encoding="utf-8"?>
<LinearLayout xmlns:android="http://schemas.android.com/apk/res/android"   →2
    android:layout_width="match_parent"
    android:layout_height="match_parent"
    android:orientation="vertical"
    android:baselineAligned="false">

    <Toolbar                                                                →8
        style="?android:actionBarStyle"
        android:layout_width="match_parent"
        android:layout_height="wrap_content"
        android:title="@string/app_name"
        android:id="@+id/toolbar"/>

    <LinearLayout                                                           →15
            android:layout_width="match_parent"
            android:layout_height="match_parent"
            android:orientation="horizontal"
            android:baselineAligned="false">

        <fragment                                                           →21
            android:id="@+id/list_fragment"
            android:name="com.dummies.tasks.fragment.TaskListFragment"
            android:layout_width="0dp"
            android:layout_height="match_parent"
            android:layout_weight="1"/>

        <FrameLayout                                                        →28
            android:id="@+id/edit_container"
            android:layout_width="0dp"
            android:layout_height="match_parent"
            android:layout_weight="2"/>

    </LinearLayout>

</LinearLayout>
```

This layout consists of three main parts:

- ✔ A toolbar
- ✔ The list fragment
- ✔ A `framelayout` which holds your edit fragment

If you look back to Listing 16-1at the beginning of the chapter, you'll see that the layout is pretty similar, but instead of having two fragments in the layout, it has one fragment and one placeholder. The reason the second fragment needs to be a placeholder is because the edit fragment cannot be instantiated without knowing the ID of the task that needs to be edited. Because the ID isn't known at the time the layout is created, you must inflate the fragment manually so that you can specify the ID. Look back at Chapter 10 and you'll see you needed to do the same thing there for the TaskEditFragment.

Discussion of the previous code in more detail:

→ 2   A vertical LinearLayout that holds the two fragments for your tablet layout. Set baselineAligned to false as recommended by Android lint to get a tiny bump in performance. See Chapter 17 for more information about Android lint.

→ 8   The toolbar for the activity. It won't be styled automatically, so set its style to the theme's actionBarStyle. Also set its title to the app's name.

→ 15   A second LinearLayout, this one arranged horizontally. This LinearLayout is used to hold the two side-by-side fragments.

→ 21   The list view fragment, which occupies the leftmost third of the screen. It is using one-third of the screen because its layout_weight is set to 1, whereas the layout_weight of the other fragment on line 28 is set to 2, and 1 out of 3 is one-third. Remember, when using layout_weight, you must set your layout_width to 0.

→ 28   The edit view fragment, which occupies the remaining two of three parts of the screen.

Building the Tablet App

The tablet app isn't quite done yet, but it's time to run it and see what happens. How do you choose whether to build the phone app or the tablet app? Android Studio gives you a simple way to choose.

Choose View⇨Tool Windows⇨Build Variants. You should see a tool window, listing the build types for each of your apps. Click the build variant for Tasks and change it to say tabletDebug (see Figure 16-4):

There are four build variants listed for the Tasks app. These correspond to the two buildTypes and the two productFlavors in your build.gradle as shown in Table 16-1.

Figure 16-4:
The Build
Variants
tool window
with the
`tablet`
`Debug`
flavor
selected.

Table 16-1	The Four Build Configurations for the Tasks App	
buildTypes / productFlavors	*Debug*	*Release*
Phone	phoneDebug	phoneRelease
Tablet	tabletDebug	tabletRelease

Your `build.gradle` may not explicitly list a debug `buildType`, but it is always there by default.

You can add additional `buildTypes` or `productFlavors` if you want, but be careful! The number of build configurations can explode very quickly if you add a bunch of new `productFlavors` or `buildTypes`.

Now choose Build⇨Make Project and build the tablet app. Then choose Run⇨Run 'Tasks' to run your app, and choose the tablet emulator you created earlier in this chapter. You should see a list view but no editor view, as in Figure 16-5.

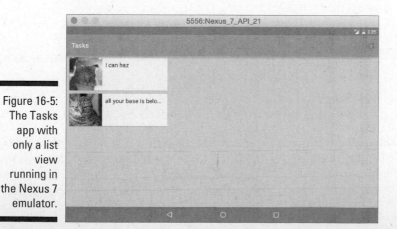

Figure 16-5:
The Tasks
app with
only a list
view
running in
the Nexus 7
emulator.

The emulator has several special keys that control it. To rotate the emulator, use Ctrl-F11 or Ctrl-F12. Note that, if you're on a Mac, you may also need to hold down the Fn key depending on how your keyboard is set up.

It looks great! But the problem is that there is no way add or edit tasks. You need to fill out the `editTask()` and `finishEditingTask()` methods.

Adding the App Callbacks

Recall from Chapter 10 that, on phones, the `editTask()` method started a new `TaskEditActivity` as shown in Listing 16-2 (do not add this code to your tablet app!):

Listing 16-2:   The editTask() Method for Phones (Not Tablets)

```
@Override
public void editTask(long id) {
    // When we are asked to edit a reminder, start the
    // TaskEditActivity with the id of the task to edit.
    startActivity(new Intent(this, TaskEditActivity.class)
            .putExtra(TaskEditActivity.EXTRA_TASKID, id));
}
```

Instead of starting a new activity on tablets, it makes more sense to use some of the empty real estate on the right-hand side of the page as a task editor. So for tablets, you'll use a different version of `editTask()`, which opens the editor fragment inside the current activity.

Add the following code to `TaskListAndEditorActivity.java`:

```
@Override
public void editTask(long id) {
    TaskEditFragment fragment = TaskEditFragment.newInstance(id);       →3

    FragmentTransaction ft = getFragmentManager()                       →5
            .beginTransaction();
    ft.replace(R.id.edit_container, fragment,
            TaskEditFragment.DEFAULT_FRAGMENT_TAG);

    ft.addToBackStack(null);                                            →10

    ft.commit();                                                        →12
}
```

This code should look familiar. It's very similar to the code you used in Chapter 10 to instantiate the `TaskEditFragment` there. As a recap:

→ **3**   Creates the fragment for the given task id.

→ **5**   Adds the fragment to the activity. If there's one already there (for example, the user clicks on another task), then replace it. Tag the fragment with a name (`DEFAULT_FRAGMENT_TAG` in this case) so that you can find it again later.

→ **10**   Adds this change to the backstack, so that when the user clicks the Back button you'll pop this editor off the stack. If you don't do this, the whole activity closes when the user clicks the Back button, which will be disruptive and unexpected.

→ **12**   Make it so!

Now the only thing left to do is implement `finishEditingTask()`. All this method needs to do is remove the fragment you just created, so add the code in bold:

```
@Override
public void finishEditingTask() {
    FragmentManager fm = getFragmentManager();
    FragmentTransaction transaction = fm.beginTransaction();

    // Find the edit fragment using the tag,
    // and remove it from the activity.
    Fragment fragment = fm.findFragmentByTag(
                TaskEditFragment.DEFAULT_FRAGMENT_TAG);
    transaction.remove(fragment);

    transaction.commit();
}
```

Run the app again and you should be able to add and edit tasks.

One More Thing ...

Do you remember adding that super cool code in Chapter 10 to change the colors of your window based on the color of the image being displayed? Well, that was pretty cool back then, but it looks a bit goofy now. For phones, the colors take over the entire window, but here in the tablet they only cover the right half of the page.

Let's disable the color change for tablets but keep it there for phones.

First, define a SHOULD_USE_PALETTE field in your build configuration. Open build.gradle and add the lines in bold:

```
productFlavors {
    phone {
        buildConfigField 'boolean', 'SHOULD_USE_PALETTE', 'true'
    }
    tablet {
        buildConfigField 'boolean', 'SHOULD_USE_PALETTE', 'false'
    }
}
```

This creates a new field named SHOULD_USE_PALETTE in the BuildConfig class. The field is set to true for the APK built for phones, and to false for the APK built for tablets.

The next step is to use the field in your code. Open TaskEditFragment .java and add the code in bold:

```
@Override
public void onLoadFinished(Loader<Cursor> loader, Cursor task) {
    ...

    // Set the thumbnail image
    Picasso.with(getActivity())
        .load(TaskListAdapter.getImageUrlForTask(taskId))
        .into(
            imageView,
            new Callback() {
                @Override
                public void onSuccess() {
                    Activity activity = getActivity();

                    if (activity == null)
                        return;

                    // Don't do this for tablets, only phones,
                    // since it doesn't really work with a split
                    // screen view.
                    if( !BuildConfig.SHOULD_USE_PALETTE )
                        return;

                    ...
}
```

Now run your app again on the tablet; the Palette behavior should be disabled. Verify that you haven't broken anything on phones by changing your build variant to phoneDebug and running the app again on your Nexus 5 phone emulator. The Palette behavior should still be present on your phone app.

Congratulations! You now have a fully implemented version of your Tasks app designed for tablets!

Chapter 17

Supporting Older Versions of Android

*I*t's always nice to be able to write apps for the latest and greatest version of Android. You can reduce the complexity of your app by targeting a single version. It also makes testing your app much easier because there are fewer devices you need to test every new feature on.

Unfortunately, most of us (maybe not Uncle Jimmy) live in the real world. In the real world, not everyone who wants to use your app is necessarily using the latest version of Android.

Why is this? Because the economics of device production make it profitable for manufacturers to produce a wide range of Android handsets, but not necessarily to keep upgrading those devices after they've been on the market for a few years. Invariably, some devices stop getting updates, and users on those phones are stuck with whatever version of Android they can get.

Although it can be useful to support older versions of Android, it's also important to know where to draw the line. The older you go, the more difficult your job of developing and testing your app will become. Figure 17-1 shows you the distribution of Android versions across all devices in the world as of the time of this writing.

Figure 17-1:
Percentage
of Android
devices by
OS version.

To find the latest data, visit `https://developer.android.com/about/dashboards`.

Using the data in the figure, you can see that about 80 percent of the market is covered by Android 4.1 and later. Knowing that the 80/20 rule says that covering the last 20 percent of the market will take 80 percent of the work, it makes sense to draw the line at Android 4.1.

For more about the 80/20 rule (also known as the Pareto Principle), visit `http://en.wikipedia.org/wiki/Pareto_principle`.

This chapter will show you how to make the Tasks app backward compatible to Android 4.1 Jelly Bean (API 16).

Understanding AppCompat

Google provides a library, called `AppCompat`, that emulates many of the features of later versions of Android on earlier versions. For example, features that were introduced in Android 5.0, such as the Toolbar and Material Design, have become available to Android 4.1 users using the `AppCompat` library.

You use the `AppCompat` library in this chapter to make your app work on Android 4.1.

For more information about the `AppCompat` library, visit `https://developer.android.com/tools/support-library/features.html` and `http://android-developers.blogspot.com/2014/10/appcompat-v21-material-design-for-pre.html`.

Updating the build File

The first step is to update your `build` file to indicate that your app supports Android 4.1 (API level 16).

Open the `build.gradle` file in the `Tasks` directory and make the following changes:

```
android {
    compileSdkVersion 21

    ...

    defaultConfig {
        applicationId "com.dummies.tasks"
        minSdkVersion 16                                              →8
        targetSdkVersion 21
        versionCode 1
        versionName "1.0"
    }

...

dependencies {
    ...


    // For backward compatibility to 16
    compile "com.android.support:appcompat-v7:21.0.0"                 →20

    ...
}
```

The following explains the code:

→ 8   You changed the `minSdkVersion` from 21 to 16. This means that your app can be installed on versions of Android as old as Android 4.1 Jelly Bean (rather than Android 5.0 Lollipop). You will leave the `targetSdkVersion` and the `compileSdkVersion` alone.

It's important to keep the `targetSdkVersion` as close to the latest Android version as possible. Whenever a new version of Android comes out, you should increase the `targetSdkVersion` (and possibly the `compileSdkVersion` if you want to use any new features), and then build and test your app. See Chapter 3 for more information about the `minSdkVersion`, `compileSdk Version`, and `targetSdkVersion`.

→ 20   You added the `AppCompat` library to your project. As mentioned
in the previous section, `AppCompat` provides most of what you
need to support the features of the newest Android OS on earlier
versions of Android. It won't do everything under the sun, but it
does support everything you need for the Tasks app.

Adding the Toolbar

In Chapters 9 and 10 you used the Toolbar widget to create both visible and
invisible action bars on the various pages of the Tasks app. You may not
have realized it then, but Toolbar was introduced in Android 5.0 and is not
available on Android 4.1.

Luckily, the `AppCompat` library supplies its own implementation of Toolbar
which works on 4.1 and later. You just need to switch over to it.

Open the following layout files:

✔ `activity_task_edit.xml`

✔ `activity_task_list.xml`

✔ `activity_task_list_and_editor.xml`

In each file, change the Toolbar view to the `android.support.v7.`
`widget.Toolbar`, as in the following example:

```
<android.support.v7.widget.Toolbar
    android:layout_width="match_parent"
    android:layout_height="wrap_content"
    . . .
    />
```

This changes your layouts to use the `AppCompat` version of Toolbar. The
next step is to change your Java code to also use the `AppCompat` version
of Toolbar.

Open the following Java files:

✔ `TaskEditActivity.java`

✔ `TaskListActivity.java`

✔ `TaskListAndEditorActivity.java`

In each file, make the following changes:

```
import android.widget.Toolbar;                                        →1
import android.support.v7.widget.Toolbar;                             →2

...

public class ... extends ActionBarActivity                           →6
{
    @Override
    protected void onCreate(Bundle savedInstanceState) {
        super.onCreate(savedInstanceState);
        ...
        setSupportActionBar((Toolbar) findViewById(R.id.toolbar));   →12
        ...
    }
}
```

Here is a description of each of the changes above:

→ 1   Previously, you used the Toolbar that ships as part of Android 5.0.
       Remove the reference to this Toolbar; you replace it on the next
       line.

→ 2   Import the `AppCompat` version of Toolbar rather than the Android
       5.0 version. This ensures that your app won't crash on versions of
       Android older than 5.0.

→ 6   The `Activity` class that comes with Android 5.0 knows about the
       Android 5.0 Toolbar, but it does not know about the `AppCompat`
       version of Toolbar. Instead of using the built-in version of the
       `Activity` class, use the `ActionBarActivity` that comes with
       `AppCompat`. The `ActionBarActivity` class knows about the
       `AppCompat` Toolbar.

→ 12   Similarly, the `setActionBar()` method you used in the old
       `Activity` class does not know about the `AppCompat` version of
       Toolbar, so change that method call to one that does.

Using the AppCompat Theme

Open the Tasks `styles.xml` file. You'll notice that the Tasks app theme
inherits from the Material Design theme:

```
<style name="AppTheme"
       parent="android:Theme.Material.NoActionBar">
```

This is a beautiful theme, but the problem is that the Material Design theme did not exist prior to Android 5.0. You must use a different theme if you want to support Android 4.1.

Luckily, AppCompat ships with a backward-compatibility version of the Material Design theme. This theme looks the same as the Material Design theme on Android 5.0, and looks close to the same on older devices. You need to update your theme to use the AppCompat theme.

Make the changes in bold to your styles.xml file as shown in Listing 17-1.

Listing 17-1: Making the styles.xml File Backward Compatible

```
<style name="AppTheme"
       parent="Theme.AppCompat.NoActionBar">                        →2

    <item name="colorPrimary">@color/primary</item>                →4
    <item name="colorPrimaryDark">@color/primary_dark</item>       →5
    <item name="colorAccent">@color/accent</item>                  →6

    <!--<item name="android:navigationBarColor">@color/primary_
          dark</item>-->                                           →8

    . . .
</style>

<style name="AppTheme.TransparentActionBar" parent="AppTheme">
    <!--<item name="android:windowTranslucentStatus">true</item>-->   →14
    <!--<item name="android:windowTranslucentNavigation">
          true</item>-->`                                          →15
    . . .
</style>

<style name="TransparentActionBar" parent="Theme.AppCompat">       →19
    . . .
</style>
```

Here is what the changes do:

→ **2**   Change your AppTheme to inherit from the AppCompat Theme. AppCompat.NoActionBar rather than from Android 5.0's Theme.Material.NoActionBar.

→ **4-6** Remove the android: namespace from the various theme color definitions. These three color definitions were introduced in Android 5.0, so they did not exist in 4.1. The AppCompat theme will find them without the android: namespace.

→ 8   Comment this line out. `navigationBarColor` isn't supported on 16. You fix this in a later section.

→ 14   Comment this line out. `windowTranslucentStatus` isn't supported on 16. You fix this in a later section.

→ 15   Comment this line out. `windowTranslucentNavigation` isn't supported on 16. You fix this in a later section.

→ 19   Replace Android 5.0's `Theme.Material` with `AppCompat`'s equivalent `Theme.AppCompat`.

Testing Your App

At this point, you should be able to try running your app. However, I have bad news: Your life just got a whole lot more complicated.

To thoroughly test your app, you should create the following 12 emulators, shown in Table 17-1:

Table 17-1	One. MILLION. Emulators . . .	
	Phone	*Tablet*
16	Nexus 5 API 16	Nexus 7 API 16
17	Nexus 5 API 17	Nexus 7 API 17
18	Nexus 5 API 18	Nexus 7 API 18
19	Nexus 5 API 19	Nexus 7 API 19
20	Nexus 5 API 20	Nexus 7 API 20
21	Nexus 5 API 21	Nexus 7 API 21

Go ahead, I'll wait. And while you're doing that, maybe you want to create another 12 emulators to test out the Nexus 4 and Nexus 9? But that wouldn't be fair to all the other Android manufacturers, so maybe you want to create a few emulators for Samsung, Motorola, HTC, LG, and other manufacturers . . .

As you can see, this can quickly get out of hand. For simplicity, it's best to just pick a few representative extremes on the device matrix and test those thoroughly. Then you can spot-check other devices as necessary.

For this section, let's test with the following 4 emulators (or are you an over-achiever? Go ahead and create the 12 emulators from Table 17-1):

- ✔ Nexus 5 API 16
- ✔ Nexus 5 API 21
- ✔ Nexus 7 API 16
- ✔ Nexus 7 API 21

Choose Tools➪Android➪AVD Manager and create the four emulators. See Chapter 3 for more information about how to create emulators.

After your emulators are available, try running the app on each, one at a time. You should see something like what's in Figure 17-2.

Poke around in the app a bit. As you can see, the app seems to work fine on Android 5.0 phones and tablets, but there are some bugs on Android 4.1 devices.

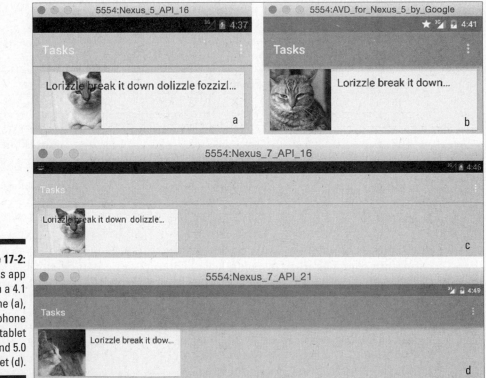

Figure 17-2:
Tasks app on a 4.1 phone (a), 5.0 phone (b), 4.1 tablet (c), and 5.0 tablet (d).

Working with Right-to-Left Languages

Looking at Figure 17-2a, it appears that the Tasks app does not lay out the text on its cards correctly for Android 4.1 devices.

The reason is that we used some features in our layouts that added support for right-to-left languages (such as Hebrew and Arabic) in Chapter 9. However, right-to-left languages were not added to Android until Android 4.2, so these layouts do not render properly on Android 4.1.

To fix this, you need to change your layouts to have the proper right-to-left directives, but add the older non-right-to-left directives as well.

For the next set of code changes, it's helpful to look at the next two figures. Figure 17-3 illustrates how to configure things for left-to-right languages.

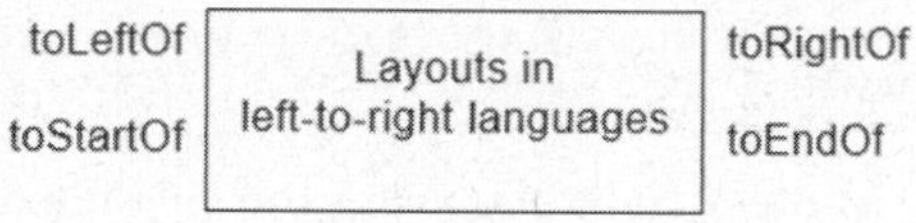

Figure 17-3:
Laying out left-to-right languages like English.

```
toLeftOf                          toRightOf
            Layouts in
toStartOf   left-to-right languages  toEndOf
```

Because you are reading this book in English, presumably you are accustomed to read in left-to-right languages. For left-to-right languages, things that are on the left of something can be thought of as at the start of the item. Things to the right can be thought of as at the end of the item.

For right-to-left languages, this is reversed, as you can see in Figure 17-4.

In the next few code blocks, you will add `toLeftOf` directives to anything that is currently using `toStartOf`. Similarly, you will add `toRightOf` anywhere that `toEndOf` is currently being used.

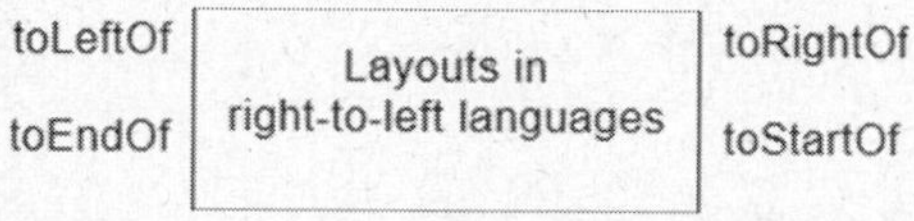

Figure 17-4:
Laying out right-to-left languages like Hebrew and Arabic.

```
toLeftOf                          toRightOf
            Layouts in
toEndOf     right-to-left languages  toStartOf
```

Open `card_task.xml` and make the following additions:

```
    <ImageView
        android:id="@+id/image"
        ...
        android:layout_alignParentStart="true"
        android:layout_alignParentLeft="true"                    →5
        />

    <TextView
        android:id="@+id/text1"
        ...
        android:layout_toEndOf="@id/image"
        android:layout_toRightOf="@id/image"/>                   →12

    <TextView
        android:id="@+id/text2"
        ...
        android:layout_alignStart="@id/text1"
        android:layout_alignLeft="@id/text1"                     →18
        />
```

These changes do the following:

→ 5   The `ImageView` is intended to align with the left side of the parent view. The way to indicate this in a non-directional way is to say that it is aligned with the parent start, as shown on the previous line. However, for older Android versions that don't have a non-directional way to specify parent start, you must add the `alignParentLeft` directive.

→ 12 Similarly, this text view is intended to be laid out to the right of the image on left-to-right devices, and to the left of the image on right-to-left devices. Hence, it uses `layout_toEndOf` on the previous line to indicate this. For older versions of Android, you must add the `layout_toRightOf`, which means the same thing in left-to-right languages.

→ 18 Adds `layout_alignLeft` to the `TextView` that is already using `layout_alignStart`.

Next, open `fragment_task_edit.xml` and make the following additions:

```
    <TextView
        android:id="@+id/task_time"
        ...
        android:layout_marginEnd="3dp"
        android:layout_marginRight="3dp"
        android:layout_alignEnd="@id/title"
        android:layout_alignRight="@id/title"/>
```

```
<TextView
    android:id="@+id/task_date"
    ...
    android:layout_marginEnd="10dp"
    android:layout_marginRight="10dp"
    android:layout_toStartOf="@id/task_time"
    android:layout_toLeftOf="@id/task_time"/>

<EditText
    android:id="@+id/notes"
    ...
    android:layout_alignStart="@id/title"
    android:layout_alignLeft="@id/title"
    android:layout_marginEnd="@dimen/gutter"
    android:layout_marginRight="@dimen/gutter"/>
```

Now when you rerun the app, the text on the list card and the edit fragment should be where you expect them to be.

Fixing the Add Task Menu

If you look at the screen shots in Figure 17-2, you may notice that the Add Task menu icon is missing.

Where did it go? The answer is in the `menu_list.xml` file. Open it now and look at the lines that use `showAsAction`.

The problem is that `android:showAsAction` was not available on very old versions of Android, so the `AppCompat` library doesn't look for it. Instead, it looks in its own namespace.

Open `menu_list.xml` and add the lines in bold:

```
<menu xmlns:android="http://schemas.android.com/apk/res/android"
    xmlns:app="http://schemas.android.com/apk/res-auto">          →2

    <item
        android:id="@+id/menu_insert"
        android:showAsAction="always"
        app:showAsAction="always"                                 →7
        ... />
```

```
<item
    android:id="@+id/menu_settings"
    android:showAsAction="never"
    app:showAsAction="never"                                    →13
    ... />

</menu>
```

Lines 7 and 13 add a second `showAsAction` directive in the `app:` namespace in addition to the one that's already there in the `android:` namespace. But before you can use the `app` namespace, you have to declare it as on line 2.

The `http://schemas.android.com/apk/res-auto` namespace (also known as the `res-auto` namespace) is a special placeholder namespace that Android replaces with a namespace containing your app's package name. You use it whenever you want custom attributes, which you can create for the custom views in your app. You also use it when you need custom attributes defined by a third-party library, such as the `showAsAction` attribute which is defined in the `AppCompat` library.

If you rerun the app on your 4.1 and 5.0 emulators, you should see that the Add Task menu has now returned.

Fixing the Window Options

If you run the app on a 5.0 phone emulator and click an item, you will notice some differences from how you built the app in Chapter 10, shown in Figure 17-5.

The differences are

- The status bar at the top is no longer translucent.
- The navigation bar at the bottom is no longer translucent.
- The Save button has been pushed down.

The problem is that Android 4.1 does not support transparent/translucent action, status, and navigation bars. You commented out these lines in Listing 17-1, and that's why they're broken now. You will need to add back in this functionality, but do it in a way that won't break Android 4.1.

The solution is to create a new style specific to API level 21 (Android 5.0) but otherwise leave the existing style alone. In order to avoid copying and pasting code everywhere, share as much of the style as possible between the existing and the 5.0 styles by using inheritance.

Figure 17-5:
The Edit
Task page
on a 5.0
phone
emulator.

Open `styles.xml` now and make the following changes:

```
<!-- This theme will be overridden in newer SDKs -->
<style name="AppTheme" parent="AppTheme.Base"/>                →2

<style name="AppTheme.Base"                                   →4
       parent="Theme.AppCompat.NoActionBar">
  ...
</style>

<!-- This theme will be overridden in newer SDKs -->
<style name="AppTheme.TransparentActionBar"
       parent="AppTheme.TransparentActionBar.Base" />         →11

<style name="AppTheme.TransparentActionBar.Base" parent="AppTheme">  →13
  ...
</style>
```

Here is a description of the changes you just made:

→ 2   Adds a new style, named `AppTheme`, which inherits from the
       `AppTheme.Base`. `AppTheme.Base` is the old style you had for
       the app (previously it was called `AppTheme`). By separating

them out, you created a new "base" theme with all your app's style definitions, and a new theme that inherits from that base. Practically speaking, this code will still behave exactly the same as the old code. But by doing it this way, you can override values for Android 5.0 later in this section.

→ **4**   Renames the old `AppTheme` theme to `AppTheme.Base`.

→ **11**   Do the same thing here as you did on line 2. Create a new theme named `AppTheme.TransparentActionBar` for the edit task page, and make it inherit from `AppTheme.TransparentActionBar.Base`, which you create on line 13.

→ **13**   Renames the old `AppTheme.TransparentActionBar` to `AppTheme.TransparentActionBar.Base`.

If you run the app now, it still behaves exactly as it did before.

The next thing to do is to add the special 5.0-specific overrides to a style definition that is applied only to Android 5.0. Create a new directory in the `res` folder named `values-v21`, and then create a new file named `styles.xml`:

```
<?xml version="1.0" encoding="utf-8"?>
<resources>

    <style name="AppTheme" parent="AppTheme.Base">
        <item name="android:navigationBarColor">@color/primary_dark</item>   →5
    </style>

    <style name="AppTheme.TransparentActionBar"
               parent="AppTheme.TransparentActionBar.Base">
        <item name="android:windowTranslucentStatus">true</item>   →9
        <item name="android:windowTranslucentNavigation">true</item>   →10
    </style>

</resources>
```

This file contains the style items that you commented out from Listing 17-1. By putting them in the `values-v21` directory, you are telling Android to use resource directories to apply them only on Android 21 (also known as 5.0) or later. See Chapter 6 for more information about resource directories.

Here is more information about the previous code:

→ **5**   Sets the `android:navigationBarColor` in the `AppTheme`. This fixes the bug that caused the navigation bar to not be colored correctly on tablets. And because this change is in the `values-v21` directory, it applies only to Android 5.0 or later.

→ 9   Tells Android 5.0 or later to set the `android:windowTranslucent Status` to `true`, which makes the status bar translucent on the Edit page.

→ 10 Tells Android 5.0 or later to set the `android:windowTranslucent Navigation` to `true`, which makes the navigation bar translucent on the Edit page.

Using Newer APIs

Every version of Android introduces some new APIs. For example, as you saw earlier in this chapter, Android 5.0 introduced the new Toolbar API. To use the Toolbar, the `AppCompat` library provides an alternative version of Toolbar that works on older versions of Android.

But what do you do if you have no equivalent for a new API in `AppCompat`? After all, `AppCompat` can't be expected to provide ports of new functionality for every single old version of Android.

In cases where a new API isn't available on older versions of Android, and you have no support for it in the `AppCompat` or other Android support libraries, you must disable that functionality in your app when it is run on versions of Android that do not support that feature.

See `https://developer.android.com/tools/support-library/ features.html` for more information about the various Android support libraries, including `AppCompat`.

The way to do this is to check the version of Android before you attempt to use one of these APIs. If you're running on a version of Android that is too old, then disable that feature; otherwise, let it go through. For example, if your app uses the new Advanced Camera APIs introduced with Android 5.0, you could do something like the following:

```
if(Build.VERSION.SDK_INT >= Build.VERSION_CODES.LOLLIPOP ) {
    String[] ids = cameraManager.getCameraIdList();
    ...
} else {
    Toast.makeText(this,
        "Sorry, that feature is not available on this " +
            "version of Android",
        Toast.LENGTH_SHORT).show();
}
```

You won't need to do this for any of the APIs that the Tasks app uses, but it's good to know what to do should you ever need it.

Using Android Lint

When dealing with backward compatibility, it's very easy to accidentally use some APIs that are available on your current API version, but weren't available a few years ago on older versions of Android. If you're not paying attention and do this, everything will seem to work fine on your latest-and-greatest phone, but your users will see crashes on their older phones.

A great tool is available to help you find these sorts of situations before they happen. It's called Android lint.

If you are familiar with the lint tool on other programming platforms, Android lint is very similar. Android lint examines the source code for your project and finds anything that looks suspicious and could possibly be a bug. Not all these warnings may, in fact, turn out to be bugs, but it's important to go through each one and make sure you know whether they are or aren't.

The reason that Android lint is so useful when working with backward compatibility is that it automatically flags any use of older APIs that haven't been wrapped in build version checks.

To run Android lint, open a file in the Tasks project and then choose Analyze⇨Inspect Code. Click Module 'Tasks' as in Figure 17-6 and click OK.

After Android lint has finished running, you see a report similar to what's in Figure 17-7.

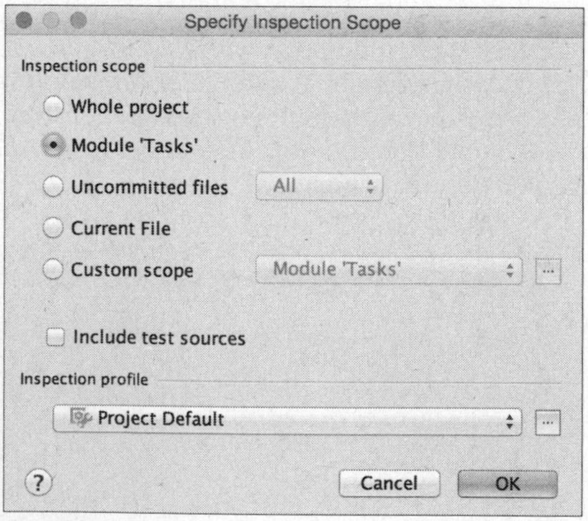

Figure 17-6: Choosing which modules to inspect using Android lint.

Figure 17-7:
The Android
lint report
for the
Tasks app.

This report gives you a list of warnings that may or may not be bugs in your app. You click each warning to view a description of it. If it's a bug, then you should fix it. If it's not in this particular case, you are given the option to suppress the warning. By suppressing the warning, you indicate to the lint tool that you acknowledge the warning, you have checked it, and you know it's not an error.

Android lint can be a very powerful tool to find potential problems with your code before you release it. Make sure you run it frequently and keep your codebase clean and lint free! For more information about Android lint, visit http://d.android.com/tools/help/lint.html.

Chapter 18

Wearing the Tasks App

Android Wear extends the Android platform to a new generation of devices, with a user experience that's designed specifically for wearables.

Android Wear devices (usually watches) are designed to complement your existing Android phone or tablet (see Figure 18-1). They are not designed to be standalone and usually do not have their own Wi-Fi or LTE radios, but instead communicate with the Internet through your phone over Bluetooth. Any Android phone running Android 4.3 or later can easily pair with an Android Wear watch.

Users typically interact with Android Wear in one of three ways:

✔ **The Context stream:** This is a vertically scrolling list of cards much like you might find in the Google Now app. The Context stream is a list of notifications that are relevant to you right now. They might include the current weather in your area, the traffic report for your evening commute, notifications from apps on your phone, or just about anything else. These notifications are usually the same notifications that show up on your Android phone.

✔ **Voice control:** Android Wear allows you to do many things simply by speaking to your watch. (To learn how to add voice control to your wearable app, visit the book's online web extras at www.dummies.com/extras/androidappdevelopment).

✔ **Apps:** You can install specially designed Android Wear apps on your watch. These are usually not the same as regular Android phone apps because they need to run on much smaller screens and use much less memory.

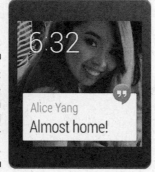

Figure 18-1:
A notifica-
tion on an
Android
Wear
watch.

By default, any Android phone app that posts notifications automatically displays its notifications in the Context stream on your Android Wear watch. If you have an Android Wear device, you can try it now with the reminders from Part III!

Developers interested in bringing a richer experience to their apps on Android Wear devices have two main options:

✔ You can leave the app running on the phone, and improve the notifications to allow them to do more stuff on the watch. For example, you might enable users to snooze reminders for the Tasks app right from their watch without having to open the app on the phone. In this scenario, the app stays on the phone, but provides rich notification actions that can be used on the watch. See `https://developer.android.com/training/wearables/notifications/` for more information about building rich Android Wear notifications.

✔ You can build a second app that runs directly on the watch, and synchronizes data with the app on your phone via Bluetooth.

This chapter focuses on building a second app that runs directly on the watch.

You can do much with Android Wear, much more than this chapter or book can explore. In many ways, Android Wear is its own platform. To learn more about it, visit `https://developer.android.com/wear/`.

At the time of this writing, you must have a real Android phone to develop for Android Wear. This is because you must install the Android Wear app on your phone, and the app is not currently available on the Android emulator. You do not need to have a real Android Wear watch though. It is possible to develop for Android Wear using a watch emulator.

Preparing Your Development Environment

Because Android Wear is a companion to your phone rather than a completely standalone product, the development environment is familiar but slightly different from developing on regular Android.

Prepping your Android phone

Before you create the Android Wear emulator, you should prepare your phone.

Checking for system updates

Android Wear is an evolving platform, and it requires that certain services be up to date on your phone. Go to your phone's Settings page, scroll down to About phone, and click System updates to make sure your phone has the latest software.

Installing Android Wear on your phone

Visit the Google Play Store and search for Android Wear. Install the app and then run it. You should see something like Figure 18-2.

Setting up an Android Wear emulator

The next step is to create your Android Wear emulators. These are the devices on which you will develop your Wear apps.

1. **In Android Studio, choose Tools➪Android➪AVD Manager.**

2. **Click Create Virtual Device.**

3. **Choose Wear, select Android Wear Square, and click Next.**

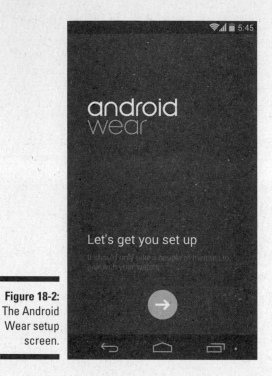

Figure 18-2:
The Android
Wear setup
screen.

4. **Choose Lollipop API 21 x86, click Next, and then click Finished.**

5. **Start the emulator by pressing the green right-pointing triangle Play button.**

   Wait until the emulator initializes and shows the Android Wear Home screen as in Figure 18-3.

Figure 18-3:
The Android
Wear
Square
emulator.

6. **Repeat the Steps 1 to 4 but create an Android Wear Round emulator.**

   You don't need to run it at this time, but you will need it later in the chapter.

Pairing your phone with the Wear emulator

Now that your phone and emulator are ready to use Android Wear, you must pair them. Every Android Wear user pairs his watch to his phone, and the Android Wear app makes this easy. Because you are using an emulator rather than a physical device, you must go through a few extra steps to pair your devices:

1. **Connect the phone to your machine through USB.**

2. **Forward the emulator's communication port to the connected phone.**

   You must do this every time the phone is connected:

   ```
   adb -d forward tcp:5601 tcp:5601
   ```

   The wearable emulator and your phone should now be listed when you run the `adb devices` command.

   ```
   $ adb devices
   List of devices attached
   emulator-5554    device
   5b44a488839e3171        device
   ```

3. **Start the Android Wear app on your phone and connect to the emulator.**

   You do this by choosing Pair with a new wearable and then choosing Pair with emulator from the overflow menu, as shown on the left and right images in Figure 18-4.

   The Android Wear app should now report that your emulator is "Connected." Your phone and emulator are now paired!

4. **Check that the pairing is working.**

   You do this by tapping the menu on the top right corner of the Android Wear app, selecting Demo cards, then clicking a Demo card. As shown in Figure 18-5, the card you select (left) appears as a notification(s) on the Home screen (right). You can dismiss the card by swiping it off the screen to the right.

   Do you want to develop with a real Android device rather than the emulator? Then visit `https://developer.android.com/training/wearables/apps/creating.html` for more information.

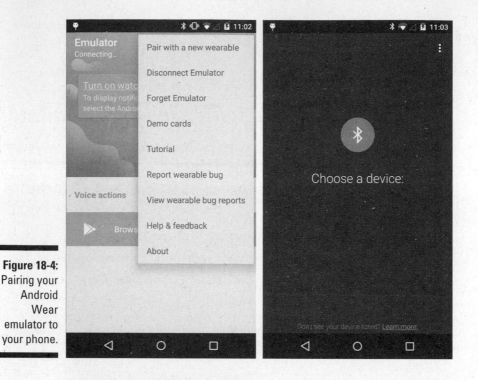

Figure 18-4:
Pairing your
Android
Wear
emulator to
your phone.

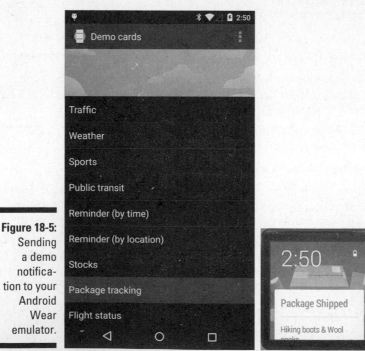

Figure 18-5:
Sending
a demo
notifica-
tion to your
Android
Wear
emulator.

Creating a New Wear App

In this section, you create a new Android Wear app that runs directly on your watch emulator, and you add the code necessary to allow it to sync with your phone.

Creating a new module

You can create a new module in your Android Studio project by following these steps:

1. **Choose File⇨New Module.**

   Select Android Wear module, and press Next.

2. **Create a new Wear module using the settings in Table 18-1.**

   The package name you use here MUST be the same as the package name you use for your Tasks app. If they're not the same, your tasks won't sync between the two apps.

3. **Press Next and add a new Blank Wear Activity.**

   Use the settings from Table 18-2 for your new activity, and then click Finish.

4. **Run your app on your Wear emulator.**

   You can do this by choosing Run⇨Run 'TasksWear' and choosing your emulator (not your phone). You should see the "Hello world" app running as shown in Figure 18-6.

Table 18-1	Settings for Creating a New Wear Module
Application Name	*Tasks*
Module name	TasksWear
Package name	com.dummies.tasks
Minimum SDK	API 21 Lollipop

Table 18-2	Settings for Creating a New Android Wear Activity
Activity Name	*MainActivity*
Layout name	activity_main
Round layout name	round_activity_main
Rectangular layout name	rect_activity_main

Figure 18-6:
The Hello
World app
running on
the Wear
emulator.

Hello Square World!

Editing MainActivity

You're now going to replace the sample code in `MainActivity` with the beginning of a real app.

Open `MainActivity.java` and replace the contents of that file with the following:

```
public class MainActivity extends Activity
{
    @Override
    protected void onCreate(Bundle savedInstanceState) {
        super.onCreate(savedInstanceState);
        setContentView(R.layout.activity_main);
    }
}
```

This code loads the `activity_main.xml` layout into your activity.

Now open `res/layout/activity_main.xml` and replace it with the following code:

```
<?xml version="1.0" encoding="utf-8"?>
<android.support.wearable.view.BoxInsetLayout                              →2
    xmlns:android="http://schemas.android.com/apk/res/android"
    xmlns:app="http://schemas.android.com/apk/res-auto"                    →4
    android:layout_height="match_parent"
    android:layout_width="match_parent"
    android:padding="15dp">                                                →7

    <android.support.wearable.view.WearableListView                        →9
```

```
        android:id="@+id/list"
        android:layout_width="match_parent"
        android:layout_height="match_parent"
        app:layout_box="all"/>                                    →13

</android.support.wearable.view.BoxInsetLayout>
```

This layout uses a few views specific to Android Wear. They are included in the Android Wear support library. Chances are you have not encountered them yet while developing regular Android apps. Here is what the code is doing:

→ 2   The outer view is the `BoxInsetLayout`. Think of this view as a fancy `FrameLayout`. Like a `FrameLayout`, the `BoxInsetLayout` lets you put other views inside it but doesn't give you any sophisticated layout options. However, unlike a `FrameLayout`, the `BoxInsetLayout` knows the difference between round and rectangular Android Wear devices, and it resizes its children appropriately to make sure that they fit on a round watch face.

Because Android Wear devices come in many different shapes and sizes, it's important to ensure your layouts work with them all. You have a few ways to make your layouts work with both round and rectangular devices. `BoxInsetLayout` is what you use in this chapter. Another useful tool is `WatchViewStub`. `WatchViewStub` is great when you want to use significantly different layouts for a round watch than a rectangular watch. For more information about `WatchViewStub`, visit `https://developer.android.com/training/wearables/apps/layouts.html`.

→ 4   You've been using the `xmlns:android` namespace for some time now and are probably quite used to it. This may be the first time you've seen a different namespace in your Android layouts. The `BoxInsetLayout` uses an additional layout parameter (`layout_box` on line 13) that is not present in the default `xmlns:android` namespace, so it must use its own namespace to add the `layout_box` parameter. I call this namespace `app`, but you can call it whatever you want as long as lines 4 and 13 agree.

→ 7   This line assigns padding to the `BoxInsetLayout` element. Because the window insets on round devices are larger than 15dp, this padding applies only to square screens.

→ 9   `WearableListView` is a Wear-specific layout very similar to the regular Android `ListView` or `RecyclerView`. It shows items one at a time in a list, and creates only as many views as will cover the screen, no matter how long the list is. `WearableListView` is optimized for ease of use on small screen wearable devices.

→ 13   This line ensures that the `FrameLayout` element and its children are boxed inside the area defined by the window insets on round screens. This line has no effect on square screens. Other options for `layout_box` are left, right, bottom, and top. See the documentation for `BoxInsetLayout` for more details.

You now have a Wear app that can theoretically show a list of data. However, you have no data yet to display. The next few sections will fix that.

Adding Google Play Services for data syncing

Android Wear apps use the Google Play Services library (which is different than the Google Play Store) for a lot of functionality. In this section you use Google Play Services to sync data between your phone and watch.

Open your `AndroidManifest.xml` and add the following `meta-data` entry to your `application` element:

```
<meta-data android:name="com.google.android.gms.version"
        android:value="@integer/google_play_services_version" />
```

This `meta-data` is necessary for apps that use the Google Play Services library.

You then open the `TasksWear` `build.gradle` and ensure that the Google Play dependency is listed there. If it's not already there, then add it to the `dependencies` section:

```
dependencies {
    ...
    compile 'com.google.android.gms:play-services-wearable:6.5.87'
}
```

Now add Google Play Services to your activity. Open `MainActivity.java` and add the code in bold:

```
public class MainActivity extends Activity                          →1
    implements DataApi.DataListener, GoogleApiClient.ConnectionCallbacks,
            GoogleApiClient.OnConnectionFailedListener
{
```

```
GoogleApiClient googleApiClient;                                    →5


@Override
protected void onCreate(Bundle savedInstanceState) {
    super.onCreate(savedInstanceState);
    setContentView(R.layout.activity_main);

    googleApiClient = new GoogleApiClient.Builder(this)            →13
        .addApi(Wearable.API)
        .addConnectionCallbacks(this)
        .addOnConnectionFailedListener(this)
        .build();
}

@Override
protected void onStart() {                                         →21
    super.onStart();

    googleApiClient.connect();                                     →24
}

@Override
protected void onStop() {
    super.onStop();

    googleApiClient.disconnect();                                  →31
}

@Override
public void onConnected(Bundle bundle) {                           →35
    Log.d("MainActivity", "onConnected");                          →36

    Wearable.DataApi.addListener(googleApiClient, this);           →38

    updateList();                                                  →40
}

@Override
public void onDataChanged(DataEventBuffer dataEvents) {
    Log.d("MainActivity", "onDataChanged");

    dataEvents.release();                                          →47

    updateList();                                                  →49
}

@Override
public void onConnectionSuspended(int i) {                         →53
```

```
        Log.d("MainActivity", "onConnectionSuspended");          →54
    }

    @Override
    public void onConnectionFailed(ConnectionResult connectionResult) {   →58
        Log.d("MainActivity", "onConnectionFailed");
    }

    private void updateList() {                                  →62
        // TBD
    }
}
```

This code adds support for Google Play data syncing. How does it do it? It basically connects to the Google Play service, subscribes to updates, and then calls `updateList()` whenever there is new data. Here is more detail about the code:

→ 1   The main activity for this app. This activity implements the `DataApi.DataListener` interface to be notified of sync events. It also implements the `GoogleApiClient` `ConnectionCallbacks` and `OnConnectionFailedListener` to handle connectivity events. If you're writing an app that needs to sync in the background (this one doesn't), then consider using a `WearableListenerService` to run continuously in the background.

→ 5   Wearables use the `GoogleApiClient` to communicate with their host devices (usually your phone).

→ 13   This sets up the `GoogleApiClient`. You tell it you need the `Wearable.API`, and also that it should call you back on `this` for any connectivity notifications.

→ 21   The `onStart` method is an Android callback (not Google Play) that happens after `onCreate`. `onStart` is called when the activity is visible on the screen, although it may not necessarily be the frontmost activity. You want to make sure that you are connected to Google Play any time the activity is visible (and disconnect from Google Play after the activity is no longer visible), so you connect to Google Play in `onStart` and disconnect in `onStop`. For more information about `onStart` and `onStop`, refer to Chapter 5.

→ 24   Connects to the `GoogleApiClient`. Upon connection, you will receive a callback on `onConnected()`.

→ 31   We're done, so disconnect from the `GoogleApiClient`.

→ 35   `onConnected` is a Google Play callback that is called after a connection has been established (which was initiated on line 24). It is defined in the `ConnectionCallbacks` interface. This method needs to do two things: It needs to start listening for data changes on line 38, and it needs to update the list with whatever data has already been cached on the watch on line 40.

→ 36   Logs a simple message to let you know that `onConnected` has been called. This may be helpful later when you're debugging your app and need to know whether a connection between the phone and the wearable has been established.

→ 38   Subscribes for any more data updates. You will be called back on `onDataChanged` if anything is updated.

→ 40   Updates the adapter as soon as you're connected.

→ 47   Always release the `dataEvents` when you're done. In this case, you don't use the `dataEvents` directly, so release them right away.

→ 49   You were told there was an update, so this line updates your adapter.

→ 53   `onConnectionSuspended` is also defined in the `Connection Callbacks` interface, and it is called whenever the Google Play connection has been shut down.

→ 54   Just logs a message. You don't have to do anything at all, but a log message can help you debug any issues.

→ 58   `onConnectionFailed` is defined in `OnConnectionFailed Listener`. It is called if there was an error connecting to the device. There is nothing that you need to do here, but again you should log a message as an aid during debugging.

→ 62   The `updateList` refreshes the UI with the latest data. At this time it doesn't do anything yet, but you will implement it in the next section.

Creating the adapter

Recall that an adapter is responsible for taking data from a data source (such as a database) and creating views for each item in the list. See Chapter 9 for more information about adapters.

You created a list view earlier in the chapter. Now you just need an adapter to feed it data.

Create a new file `WearableTaskListAdapter.java` in the same directory as your `MainActivity.java`, and add the following to it:

```
/**
 * A WearableListAdapter that knows how to display our Task items in a
 * list.
 */
public class WearableTaskListAdapter
    extends WearableListView.Adapter                                    →6
{
    static final String COLUMN_TITLE = "title";                         →8

    List<DataItem> dataItems;                                           →10

    LayoutInflater inflater;                                            →12

    public WearableTaskListAdapter(Context context) {
        inflater = LayoutInflater.from(context);                        →15
    }

    @Override                                                           →18
    public WearableListView.ViewHolder onCreateViewHolder(
        ViewGroup viewGroup, int i) {

        return new ViewHolder(                                          →22
            inflater.inflate(R.layout.item_task, null));
    }

    @Override                                                           →26
    public void onBindViewHolder(
        WearableListView.ViewHolder viewHolder, int i) {

        DataItem dataItem = dataItems.get(i);                           →30

        DataMap map                                                     →32
            = DataMapItem.fromDataItem(dataItem).getDataMap();

        ((ViewHolder) viewHolder).titleView.setText(                    →35
            map.getString(COLUMN_TITLE)
        );
    }

    @Override
    public int getItemCount() {                                         →41
        return dataItems != null ? dataItems.size() : 0;
    }

    public void setResults(List<DataItem> dataItems) {                  →45
        this.dataItems = dataItems;
        notifyDataSetChanged();                                         →47
    }
```

```
static class ViewHolder extends WearableListView.ViewHolder {          →51
    TextView titleView;

    public ViewHolder(View itemView) {
        super(itemView);
        titleView = (TextView) itemView.findViewById(R.id.title);
    }
  }
}
```

This adapter takes a list of `DataItems` and creates views for each one from `item_task.xml`. Here is a look at the code in detail:

→ **6**   All adapters used by the `WearableListView` must inherit from `WearableListView.Adapter`. The `WearableListView.Adapter` is pretty similar to the `RecyclerView.Adapter` you used in Chapter 9.

→ **8**   The name of the column containing the data you are looking for. The only column shown in this list view is the title, due to the limited screen real estate. This string must match the name used in the phone app.

→ **10**   The current list of `dataItems`. May be `null`.

→ **12**   The layout inflater used to inflate the views.

→ **15**   Retrieves a `LayoutInflater` from the current context.

→ **18**   Creates a `ViewHolder` that holds a reference to the views that you will need to update for each new item in the list.

→ **22**   Returns a new `ViewHolder` (see line 51 for class `ViewHolder`). Each view in your list will use the `item_task.xml` layout. Note that you haven't created `item_task.xml` yet, but you will shortly.

→ **26**   Updates the views in the `ViewHolder` using the information in the item in position i.

→ **30**   Finds the `DataItem` for the item in position i.

→ **32**   Reconstructs the original `DataMap` for that item.

→ **35**   Sets the title view text based on the `COLUMN_TITLE` in the `DataMap`.

→ **41**   As in Chapter 13, `getItemCount` returns the count of items in the list. In this case it is equal to `dataItems.getCount()`, or zero if `dataItems` is null.

→ **45**   Updates the items in the list, and notifies listeners (particularly the `ListView`) that the data in the adapter has changed.

→ **47**   `notifyDataSetChanged` works the same way here as it did in Chapter 9. It notifies any listeners (in particular, the `WearableListView`) that the data has been updated and that the listener should be refreshed.

→ **51**   A simple `ViewHolder` that just holds the `titleView` for the list item. See Chapter 9 for more information about `ViewHolders`.

The previous code used a layout called `item_task` for each item in the list, so add a new layout file in `res/layouts` and call it `item_task.xml`:

```xml
<?xml version="1.0" encoding="utf-8"?>
<TextView
    xmlns:android="http://schemas.android.com/apk/res/android"
    android:id="@+id/title"
    android:gravity="center_vertical|start"          →5
    android:layout_width="wrap_content"
    android:layout_marginEnd="16dp"                  →7
    android:layout_height="80dp"                     →8
    android:fontFamily="sans-serif-condensed-light"  →9
    android:lineSpacingExtra="-4sp"                  →10
    android:textSize="16sp"/>                        →11
```

This layout is just a single, simple `TextView`.

→ **5**   Positions the text to the far left and centers it vertically in the view.

→ **7-11**   These lines represent some styling choices to make sure the text fits on the screen and is readable. Feel free to play around with these values to find the right look for your app.

Now you need to hook the adapter up to the list view. Open `MainActivity.java` and add the code in bold:

```java
public class MainActivity extends Activity
    implements DataApi.DataListener, GoogleApiClient.ConnectionCallbacks,
            GoogleApiClient.OnConnectionFailedListener
{

    WearableTaskListAdapter adapter;                        →5


    @Override
    protected void onCreate(Bundle savedInstanceState) {
        super.onCreate(savedInstanceState);
        setContentView(R.layout.activity_main);
```

```
    . . .

        adapter = new WearableTaskListAdapter(this);              →15

        WearableListView listView =                               →17
            (WearableListView) findViewById(R.id.list);

        listView.setAdapter(adapter);                             →20
    }

private void updateList() {
    Wearable.DataApi.getDataItems(googleApiClient).setResultCallback(   →25
        new ResultCallback<DataItemBuffer>() {
            @Override
            public void onResult(DataItemBuffer dataItems) {      →28
                try {
                    List<DataItem> items                          →30
                        = FreezableUtils.freezeIterable(dataItems);

                    adapter.setResults(items);                    →33

                    Log.d("MainActivity", "adapter.setResults");  →35
                } finally {
                    dataItems.release();                          →38
                }
            }
        });
    }
}
```

If you run the app now, you won't see anything because you haven't published any data to the watch yet.

→ 5 The adapter you just created.

→ 15 Creates the adapter.

→ 17 Finds the WearableListView in the view hierarchy.

→ 20 Links the adapter and the ListView.

→ 25 Retrieves the complete list of dataitems using DataApi getDataItems. Because this may involve a network sync and may take some time, you get the results back in a ResultCall back at a later time.

→ 28 The onResult method of your callback is called when data is received. It returns to you the list of items that resulted from your query.

→ 30   Before you start using `dataItems`, you must "freeze" them to make sure they don't change while you are iterating over them.

→ 33   Updates the adapter with the new items.

→ 35   Logs a message to logcat to assist with debugging.

→ 38   Always releases the `dataItems` when you are through.

Your Android Wear app is now complete! However, if you run it, you will see just a blank screen. This is because it does not yet have any data to show. You will fix that in the next section.

Publishing the Data from Your Phone

Now that you've created a Wear app, it's time to publish the tasks from your phone so they can be synced to your Wear app. This involves adding the Google Play sync services to your phone and then testing the sync between your phone and Wear app. But before you do that, you need to do a little setup work.

Configuring the phone's build

Open `build.gradle` in your original Tasks (not `TasksWear`) directory, and add the following dependency:

```
compile 'com.google.android.gms:play-services-wearable:6.5.87'
```

Make sure the version you use agrees with the version in your `Tasks Wearbuild.gradle` from earlier in this chapter.

Next, open `AndroidManifest.xml` for your Tasks app and add the required `meta-data` tag to your application element (like you did for `TasksWear`):

```
<meta-data android:name="com.google.android.gms.version"
        android:value="@integer/google_play_services_version" />
```

Publishing the data from the phone

With those preliminaries over, it's time to add Google Play data syncing to your phone's `TaskProvider`. Go back to `TaskProvider.java` in your Tasks app, and add the code in bold:

```
/**
 * A Content Provider that knows how to read and write tasks from our
 * tasks database.
 */
public class TaskProvider extends ContentProvider
    implements GoogleApiClient.ConnectionCallbacks,
        GoogleApiClient.OnConnectionFailedListener          →7
{
            ...

    // Google Play Constants
    private static final String PLAY_BASE_URL = "/" + DATABASE_TABLE;    →12

    GoogleApiClient googleApiClient;                        →14

    @Override
    public boolean onCreate() {
        ...

        googleApiClient = new GoogleApiClient.Builder(getContext())   →20
                .addApi(Wearable.API)
                .addConnectionCallbacks(this)
                .addOnConnectionFailedListener(this)
                .build();
        googleApiClient.connect();                          →25

        ...

    }


    @Override
    public Uri insert(Uri uri, ContentValues values) {

        ...


        // Save to google Play for wearable support
        PutDataMapRequest dataMap = PutDataMapRequest.create(
                PLAY_BASE_URL + "/" + id);                  →38
        DataMap map = dataMap.getDataMap();                 →39
        map.putLong(COLUMN_TASKID, id);                     →40
        map.putString(COLUMN_TITLE, values.getAsString(COLUMN_TITLE));
        map.putLong(COLUMN_DATE_TIME, values.getAsLong(COLUMN_DATE_TIME));
        map.putString(COLUMN_NOTES, values.getAsString(COLUMN_NOTES));   →43
        PutDataRequest request = dataMap.asPutDataRequest();   →44
        Wearable.DataApi.putDataItem(googleApiClient, request);   →45

        ...

    }

    /**
     * This method is called when someone wants to delete something
```

```
        * from our content provider.
        */
       @Override
       public int delete(Uri uri, String ignored1, String[] ignored2) {

           ...

           // Delete from google Play for wearable support
           long id = ContentUris.parseId(uri);                              →60
           Uri wearUri
               = new Uri.Builder().scheme(PutDataRequest.WEAR_URI_SCHEME)
               .path(PLAY_BASE_URL + "/" + id).build();                     →63
           Wearable.DataApi.deleteDataItems(googleApiClient, wearUri);      →64

           ...
       }

       /**
        * This method is called when someone wants to update something
        * in our content provider.
        */
       @Override
       public int update(Uri uri, ContentValues values, String ignored1,
                         String[] ignored2) {
           ...

           // Update to google Play for wearable support
           long id = ContentUris.parseId(uri);                              →79
           PutDataMapRequest dataMap = PutDataMapRequest.create(
                   PLAY_BASE_URL + "/" + id);
           DataMap map = dataMap.getDataMap();
           map.putLong(COLUMN_TASKID, values.getAsLong(COLUMN_TASKID));
           map.putString(COLUMN_TITLE, values.getAsString(COLUMN_TITLE));
           map.putLong(COLUMN_DATE_TIME, values.getAsLong(COLUMN_DATE_TIME));
           map.putString(COLUMN_NOTES, values.getAsString(COLUMN_NOTES));

           PutDataRequest request = dataMap.asPutDataRequest();
           Wearable.DataApi.putDataItem(googleApiClient, request);         →88

           ...
       }


       @Override
       public void onConnected(Bundle bundle) {
           Log.d("TaskProvider", "connected to Google Play");

       }

       @Override
       public void onConnectionSuspended(int i) {
           Log.d("TaskProvider", "Google Play connection suspended");
```

```
        }

        @Override
        public void onConnectionFailed(ConnectionResult connectionResult) {
            Log.e("TaskProvider", "Google Play connection failed");
        }
    }
}
```

You recall that the `TaskProvider` manages all of your database access for
you. This code added the ability to sync data to Google Play whenever your
database changes. Here is more detail about how this code works:

→ 7   As you did for the Wear app, add the `ConnectionCallbacks`
       and `OnConnectionFailedListener` interfaces to get noti-
       fied when you connect and disconnect from Google Play.

→ 12   Every item that is to be synced with Google Play must have a
       unique URI. This URI must be unique for all items within your
       app, but does not have to be unique globally across all apps.
       For this reason, you use a very simple URI which looks like /
       `tasks` to reference all tasks, or `/tasks/<id>` to reference a
       specific task by id.

→ 14   Google Play API client, used for Android Wearable syncing.

→ 20   This block of code connects to Google Play. It is identical
       to the connection you made for the Wear app earlier in this
       chapter.

→ 25   Connects to the Google Play services. In the `TaskWear` app,
       you waited to connect to Google Play until the `onStart`
       method. `TaskProviders` do not have an `onStart` method,
       so they connect right away.

→ 38   Lines 38–45 sync a new task to Google Play. `PutDataMap`
       `Request.create()` on line 37 creates a new `PutDataMap`
       `Request` that requests that you sync a `DataMap` to Google
       Play. The `DataMap` is basically a hashmap that contains all the
       data for the task.

→ 39   Gets the `DataMap` from the `PutDataMapRequest` so you can
       put your data in it.

→ 40–43 These lines insert all the task data into the hashmap. This
       includes the task ID, title, notes, and date/time.

→ 44   Converts the `PutDataMapRequest` to a `PutDataRequest` so
       that it can be sent to Google Play.

→ 45   Finally, this line sends the request to Google Play. The call to
       `Wearable.DataApi.putDataItem` is what actually does the
       syncing to the watch.

→ 60   Lines 60–64 delete a task from Google Play. First you must determine the task ID from the task provider URI.

→ 63   Once you have the task ID from line 60, you must determine the Google Play URI for that task. This is done by using a `URI.Builder` to create a new URI with the `PutDataRequest.WEAR_URI_SCHEME` scheme, followed by the path to your task. The path to the task is `/tasks/<id>` as was indicated in the description for line 12.

→ 64   Deletes the task identified by the `wearUri`.

→ 78–87   These lines update a task. The code is identical to lines 38–45 when you inserted a task into Google Play. If the task already exists, it is updated with the new data.

Testing the sync

Congratulations, you should now have a working sync between your Tasks phone app and your Tasks Wear app!

To test it out, follow these steps:

1. **Uninstall the app from your phone and watch emulator.**

   This is important to clear out the database.

   ```
   adb -e uninstall com.dummies.tasks    # uninstall from the emulator
   adb -d uninstall com.dummies.tasks    # uninstall from your phone
   ```

2. **Run the Android Wear app and make sure that it still says "Connected" at the top.**

   If not, go back to the section "Preparing Your Development Environment" and reconnect your emulator to your phone.

3. **Run the app on your phone and add a few new tasks.**

4. **Run the `TasksWear` app on your emulator.**

   You should see the items you just added in your emulator, as in Figure 18-7. If you add more items, they should appear immediately on your emulator.

5. **Shut down the Android Wear Square emulator, then start up the Android Wear Round emulator that you created earlier in this chapter.**

   Connect the round emulator to your phone using the Android Wear app. Then run the app on that emulator to make sure that all the text is visible on a round display. You should see something like Figure 18-8.

Figure 18-7:
The Tasks app showing one item on the rectangular emulator.

meow is a verb and noun

Figure 18-8:
The Tasks app on the round emulator.

meow is a verb and a noun

Running the App without Android Studio

So far, you've been using Android Studio to run your Android Wear app. Most users are not developers, of course, and will not have Android Studio handy.

Unlike regular Android, you have no launcher on Android Wear, which can make it hard to find the app that you installed on your watch. How do you run your app without a launcher or Android Studio?

You have two ways:

✔ You can tap on your watch face and wait until it says Speak Now, and then say "Start tasks." Your watch will launch the Tasks app.

✔ If you prefer the long way, you can tap on your watch face and wait until it says Speak Now, and then scroll down to the Start option. Then choose the Tasks app.

Packaging the App

One more difference between Android and Android Wear is that you have no Google Play Store for Android Wear. Wait, there's no Play Store for Android Wear? How are people supposed to download and install your app?

The answer is that you need to bundle your Android Wear app into your phone app so that it automatically installs when your phone app does.

To bundle your Wear app inside your phone app, add the following line to your `build.gradle` in Tasks (not `TasksWear`):

```
dependencies {
    ...
    wearApp project(':TasksWear')
}
```

Now, choose Build⇨Generate Signed APK and generate a signed APK for your Tasks app (not `TasksWear`). Now if you install the signed APK, the Wear app automatically installs on your Wear watch.

What's Next?

This is just the tip of the iceberg. There are plenty of additional things you can do with your new Android Wear app. Consider making a few of the following changes:

- ✔ Improve your phone's notifications to make them actionable from your watch.
- ✔ Allow users to be able to click into individual tasks and view them.
- ✔ Add voice control so users can edit tasks or search them.
- ✔ Use `GridViewPager` and `CardFragment` to add images and make a more visually appealing interface.
- ✔ Create a `WearableListenerService` to sync data from your phone while the `MainActivity` isn't running.

Visit `https://developer.android.com/wear` for more information about how to add some of these exciting features.

To learn how to add voice control to your Android Wear apps, visit the book's online web extras at `www.dummies.com/extras/androidappdevelopment`.

Chapter 19

Look Ma, I'm on TV!

I wish there was a knob on the TV so you could turn up the intelligence.
They got one marked "brightness" but it don't work, does it?

— *Leo Anthony Gallagher*

Smart TVs are changing the living room. Up until now, every TV manu-facturer has developed their own unique interfaces for their TVs. Now Android is available on TVs to consolidate those interfaces and bring devel-oper apps to your living room. Android is available in set top boxes such as the Android TV, which you can plug into any modern TV, and it's being built directly into televisions shipping from Sony, Sharp, and Phillips.

As a developer, this is an opportunity for you to bring your apps to a whole new audience. In this chapter, you will port the Tasks app to Android TV.

Understanding Guidelines for Building TV Apps

It goes without saying that the way people use their TVs is different from the ways they use their phones. TVs are good for browsing information, but they're not as great for entering information, given their lack of a keyboard and touchscreen. Android TV is designed for casual consumption, simplicity, and a beautiful, cinematic experience.

Consequently, you should build your TV apps differently than you build them for tablets or phones. Here are some of the differences you should take into account when building TV apps:

- ✔ Build for browsing, not for data entry.
- ✔ TVs have no touchscreen, so build your interfaces so they can be navigable with a D-pad (imagine a remote control with up, down, left, and right buttons).
- ✔ Put onscreen navigation controls on the left or right side of the screen and save the vertical space for content. Do not use an action bar.
- ✔ Don't just reuse your phone or tablet activities; they will be hard to use and won't look good on the TV.

For more information about designing for Android TV, visit `https://developer.android.com/design/tv`. For more information about developing for Android TV, visit `https://developer.android.com/training/tv`.

You will use these techniques to transform your Tasks app into a TV-like browsing experience.

Building and Manifesting Changes

To build an app for TVs, you must make some changes to your build settings and your `AndroidManifest.xml`.

Open the `build.gradle` file in the `Tasks` directory, and add the line in bold:

```
dependencies {
    ...
    compile 'com.android.support:leanback-v17:21.0.3'
}
```

If you set your `minSdkVersion` to 16 in Chapter 17, you will receive an error message when you add the `leanback-v17` dependency from the previous code. This is because the leanback library requires platform API 17 or later, as the name implies. To continue, change your `minSdkVersion` to 17 in your `build.gradle` file.

This adds the Android TV dependency (also known as the "leanback" library, because that's what you do when you watch TV) to your Tasks project.

Now open the `AndroidManifest.xml` file in your `src/main` directory and add the two sections in bold:

```
<manifest xmlns:android="http://schemas.android.com/apk/res/android"
        package="com.dummies.tasks">

    <!-- For Android TV -->
    <uses-feature android:name="android.hardware.touchscreen"          →5
                android:required="false" />
    <application ... >

        ...

        <activity android:name="com.dummies.tasks.tv.BrowseActivity"   →11
                android:theme="@style/Theme.Leanback"                  →12
                android:screenOrientation="landscape" >                →13
            <intent-filter>
                <action android:name="android.intent.action.MAIN" />   →15
                <category
                    android:name ="android.intent.category.LEANBACK_LAUNCHER"/>
                                                                       →17
            </intent-filter>
        </activity>

        ...

    </application>

</manifest>
```

Here is a description of what these lines do:

→ 5   Your Android TV is not going to have a touchscreen, because most couch potatoes do not have a long enough backscratcher that can reach the screen from their La-Z-Boy. You must tell the Google Play Store that a touchscreen is not required to install this app if you want the app to be displayed to users browsing the store from their TVs.

→ 11   Declares a new activity for the TV. This activity will be your "browse" activity, which users will use to browse their tasks on your TV.

→ 12   All TV activities should use the `Theme.Leanback` style, which among other things disables the action bar (which is really hard to use on a TV).

→ 13   This line forces Android to display this activity in landscape mode. There are very few TVs out there that display in portrait mode.

→ 15   Every launcher activity should also be a `MAIN` activity. You did the same thing for your phone and tablet activities.

→ 17   Unlike your phone and tablet, Android TV uses a different launcher. Thus, the category will be `android.intent.category.LEANBACK_LAUNCHER` rather than `android.intent.category.LAUNCHER`. This is convenient because it means you can have two `MAIN` activities in your app, and Android can automatically pick the appropriate one depending on whether your app is running on a phone/tablet or a TV.

Adding the BrowseActivity

In the previous section, you added a new activity to your manifest. In this section, you will create the activity.

The `BrowseActivity` is just a simple activity wrapper around a fragment, which you will write in the next section. It consists of two parts:

- The `BrowseActivity` class
- The `activity_browse.xml` layout

Create a new package in `src/main/java/com/dummies/tasks` named `tv`, then create a new file named `BrowseActivity.java` in the `tv` directory and add the following code to it:

```
public class BrowseActivity extends Activity {

    @Override
    protected void onCreate(Bundle savedInstanceState) {
        super.onCreate(savedInstanceState);
        setContentView(R.layout.activity_browse);
    }
}
```

Then add the following layout to `res/layout` in a file named `activity_browse.xml`:

```
<?xml version="1.0" encoding="utf-8"?>
<fragment xmlns:android="http://schemas.android.com/apk/res/android"
          android:id="@+id/main_browse_fragment"
          android:name="com.dummies.tasks.tv.MainFragment"
          android:layout_width="match_parent"
          android:layout_height="match_parent"/>
```

This layout is similar to the one you created in Listing 9-2. It declares that this layout consists of one element, a fragment with code defined in `com.dummies.tasks.tv.MainFragment`, which you will create next.

Creating the TV Browse Fragment

As you can see, the `BrowseActivity` does very little. All it does is create the `MainFragment`, which is where most of your TV code is going to go.

The `MainFragment` is an instance of an Android TV's `BrowseFragment`. The built-in `BrowseFragment` consists of three parts:

- ✔ A column of headings, or categories, on the left
- ✔ Rows of content on the right, divided into the appropriate heading
- ✔ A transparent title bar at the top containing a title and an optional search icon

You can see how these parts are arranged in Figure 19-1.

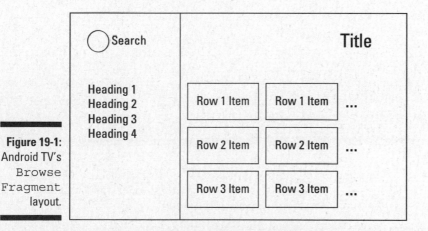

Figure 19-1: Android TV's `Browse Fragment` layout.

Creating the MainFragment outline

Let's focus first on putting your tasks into the section on the right.

Create a new class named `MainActivity` in the `com.dummies.tasks.tv` package, and add the following code to it:

```
public class MainFragment extends BrowseFragment
        implements LoaderManager.LoaderCallbacks<Cursor>                →2
{
    @Override
    public void onActivityCreated(Bundle savedInstanceState) {         →5
        super.onActivityCreated(savedInstanceState);

        setTitle(getString(R.string.app_name));                        →8
        setBrandColor(getResources().getColor(R.color.primary));       →9

        ArrayObjectAdapter adapter
            = new ArrayObjectAdapter(new ListRowPresenter());          →12

        setAdapter(adapter);                                           →14
    }

    @Override                                                          →18
    public Loader<Cursor> onCreateLoader(int id, final Bundle args) {
    }

    @Override
    public void onLoadFinished(Loader<Cursor> loader, Cursor cursor) {
    }

    @Override
    public void onLoaderReset(Loader<Cursor> loader) {
    }                                                                  →28
}
```

This class creates a new `BrowseFragment` named `MainFragment`, sets
some properties on the fragment, creates an adapter, and then sets up the
loader callbacks needed to populate the adapter. For a refresher on how
loaders and adapters work, see Chapter 13.

Here is more information about the previous listing:

→ 2   This line creates the `MainFragment`, declares that it extends
      `BrowseFragment`, and implements the loader callbacks that
      you'll need to load data into your adapter.

→ 5   These lines override the `onActivityCreated()` method, and call
      `super.onActivityCreated()` to make sure that the fragment is
      initialized properly. `onActivityCreated` is called when the activ-
      ity has been created and the fragment has been attached to it. This
      is where you'll do most of your initialization code for the fragment.
      See Chapter 9 for more examples of using `onActivityCreated`.

→ 8   Sets the title of the activity. This will be displayed in the upper
      right-hand side of the screen, as in Figure 19-1.

→ 9   Sets the "brand" color of the activity. This is the color that will be used for the background of the left half of Figure 19-1 containing your headers. For phones and tablets, you used this color in your action bar, but because TVs have no action bar, you will use this color on the left side of the screen.

→ 12   Creates a new `ArrayObjectAdapter` which will be the main adapter used by the `BrowseFragment`. Recall from Chapter 13 that an adapter knows how to read a list of items (usually from a database) and create views for them. In this case, an `ArrayObjectAdapter` knows how to read a list of items from an array and create views for them.

Why an array rather than a database? The array contains one entry for each row in the grid in Figure 19-1. Each row has its own adapter, and *that* adapter reads items from the database. So you'll still be reading from the database, but not directly from this adapter.

Android TV adapters require a `Presenter` object to create views from objects. Presenters are very similar to the `RecyclerView.Adapters` you used in Chapter 13, but they are not position based (their methods take objects rather than positions). In this case you are using the built-in `ListRowPresenter`, which knows how to take `ListRow` objects (which you will create in the next section) and create views for them.

→ 14   Tells the `BrowseFragment` to use the adapter you just created.

→ 18-28   Adds the loader callback methods that you'll need to use a loader. See Chapter 13 for more information about loaders. These callbacks are not fully implemented yet.

Reading data from the database

The next step is to actually read your tasks from the database. You will use a `CursorObjectAdapter` with a loader to load your tasks.

First you will need a simple model class to represent a task. Create a new file named `Task.java` in `com.dummies.tasks.tv` and add the following:

```java
public class Task {
    long id;
    String title;
    String notes;
}
```

This class will hold the data that you read out of the database.

Displaying tasks using loaders and CardPresenters

Now that you have the Task model, you need to set up your fragment so that it can read items from the database and present them to the user. This is similar to using the loaders and adapters you used in Chapter 9, except for Android TV you will also use a `Presenter` and a `CursorMapper`.

Open `MainFragment.java` again and add the lines in bold:

```
public class MainFragment extends BrowseFragment
    implements LoaderManager.LoaderCallbacks<Cursor>
{
    @Override
    public void onActivityCreated(Bundle savedInstanceState) {
        super.onActivityCreated(savedInstanceState);

        setTitle(getString(R.string.app_name));
        setBrandColor(getResources().getColor(R.color.primary));


        ArrayObjectAdapter adapter
            = new ArrayObjectAdapter(new ListRowPresenter());          →13

        CardPresenter cardPresenter = new CardPresenter();            →15
        CursorMapper simpleMapper = new CursorToTaskMapper();         →16

        HeaderItem header = new HeaderItem(0,"All", null);            →18
        CursorObjectAdapter cursorObjectAdapter
            = new CursorObjectAdapter(cardPresenter);                 →20
        cursorObjectAdapter.setMapper(simpleMapper);                  →21

        adapter.add(new ListRow(header, cursorObjectAdapter));        →23


        setAdapter(adapter);

        LoaderManager loaderManager = getLoaderManager();             →28
        loaderManager.initLoader(0, null, this);                      →29

    }


    @Override
    public Loader<Cursor> onCreateLoader(int id, final Bundle args) { →35
        return new CursorLoader(getActivity(),                        →36
            TaskProvider.CONTENT_URI,
            null, null,null,null);
    }
```

```
    @Override
    public void onLoadFinished(Loader<Cursor> loader, Cursor cursor) {
        ListRow row = (ListRow) getAdapter().get(0);                    →43
        CursorObjectAdapter rowAdapter
            = (CursorObjectAdapter) row.getAdapter();                   →45
        rowAdapter.swapCursor(cursor);                                  →46
    }

    @Override
    public void onLoaderReset(Loader<Cursor> loader) {
        // This is called when the last Cursor provided to
        // onLoadFinished()
        // above is about to be closed. We need to make sure we are no
        // longer using it.
        ListRow row = (ListRow) getAdapter().get(0);                    →55
        CursorObjectAdapter rowAdapter
            = (CursorObjectAdapter) row.getAdapter();                   →57
        rowAdapter.swapCursor(null);                                    →58
    }
}
```

Here is what the code is doing:

→ 15   In the previous section you used a `ListRowPresenter` to
        convert rows into views. Similarly, on this line you will use
        a `CardPresenter` to convert each task into a card. The
        `CardPresenter` does not exist yet; you will write it in the next
        section.

→ 16   Every `CursorObjectAdapter` must have a `CursorMapper`
        that knows how to map rows in the database to objects
        that the adapter can read. You will create one called
        `CursorToTaskMapper` a little later.

→ 18   Each row in the grid needs to have a header associated with it.
        For your first header, the row will contain all the tasks in the data-
        base, so name this header `"All"` and give it an id of `0`.

→ 20   On this line you finally get to meet the `CursorObjectAdapter`
        that we've been referring to throughout this section. The
        `CursorObjectAdapter` is an adapter that knows how to read
        rows from the database and convert them into views. To do that,
        it uses the mapper and the presenter that you configured earlier
        and are added to the `CursorObjectAdapter` on lines 20 and 21.
        Remember that the `CursorObjectAdapter` is the second adapter
        you've created for this fragment. The first (and main) adapter is
        the `ArrayObjectAdapter` you created in the previous section.
        The `ArrayObjectAdapter` represents the rows in our grid, and
        the `CursorObjectAdapter` represents the items in the row.

→ 23   You created the `CursorObjectAdapter` on line 20, so now you need to add it to the `ArrayObjectAdapter`. Recall that the `ListRowPresenter` that you added on line 13 knows how to read `ListRow` objects, so on this line you create a new `ListRow` object and add it to the adapter. The `ListRow` object represents one row in the grid, so it will have the "All" header you created on line 19 and the `CursorObjectAdapter` that you created on line 20. Together, those two objects contain all the data (the header and the items) needed to construct one row in the grid.

→ 28–29 Kicks off the loader so that it starts running. `initLoader` will call your `onCreateLoader` callback on line 35 to create the loader, and then it will call the `onLoadFinished` callback when the data is done loading. Refer to Chapter 13 for more information about `initLoader`.

→ 36   `onCreateLoader` is called when the fragment has been asked to create a loader, so create a new `CursorLoader` that knows how to load tasks from the `TaskProvider`. This code is the same as what you used in Chapter 13 to load tasks from the database.

→ 43–47 `onLoadFinished` is called when the database has finished loading data and has a cursor to give you. You need to take that cursor and hand it to the adapter. But remember there are two adapters, so which one? Call `getAdapter()` to get the main adapter from the fragment, which in this case is the `ArrayObjectAdapter`. Then get the first object from that adapter (which you added on line 23). That object is a `ListRow`, so call `getAdapter()` on the `ListRow` and that will return to you the `CursorObjectAdapter` that you set on line 23.

Now that you have the `CursorObjectAdapter`, call `swapCursor()` to set the cursor that the loader just gave you. This is similar to how you implemented `onLoadFinished` in Chapter 13, except it requires an additional step to find the right adapter.

→ 58   Do the same thing you did above, but in this case set the cursor to `null`. `onLoaderReset` is called when the loader is reset, and it should zero-out any data that it's holding onto. In this case, that means swapping out the old cursor and setting the cursor to `null`. This is similar to what you did in Chapter 13.

Mapping database cursors to tasks

The next step is to add the `CursorToTaskMapper` referenced on line 16 in the previous code. Create a new class in `com.dummies.tasks.tv` called **CursorToTaskMapper**, and add the following to it:

```
public class CursorToTaskMapper extends CursorMapper {
    int idIndex;                                                        →2
    int titleIndex;
    int notesIndex;                                                     →4

    @Override
    protected void bindColumns(Cursor cursor) {                         →7
        idIndex =                                                       →8
            cursor.getColumnIndexOrThrow(TaskProvider.COLUMN_TASKID);
        titleIndex =
            cursor.getColumnIndexOrThrow(TaskProvider.COLUMN_TITLE);
        notesIndex =
            cursor.getColumnIndexOrThrow(TaskProvider.COLUMN_NOTES);    →13
    }

    @Override
    protected Task bind(Cursor cursor) {
        long id = cursor.getLong(idIndex);                              →18
        String title = cursor.getString(titleIndex);
        String notes = cursor.getString(notesIndex);                    →20

        Task t = new Task();                                            →22
        t.id=id;                                                        →23
        t.title=title;
        t.notes=notes;                                                  →25
        return t;                                                       →26
    }
}
```

The `CursorToTaskMapper` knows how to read a row in the cursor and convert it to a `Task` object. The following explains the way this is done:

→ **2–4**   Creates fields that store the indices of the ID, title, and notes columns in the database. Recall from Chapter 13 that you must know the index of the column you want to retrieve from the cursor.

→ **7**   Overrides the `bindColumns()` method. This method is called once when the cursor is obtained so that you can ask the cursor what the indices of the columns are. Lines 8–13 retrieve these indices and store them in the fields on lines 2–4. Refer to Chapter 13 for more information about using cursors.

→ **18–20**   The `bind()` method is called to generate a `Task` object from a cursor. Lines 18–20 get the ID, title, and notes of the task from the cursor by using the column indices that were obtained in `bindColumns` on line 7.

→ **22–26**   Creates a new `Task` object, and sets its fields based on the data you obtained from lines 18–20, then returns the object.

Now your TV app is very close to working. The only thing you still need to implement is the `CardPresenter`, which knows how to convert tasks into cards.

Creating the CardPresenter

Presenters are objects in Android TV used by adapters to convert objects (in this case, tasks) into views. They are similar to the `RecyclerView`. `Adapters` you used in Chapter 9, so they should look familiar to you.

Create a new class named `CardPresenter.java` in the `com.dummies.tasks.tv` package, and add the following code:

```
public class CardPresenter extends Presenter {                          →1
    private static int CARD_WIDTH = 313;                                →2
    private static int CARD_HEIGHT = 176;                               →3

    @Override
    public ViewHolder onCreateViewHolder(ViewGroup parent) {            →6
        Context context = parent.getContext();                          →7
        ImageCardView cardView = new ImageCardView(context);            →8
        cardView.setFocusable(true);                                    →9
        cardView.setFocusableInTouchMode(true);                         →10
        cardView.setBackgroundResource(R.color.window_background);      →11
        return new ViewHolder(cardView);                                →12
    }

    @Override
    public void onBindViewHolder(Presenter.ViewHolder viewHolder, Object item) {
                                                                        →16
        Task task = (Task)item;                                         →17

        // Update card
        ViewHolder vh = (ViewHolder) viewHolder;                        →20
        ImageCardView cardView = vh.cardView;                           →21
        cardView.setTitleText(task.title);
        cardView.setContentText(task.notes);                            →23
        cardView.setMainImageDimensions(CARD_WIDTH, CARD_HEIGHT);       →24

        Context context= cardView.getContext();                         →26
        Picasso.with(context)                                           →27
                .load(TaskListAdapter.getImageUrlForTask(task.id))      →28
                .resize(CARD_WIDTH, CARD_HEIGHT)                        →29
                .centerCrop()                                           →30
                .into(cardView.getMainImageView());                    →31
    }
```

```
    @Override
    public void onUnbindViewHolder(Presenter.ViewHolder viewHolder) {       →35
    }


    // The ViewHolder class
    static class ViewHolder extends Presenter.ViewHolder {                   →39
        ImageCardView cardView;

        public ViewHolder(View view) {
            super(view);
            cardView = (ImageCardView) view;
        }
    }
}
```

About this class:

→ 1   Every presenter class must be a subclass of the `Presenter`
       class and must implement three methods and one class:

       • `onCreateViewHolder`

       • `onBindViewHolder`

       • `onUnbindViewHolder`

       • A `ViewHolder` class

→ 2–3 The width and height of the `ImageCardView`. This needs to be
       in Java because you are creating views in Java rather than in an
       XML layout file.

→ 6   `onCreateViewHolder` is called when the `ViewHolder` is cre-
       ated. One `ViewHolder` is created for every visible card on the
       screen. So if your screen is large enough to show four cards at
       once, approximately four `ViewHolders` and `CardViews` are
       created, no matter how long your list is. See Chapter 9 for more
       information about using `ViewHolders`.

→ 7   Gets the current context from the parent view. You will need
       this later.

→ 8   Creates a new instance of Android TV's built-in
       `ImageCardView`. This view will be recycled over and over
       to display tasks in a row. You can see examples of the
       `ImageCardView` in Figure 19-1 on the right-hand side. In
       Chapter 9 you used a `LayoutInflater` to inflate an XML
       layout for the card view there, but it's also okay to create views
       directly in Java instead of using XML.

→ 9–10 Makes sure that the `ImageCardView` is focusable when using a
       D-pad and when using touch.

TIP

For more information on using focus for navigation on devices without touchscreens, see `http://d.android.com/guide/topics/ui/ui-events.html#HandlingFocus`.

→ 11   Sets the background of the view to the default window background color for this theme.

→ 12   Creates a new `ViewHolder`, defined on line 45, and returns it for the view you just created. See Chapter 9 for more information about using `ViewHolder`s.

→ 16   `onBindViewHolder` is called when it's time to populate a card with data from the object in the adapter. `onBindViewHolder` will get the card view from the `ViewHolder` object, and then update that card to reflect the data in the object that's passed in. As you scroll through your list, `onBindViewHolder` will be called every time an item scrolls onto the screen. Again, see Chapter 9 for more information about binding views to objects.

→ 17   The item in this case is a `Task` object (because the mapper returns tasks), so this line casts the item to a `Task`.

→ 20   Casts the `viewHolder` object to a `CardPresenter.ViewHolder` (rather than a `Presenter.ViewHolder`) so that you can access the `cardView` on line 9.

→ 21–23   Sets the title and content of the `cardView` using the data from the task.

→ 24   Sets the dimensions of the `ImageView` inside the `ImageCardView` to be the size from line 2–3.

→ 26   Gets the current context from the `cardView`.

→ 27   Uses Picasso to download the image for this task. Refer to Chapter 9 for more information about using Picasso. In this case, you will load the image using the task's image URL obtained from `getImageUrlForTask()` (line 28) into the `ImageView` that's managed by the `cardView` on line 31. In addition, on line 29 and 30, you will resize and crop the image to fit the size of the `ImageView`.

→ 35   `onUnbindViewHolder` is called whenever a view is about to be unbound from a `ViewHolder`. It's the opposite of `onBindViewHolder` on line 16. Most presenters do not need to do anything here.

→ 39   Most presenters will need to implement a `ViewHolder` that contains references to the views that need to be updated in `onBindViewHolder`. This `ViewHolder` is a simple one that has a reference to a single view, Android TV's built-in `ImageCardView`. See Chapter 9 for more information about using `ViewHolder`s.

Running Your App

Your app isn't done yet, but it should be possible to build and run it. To do that, you'll need to create an Android TV emulator.

Choose Tools ⇨ Android ⇨ AVD Manager, click Create Virtual Device, and create a new device with the settings in Table 19-1.

Table 19-1	Settings for Creating a New TV Emulator
Category	*TV*
Name	Android TV (720p)
Release name	Lollipop
API level	21
ABI	x86

See Chapter 3 for more information about creating an Android emulator.

Once the emulator has been created, click the Run icon to start it up. Be aware that because the Android TV does not have a touchscreen, many items in the interface may not be clickable. Instead, you should use the arrow keys on your keyboard to navigate the Android TV emulator interface.

Now that the emulator has been created, go to Android Studio and select Run ⇨ Run 'Tasks', then choose to run it on the emulator that you just created. You should see something like Figure 19-2.

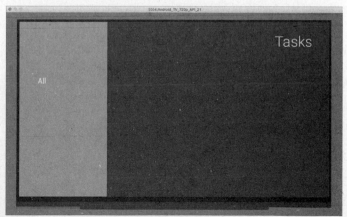

Figure 19-2:
The Tasks app running on Android TV with no data.

Well, that's fun, but there's no data to view. And there's no way to add data! Let's fix that.

Adding and Editing Items

Android TV isn't really designed for inputting data. There's no keyboard on most devices, and although there's a virtual onscreen keyboard, using it with a standard TV remote control can be a real pain.

For that reason, the `BrowseFragment` doesn't really have a built-in way for adding items to the database. But without a way to add items to the database, how are you going to test your app?

The trick is to launch the `TaskEditActivity` on your emulator, directly from Android Studio. Once the `TaskEditActivity` is running, you can use it to save tasks to the database. Your users can't launch `TaskEditActivity` directly from the app, but you can launch it from Android Studio for testing purposes.

Because TVs aren't a good way to input data, it probably doesn't make sense to have a permanent Add Item button on the Tasks app for TVs. The technique in this section is a good way to test your app, but most users will expect your TV Tasks app to sync with their apps on their phones. Cloud storage is not covered in this book, but take a look at Google Cloud Save (http://developer.android.com/google/gcs) for one potential way to sync your tasks between devices.

Using voice input can be a great way to allow your users to add data to apps on your TV. Many Android TVs support voice input either directly on the TV, or built into the Android TV remote. For more information about using Voice Input on Android, visit the book's web extras online at www.dummies.com/extras/androidappdevelopment.

To launch `TaskEditActivity`, open the `TaskEditActivity.java` file and right-click on `TaskEditActivity`, then choose Run 'TaskEditActivity', as in Figure 19-3.

The `TaskEditActivity` should run on your emulator, and you should be able to save a new task into your database. If you repeat this a few times, you should see a few items in your app, like in Figure 19-4.

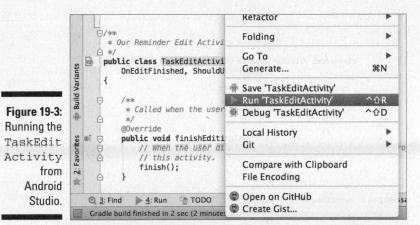

Figure 19-3:
Running the
`TaskEdit`
`Activity`
from
Android
Studio.

Figure 19-4:
The Tasks
app with
one item
selected.

Creating Backgrounds

As mentioned in the first section, Android TV apps should be a little bit more cinematic than their phone and tablet counterparts. Let's add a touch of visual flair by changing the background of the app when you select each task.

Open `MainFragment.java` and add the lines in bold:

```
@Override
public void onActivityCreated(Bundle savedInstanceState) {
    super.onActivityCreated(savedInstanceState);

    final BackgroundManager backgroundManager
        = BackgroundManager.getInstance(getActivity());          →6
```

```
        backgroundManager.attach(getActivity().getWindow());          →7

    ...

    setOnItemViewSelectedListener(                                     →11
        new OnItemViewSelectedListener() {
            @Override
            public void onItemSelected(Presenter.ViewHolder
                                        itemViewHolder,
                                Object item,
                                RowPresenter.ViewHolder
                                    rowViewHolder, Row row)
        {
            if( itemViewHolder==null )                                 →20
                return;

            ImageCardView cardView =
                ((CardPresenter.ViewHolder)itemViewHolder).cardView;  →24
            Drawable d = cardView.getMainImage();                     →25
            if(d!=null) {                                             →26
                Bitmap b = ((BitmapDrawable)d).getBitmap();           →27
                backgroundManager.setBitmap(b);                       →28
            }
        }
    }
);

    ...
}
```

Here is what the code does:

→ 6   Gets a `BackgroundManager` from the activity. The Android
       TV `BackgroundManager` is responsible for setting the back-
       ground of the app.

→ 7   Every time you want to use a `BackgroundManager`, you must
       make sure that it is associated with the current activity's
       window.

→ 11   Calls `setOnItemViewSelectedListener()` when you
       want to set the listener that is invoked whenever an item is
       selected. You will use this listener to change the background
       to be a scaled-up version of the image for the currently
       selected task.

→ 20   You must use the `itemViewHolder` to get the current `card
       View` for the selected item, but the `itemViewHolder` may
       sometimes be `null`. This can happen when a row header is
       selected rather than a row item. To protect against this case,
       make sure to check for `null`.

→ **24**   Gets the `cardView` from the `ViewHolder`.

→ **25–27**   Gets the bitmap from the `ImageCardView` by first getting the drawable, and then getting the bitmap from the drawable. It's possible that the drawable may be null if it hasn't been downloaded from the network yet, so make sure to check for that case.

→ **28**   Uses the `BackgroundManager` to set the background to the bitmap you got from line 27.

`BackgroundManager` has a `setDrawable()` method, so you might be tempted to call `backgroundManager.setDrawable()` using the drawable on line 25 and skipping line 26 entirely. Do not do this; it's not safe to reuse drawables in multiple places. `ImageViews` may modify their drawables, and if you're using the same drawable in two different `ImageViews`, you can get some very weird-looking behavior. `ImageViews` do not modify bitmaps, so they are safe to reuse here.

Try running the app now, and you will see that the background changes as you select different tasks.

Creating More Filters

Currently, the only header you have on the left-hand side of the app is the "All" filter. Let's add some additional filters to make it easier for users to navigate their tasks. In this section, you add the following filters:

- ✔ All
- ✔ Today
- ✔ This Week
- ✔ This Month
- ✔ This Year

The way to do this is to add one `HeaderItem` for each new filter, then add a new `CursorObjectAdapter` for each filter's row of data. You also need to create several more loaders to handle all the new `CursorObjectAdapters`.

First add the following to your `MainFragment`:

```
public static final Object[] CATEGORIES[] = {
    new Object[]{ "All",new int[]{
        Calendar.YEAR,
        Calendar.DAY_OF_YEAR,
```

```
        Calendar.HOUR_OF_DAY,
        Calendar.MINUTE,
        Calendar.SECOND
    }
    },
    new Object[]{ "Today", new int[]{
        Calendar.HOUR_OF_DAY,
        Calendar.MINUTE,
        Calendar.SECOND
    }
    },
    new Object[]{"This Week", new int[]{
        Calendar.DAY_OF_WEEK,
        Calendar.HOUR_OF_DAY,
        Calendar.MINUTE,
        Calendar.SECOND
    }
    },
    new Object[]{"This Month", new int[]{
        Calendar.DAY_OF_MONTH,
        Calendar.HOUR_OF_DAY,
        Calendar.MINUTE,
        Calendar.SECOND
    }
    },
    new Object[]{ "This Year",new int[]{
        Calendar.DAY_OF_YEAR,
        Calendar.HOUR_OF_DAY,
        Calendar.MINUTE,
        Calendar.SECOND
    }
    },
};
```

This static field defines all the categories you're going to use as headers on the left-hand side of the app. It also defines the fields that you need to zero-out if you want to take a timestamp and create a filter for it.

Let's say that you want to find all the tasks that have a reminder set for today. To do that, you would take a timestamp that represents your time right now, and zero-out the hour, minutes, and seconds to get the time at midnight this morning. Anything with a reminder after midnight would be selected by your filter.

Similarly, if you want to find all of the reminders that are set this week, you would still zero-out the hours, minutes, and seconds, but you would ALSO zero-out the day of the week. This would tell you the time that the current week started, so any reminder after that time would be for this week.

Now that you've defined your filters, you just need to use them. Edit `MainFragment` again and change the following lines in `onActivityCreated`:

```
HeaderItem header = new HeaderItem(0,"All", null);
CursorObjectAdapter cursorObjectAdapter
    = new CursorObjectAdapter(cardPresenter);
cursorObjectAdapter.setMapper(simpleMapper);

adapter.add(new ListRow(header, cursorObjectAdapter));

for( int i=0; i< CATEGORIES.length; ++i ) {                →9
    HeaderItem header = new HeaderItem(i,
        (String)CATEGORIES[i][0], null);                   →11
    CursorObjectAdapter cursorObjectAdapter
        = new CursorObjectAdapter(cardPresenter);          →13
    cursorObjectAdapter.setMapper(simpleMapper);           →14

    adapter.add(new ListRow(header, cursorObjectAdapter)); →16
}

setAdapter(adapter);

LoaderManager loaderManager = getLoaderManager();
loaderManager.initLoader(0, null, this);                   →22

for( int i=0; i<CATEGORIES.length; ++i)                    →24
    loaderManager.initLoader(i, null, this);               →25
```

You just took the previous code that created a single row in the grid, and replaced it with code that created one row for each item in the `CATEGORIES` variable. Here's how the code works:

→ 9   Loops over each item in the `CATEGORIES` array. Each of these categories will become a row in your grid.

→ 11   Creates a `HeaderItem` for each category in the `for` loop. The ID of the `HeaderItem` will be the current position in the category array (`i`), and the name of the `HeaderItem` will be set to `"All"`, `"Today"`, `"This Week"`, and so on as appropriate. The last parameter is an optional image URL which you won't use for the category headers.

→ 13   Because each category corresponds to a row in the grid, this line creates a new `CursorObjectAdapter` to load the data for that row. As before, you create the `CursorObjectAdapter` and pass in a `cardPresenter` and a `simpleMapper` (lines 13 and 14).

→ 16   Just like before, this line creates a new `ListRow` using the `HeaderItem` and the `CursorObjectAdapter`, and adds it to the `ArrayObjectAdapter`.

→ 22   Make sure you delete this line.

→ 24–25   Instead of initializing just one loader, this line calls `initLoader()` once for each row in the grid. You pass in the index of the row as the ID of the loader to initialize. You will use that ID later to find the correct loader in `onCreateLoader`.

The last step is to update the loader callbacks to know that they need to work with multiple loaders rather than just one. Replace your existing loader callbacks with the following:

```
@Override
public Loader<Cursor> onCreateLoader(int id, final Bundle args) {
    long filterTimestamp = getFilterTimeForSelectedFilter(id);        →3
    return new CursorLoader(getActivity(),                            →4
        TaskProvider.CONTENT_URI,
        null,
        TaskProvider.COLUMN_DATE_TIME + "> ?",                        →7
        new String[]{Long.toString(filterTimestamp)},                →8
        null);
}


@Override
public void onLoadFinished(Loader<Cursor> loader, Cursor cursor) {
    int id = loader.getId();                                          →14
    ObjectAdapter adapter = getAdapter();                             →15
    ListRow row = (ListRow) adapter.get(id);                          →16
    CursorObjectAdapter rowAdapter = (CursorObjectAdapter) row
        .getAdapter();                                                →18
    rowAdapter.swapCursor(cursor);                                    →19
}


@Override
public void onLoaderReset(Loader<Cursor> loader) {
    int id = loader.getId();                                          →24
    ObjectAdapter adapter = getAdapter();                             →25
    ListRow row = (ListRow) adapter.get(id);                          →26
    CursorObjectAdapter rowAdapter = (CursorObjectAdapter) row
        .getAdapter();
    rowAdapter.swapCursor(null);
}
```

The last two methods are virtually identical to their predecessors, only now they use the ID of the loader to pick the correct adapter to update. The first method requires a little more explanation:

→ 3   Calls `getFilterTimeForSelectedFilter()` to get the timestamp for the selected filter. For example, if the filter was `"Today"`, then the timestamp will correspond to midnight this morning as described previously in this section. You'll add the `getFilterTimeForSelectedFilter()` shortly.

→ **4**   As before, this line creates the `CursorLoader` using the `CONTENT_URI` for our task `ContentProvider`. The only difference is on lines 7 and 8. Line 7 specifies a filter criteria for the query. It's beyond the scope of this book to explain SQL, but the idea is that you create a query that says `"task_date_time > ?"`, and the *?* will be replaced by the time you specify on line 8. This way, each `CursorLoader` gets its own unique query (one for Today, one for This Week, one for This Month, and so on).

→ **14–16**   The functions `onLoadFinished()` and `onLoaderReset()` are nearly identical to what they were before, except instead of assuming that they should use the `CursorObjectAdapter` in index 0 of the `ArrayObjectAdapter` like they did before, they now get the ID of the loader from the `loader` object, and use that as the index into the `ArrayObjectAdapter` to find the correct `CursorObjectLoader`. You're using the loader's ID to pass around the index for the correct adapter.

→ **24–26**   The same as lines 14–16.

Finally, add the `getFilterTimeForSelectedFilter` method:

```
private long getFilterTimeForSelectedFilter(int id) {          →1
    Calendar calendar = Calendar.getInstance();                →2
    int[] calendarFieldsToZero = (int[])CATEGORIES[id][1];      →3

    for( int fieldToZero : calendarFieldsToZero )              →5
        calendar.set(                                          →6
            fieldToZero,
            calendar.getActualMinimum(fieldToZero));            →8

    return calendar.getTimeInMillis();                         →10
}
```

This method isn't really related to Android at all, but what it does is this:

→ **1**   `getFilterTimeForSelectedFilter` takes an index into the `CATEGORIES` array that indicates which filter to use. Index 0 is `"All"`, index 1 is `"Today"`, and so on.

→ **2**   Gets a new calendar instance that corresponds to "now."

→ **3**   Gets the list of fields to zero-out from the array. For example, if the selected filter is `"Today"`, then according to the `CATEGORIES` array, the fields will be `HOUR_OF_DAY`, `MINUTE`, `SECOND`.

→ 5-8   For each field that needs to be zeroed, these lines call `calendar.set()` on the field and set it to its minimum. In most cases, this will be zero or one, but in some cases it may be other values. For example, the beginning of the week is considered to be SUNDAY (1) in the U.S., but in Europe it is considered to be MONDAY (2). `Calendar.getActualMinimum()` will tell us the appropriate value for each field, given the user's current locale.

Programming dates and times in Java can get quite complicated. For more information about Java's date and time classes, visit `https://docs.oracle.com/javase/tutorial/datetime/iso`. You may also be interested in checking out ThreeTenBackport at `http://www.threeten.org/threetenbp`.

→ 10   Returns the timestamp for the result, in UNIX time (a long representing milliseconds since Jan 1, 1970 UTC).

Run the app again and create a few tasks with reminder times today, yesterday, and earlier this month, and you should see something similar to Figure 19-5.

Figure 19-5:
The completed Tasks app on Android TV.

Chapter 20

Moving beyond Google

· ·

In This Chapter

▶ Making your app work on Amazon Fire

▶ Finding out which features don't work with Fire

▶ Configuring and testing with an emulator

▶ Uploading your app to the Amazon Appstore

· ·

*F*or Android, Google may be the biggest game in town, but it isn't the only one. Because Google makes every release of Android open to the public via the Android Open Source Project, many companies produce their own, custom versions of the Android source code.

One company that you may be familiar with, Amazon, chose Android to run on its devices — the Fire OS tablet and phone.

The Android-based Fire devices can run Android apps with few or no modifications. It has no access to the Google Play Store, though, which means that if you want Fire users to be able to download your app, you have to publish it to the Amazon Appstore for Android. In this chapter, you find out how to port your application to the Fire OS and then publish it via Amazon.

 One reason you may want to port to the Fire is to reach more users. But only you can decide whether the additional users you'll acquire are worth the extra effort that's necessary. Do your homework and read relevant statistics on how many users each new platform has before you commit to expending the effort.

Working around Google Features

Because the Fire isn't a "true" Android device (it doesn't use the official Google Android source code but instead uses a modified version), it doesn't have access to any of the closed-source Google services that you might already be using. In addition, the device itself may not have certain features that you're accustomed to:

- ✔ **Google Maps:** If you're using the Google Maps library to bring maps to your Android application, you can't use this library on the Fire. If you use maps, you may be able to use Amazon's Map v2, available at `https://developer.amazon.com/public/apis/experience/maps`.

- ✔ **Google Play Store in-app purchasing:** If your app uses in-app purchasing to allow users to purchase from inside it, you can't use this same API in your Fire app. Luckily, Amazon has a version of in-app purchasing that you can use on the Fire.

- ✔ **GCM push notifications:** If you're using Google Cloud Messaging for push notifications, you won't be able to use these on the Fire. Amazon has an alternative that you can use for Fire devices.

- ✔ **Android Lollipop:** Amazon uses the version of Android source code before Lollipop was released, so the Fire has no access to any of the features in Lollipop. In particular, you'll notice that the Fire has a unique look and feel unlike any other Android tablet.

Even without these features and services, *many* Android applications work on the Fire with little or no modification. If this includes your app, read on.

The Amazon App Testing Service can inspect your Android app and tell you what, if anything, needs to be updated to support the Fire OS. You can learn more about the App Testing Service at `https://developer.amazon.com/public/resources/development-tools/app-testing-service`.

Setting Up the Fire SDK

Much like developing on Android requires the Android SDK, developing on Fire requires the Fire SDK. Because you already have the Android SDK, installing the components necessary for Fire development is simple:

1. **Open Android Studio and choose Tools⇨Android⇨SDK Manager.**

2. **In the SDK Manager, choose Tools⇨Manage Add-on Sites.**

3. **Click User Defined Sites, click New, and add the following URL:**
   `https://s3.amazonaws.com/android-sdk-manager/redist/addon.xml`.

   Click Close, and wait for the SDK to download.

4. Uncheck "Installed" to only show you SDKs that are not yet installed.

Then check the Amazon Fire Phone SDK Addon, and click Install.

After the SDK is installed, you need to modify your Gradle build file to use the new SDK.

In the `build.gradle` in the top level of your project (not the `build.gradle` in your individual app directories), change the line in bold to the following:

```
buildscript {
    repositories {
        mavenCentral()
    }
    dependencies {
        classpath 'com.android.tools.build:gradle:1.0.1'
        classpath 'com.amazon.device.tools.build:gradle:1.0.0'
    }
}
```

In the `build.gradle` for your app, change your `compileSdkVersion` to the following:

```
compileSdkVersion "Amazon.com:Amazon Fire Phone SDK Addon:17"
```

Now you should be able to rebuild your project for the Fire.

Setting Up Your Fire or Emulator

If you want to develop for the Fire, you need either the Fire itself to test your app with or an emulator that can act as a surrogate. Because the Fire is its own breed of Android, you can't use the same ADB you use with other Android devices unless you make a few configuration changes.

Creating a Fire-like emulator

If you don't have access to a Fire, you need to create an emulator for one. Follow these steps:

1. **Choose Tools ⇨ Android ⇨ AVD Manager, then click Create Virtual Device.**

2. **Click New Hardware Profile to create a new kind of virtual device.**

3. **Enter the settings from Figure 20-1 and click Finish.**

4. **Select your newly created Fire Phone virtual device and click Next.**

   Then choose Jelly Bean API level 17 for x86 devices, as in Figure 20-2.

5. **Click Next.**

   Use the default configuration and then click Finish to create your Fire Phone AVD.

	● ● ●

Create new Android Virtual Device (AVD)

AVD Name:	Fire Phone
Device:	4.65" 720p (Galaxy Nexus) (720 × 1280: xhdpi) ⇕
Target:	Android 4.2.2 – API Level 17 ⇕
CPU/ABI:	Intel Atom (x86) ⇕
Keyboard:	☑ Hardware keyboard present
Skin:	No skin ⇕
Front Camera:	None ⇕
Back Camera:	None ⇕
Memory Options:	RAM: 2048 VM Heap: 64
Internal Storage:	200 MiB ⇕
SD Card:	⦿ Size: MiB ⇕
	○ File: Browse...
Emulation Options:	☐ Snapshot ☑ Use Host GPU
	Cancel OK

Figure 20-1:
Settings
in the
Create new
Android
Virtual
Device
(AVD)
dialog.

Do you need to create an emulator for a different kind of Fire device? Visit https://developer.amazon.com/public/solutions/ devices/kindle-fire/specifications/01-device-and-feature- specifications for a list of all of the emulator settings for all of the available Fire devices.

Enabling Developer Options

If you are using a real Fire device, you need to enable Developer Options to be able to use it with ADB on your computer. To enable Developer Options

1. **Open the Settings interface.**

2. **Scroll to and expand the Device section.**

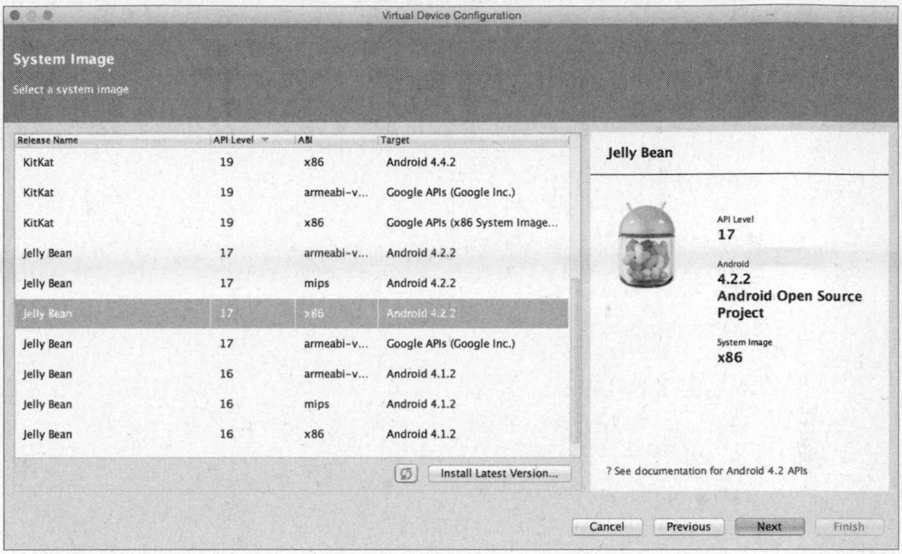

Figure 20-2:
The Virtual
Device
Configura-
tion dialog.

3. **Tap Get info about your Fire.**

4. **Now tap any item in the list repeatedly.**

   You must tap the item at least seven times within five seconds.

5. **Click the Developer Options button that appears at the bottom of the screen.**

6. **Set the Developer Options slider to the ON position.**

7. **Select USB Debugging.**

Installing the USB driver (Windows only)

On Windows, to detect the Fire phone on your development computer, you must first install a modified version of the Kindle Fire USB driver that is included with the Fire Phone SDK add-on:

1. **Run the USB driver installer at** `<ANDROID_SDK>/add-ons/ addon-fire_phone_sdk_addon-amazon-17/tools/ KindleDrivers.exe`.

2. **After installing the driver, wait a few minutes for the system to update before attempting to connect the Fire phone to your development computer.**

Connecting to ADB

You will now need to restart ADB. In a terminal, go to `ANDROID_SDK/platform-tools` and run

Windows:

- ✔ `adb kill-server`
- ✔ `adb start-server`
- ✔ `adb devices`

Mac OS X or Linux:

- ✔ `./adb kill-server`
- ✔ `./adb start-server`
- ✔ `./adb devices`

You now see your Fire in the output from the `adb devices` command.

Publishing to Amazon Appstore for Android

Publishing to the Amazon Appstore for Android is similar to publishing to the Google Play Store: You create an account, and then you may need to pay a developer fee.

Unlike the Google Play Store, apps must be reviewed on the Amazon Appstore for Android, so plan a few days between the day you submit your app and the day it becomes available on the store.

Follow these steps:

1. **Go to `https://developer.amazon.com/appsandservices` and click Sign In.**

2. **Sign in using your Amazon login, or create a new account.**

3. **Enter your developer information, such as in Figure 20-3.**

4. **Agree to the Amazon Distribution Terms by scrolling down and clicking Accept and Continue (Figure 20-4).**

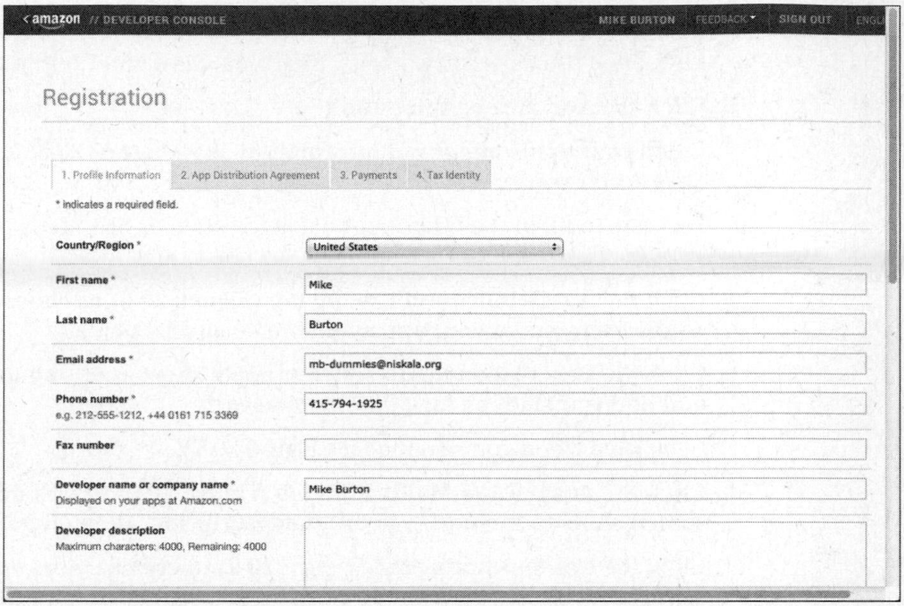

Figure 20-3:
The
Registration
window.

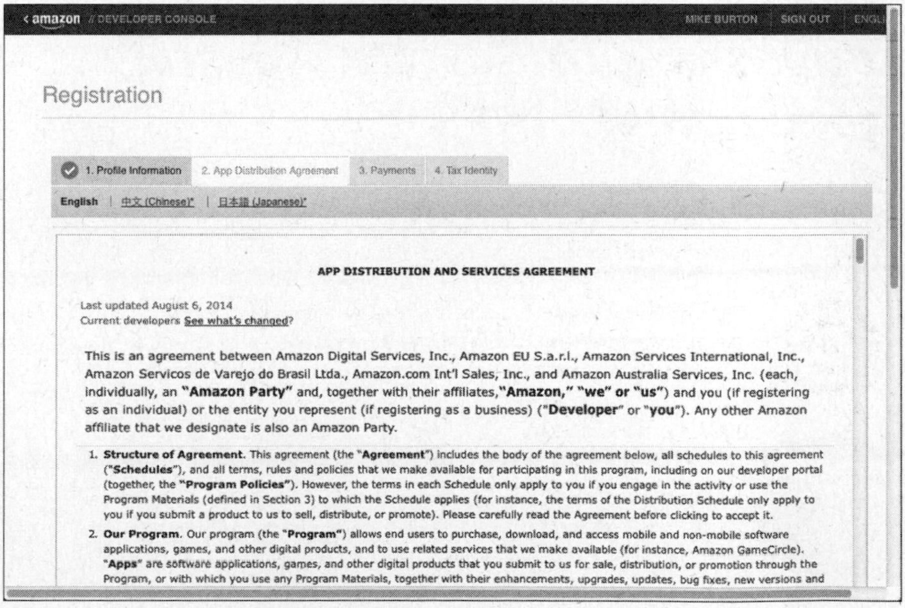

Figure 20-4:
Click to
Accept the
Distribution
Terms.

5. **Indicate whether you intend to monetize your apps.**

   If so, fill in the necessary details, then click Save and Continue.

6. **Click the Add a New App button.**

7. **Enter your app's important information as in Figure 20-5, and click Save when you're done.**

   Feel free to fill in the other optional fields such as SKU if it's useful to you; see Figure 20-5.

8. **Click the Availability and Pricing tab (Figure 20-6) to choose in which countries to make your app available — and its price.**

9. **Click the Description tab to set your app's short and long descriptions, and add translations for other languages.**

   Click Save when you're done (see Figure 20-7).

10. **Click the Images and Multimedia tab (Figure 20-8) to upload icons and screen shots to include in your app description, then click Save.**

11. **Click the Content Rating tab (Figure 20-9) to choose your app's content rating and age restrictions by clicking the appropriate radio buttons, then click Save.**

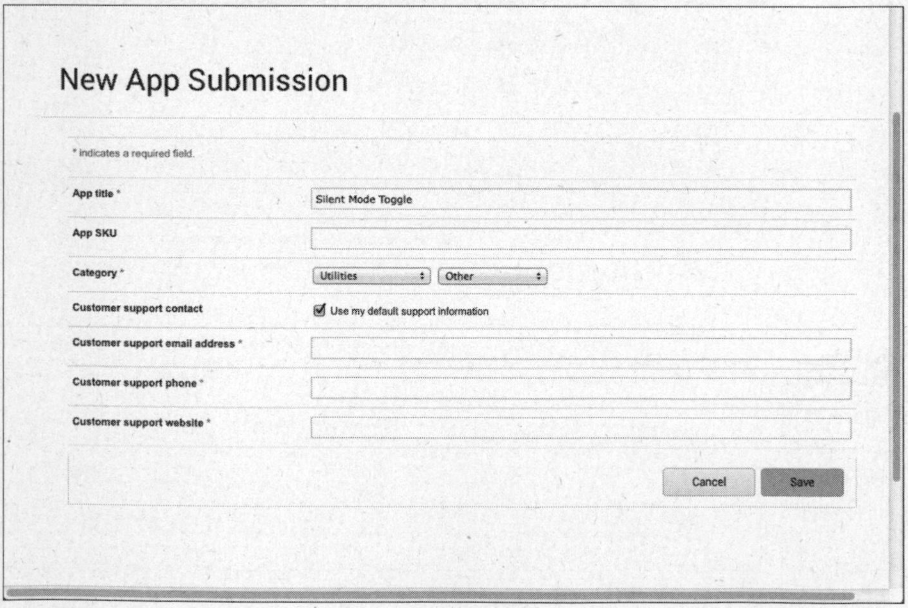

Figure 20-5:
The New
App
Submission
window.

New App Submission

* indicates a required field.

App title *	Silent Mode Toggle
App SKU	
Category *	Utilities / Other
Customer support contact	☑ Use my default support information
Customer support email address *	
Customer support phone *	
Customer support website *	

Cancel Save

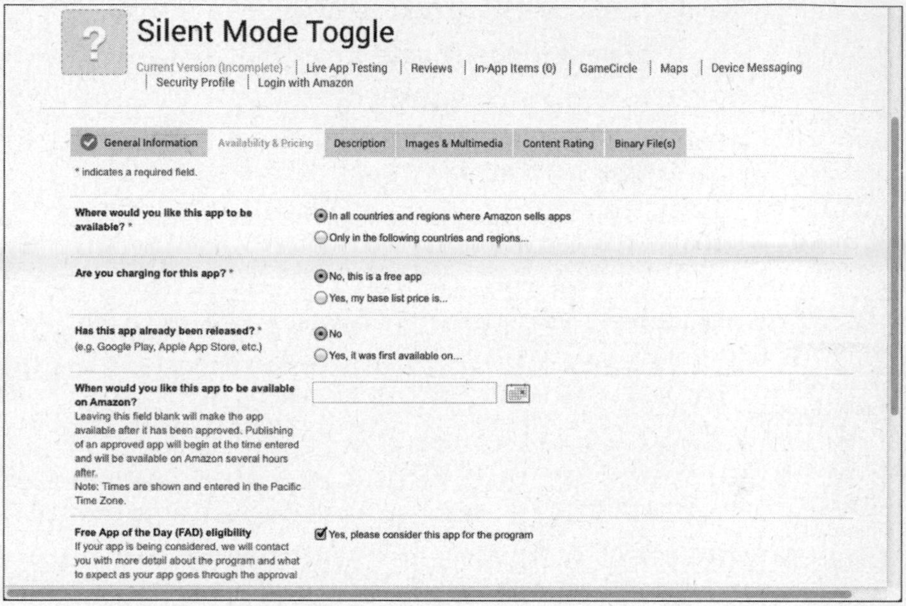

Figure 20-6:
The
Availability
and Pricing
tab for the
Silent Mode
Toggle app.

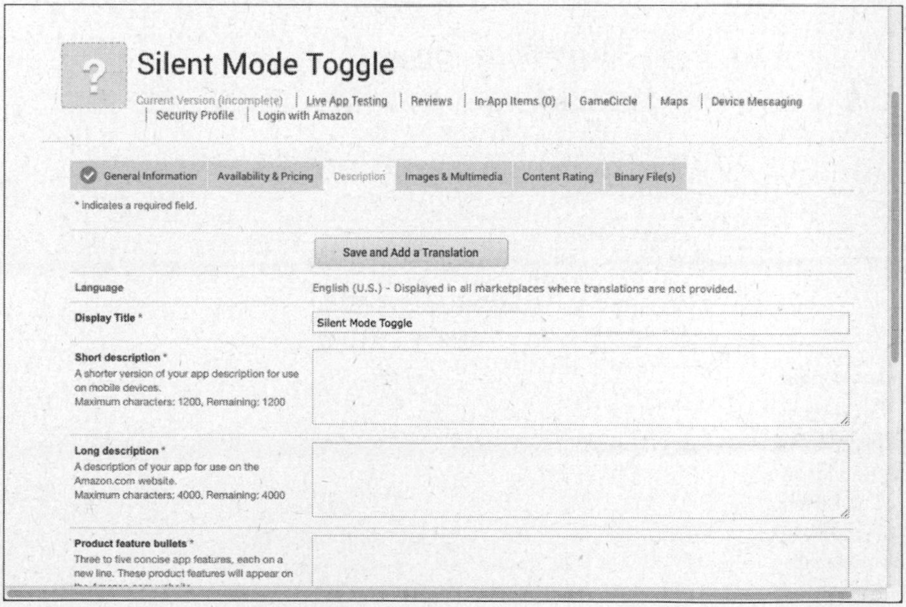

Figure 20-7:
The
Description
tab for the
Silent Mode
Toggle app.

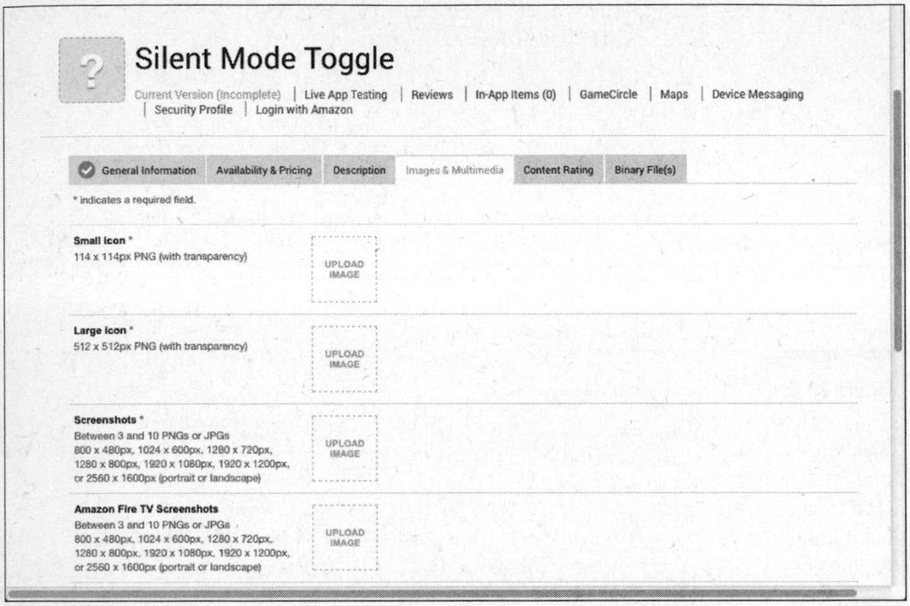

Figure 20-8:
The Images and Multimedia tab for the Silent Mode Toggle app.

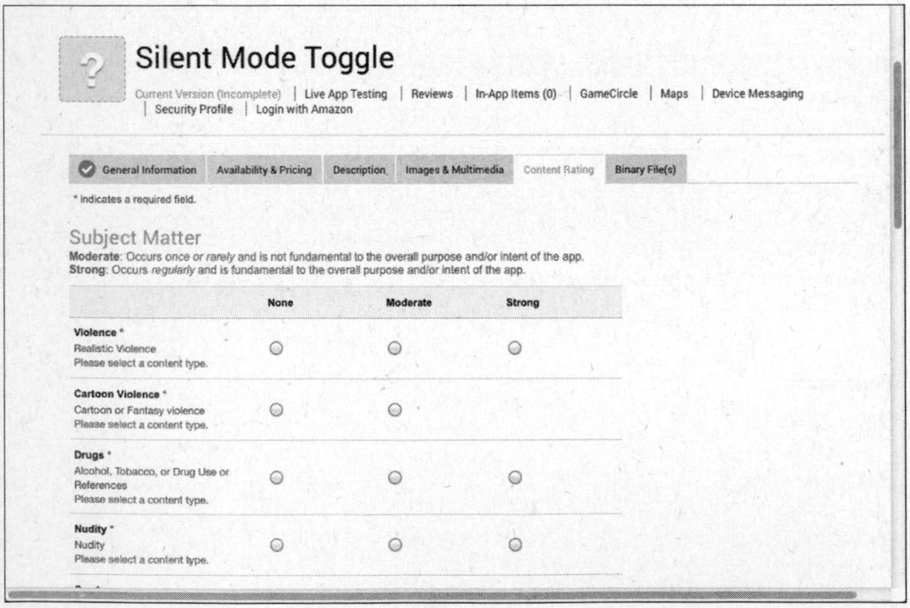

Figure 20-9:
The Content Rating tab for the Silent Mode Toggle app.

12. **Click the Binary File(s) tab (Figure 20-10) to upload your app's binary code, then click Save.**

    See Chapter 8 for more information about how to build and upload your app's APK file.

13. **Click the Submit App button.**

The review process can take anywhere from hours to days to weeks. However, when your app launches in the Appstore, you can find it in the Amazon Appstore for Android alongside other apps as shown in Figure 20-11.

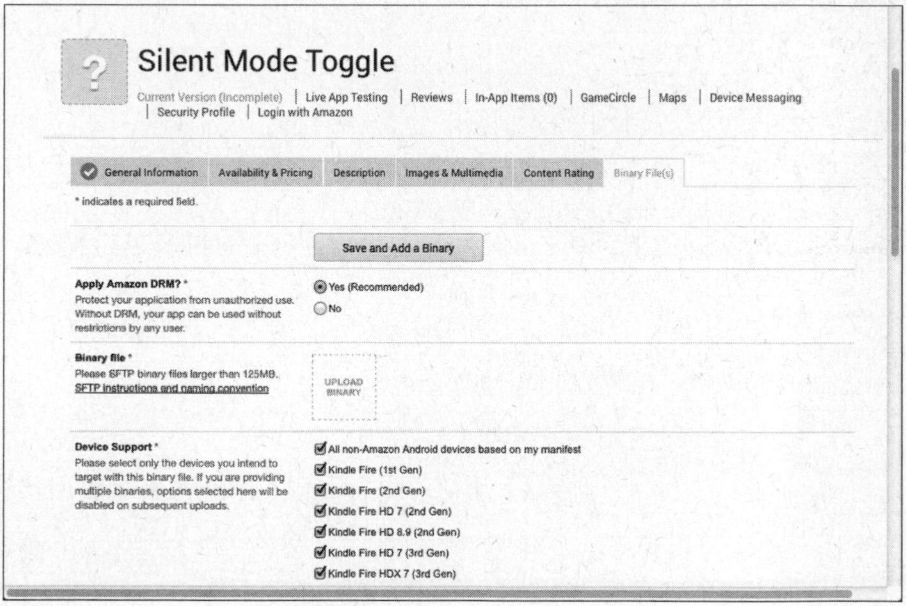

Figure 20-10:
The Binary File(s) tab for the Silent Mode Toggle app.

To find out more about the Amazon Appstore submission process, visit `https://developer.amazon.com/public/support/ submitting-your-app/tech-docs/submitting-your-app`.

Figure 20-11: The Amazon Appstore for Android.

Part V
The Part of Tens

Enjoy an additional Android Part of Tens chapter online at
www.dummies.con/cheatsheet/androidappdevelopment.

In this part . . .

Part V consists of some of the best secret-sauce-covered Android nuggets that you acquire only after having been in the development trenches for quite some time. Chapter 21 lists some of the best sample applications that can help springboard you on your way to creating the next hit application. These applications range from database-oriented apps to interactive games to applications that interact with third-party web application programming interfaces (APIs).

Part V closes with a list of professional tools and libraries that can help streamline and improve the productivity of your application development process and make your life as a developer much easier.

Chapter 21

Ten Free Sample Applications and SDKs

· ·

W hen you develop Android apps, you may run into various roadblocks based on the code. Perhaps you want an app to communicate with a third-party API that returns JSON or to perform collision detection in a game. You can usually search the web for sample code because someone else has likely already written it. Then all you have to do is review the code, alter it to fit your needs, and continue with development.

Reviewing sample code increases your knowledge even if you don't need the code in an application. In fact, a good way to find out how to program for Android is to look at sample code. Sure, it comes supplied with the Android SDK — in the API Demos, for example (see Chapter 2) — but a truly cool plethora of real-world application code is freely available on the web. You can find on the Internet plenty of high-quality open source applications to serve as examples, thanks to the open source nature of Android.

Most of the ten excellent open source applications and samples in this chapter are real-world Android applications that you can install from the Google Play Store. Try an application on your device, and then crack open its source code to see how the gears turn.

Android Samples

The `samples` folder of the Android SDK holds the source code for the various Android samples, which demonstrate how to use various Android APIs via small, digestible, working examples. You can find tons of simple, straight-to-the-point examples in the Android samples source code. Incorporating animation into your project or playing an audio file inside your app is easy because API Demos provides examples of both. If you have a lot of ideas but not a lot of time, you should definitely install this demo app on your device and play with its numerous examples to see exactly what they can do. The samples are easy to use with Android Studio: Just go to File⇨Import Sample to browse the list of available samples and import them into a new Android Studio project.

The Google I/O App

```
https://github.com/google/iosched
```

Every year, throngs of Google developer groupies descend on Moscone West in San Francisco for a multi-day conference to discuss all things Google. The official conference app is written for Android devices, and the source code serves as an example of how to write good apps for the platform.

K-9 Mail

```
http://code.google.com/p/k9mail/
```

K-9 Mail is a popular email client for Android that used to ship with Android before it became a separate app. It's an extraordinarily full-featured open source application, with functionality such as search, push, sync, flagging, signatures, and more.

GitHub Android App

```
https://github.com/github/android
```

GitHub is a popular community of open source projects that uses the Git Distributed Version Control System (DVCS). The GitHub Android App lets you view, from the palm of your hand, all your favorite GitHub repositories located on GitHub.com. The application demonstrates how to use the GitHub API as well as the RoboGuice framework.

Facebook SDK for Android

```
http://github.com/facebook/facebook-android-sdk
```

If you're feeling ambitious, you can tackle the task of creating the next popular Facebook application, even if you don't know where to begin. Use the

Facebook Android SDK to easily integrate Facebook functionality into your application — authorize users, make API requests, and much more. Integrate all the goodness of Facebook without breaking a sweat.

Notepad Tutorial

```
http://d.android.com/guide/tutorials/notepad/
```

If you're interested in understanding the basic principles of SQLite without all the fluff of services, background tasks, and other technical concepts, Notepad Tutorial is for you. Although simple in its execution and usage, the source code and tutorial that go along with it are helpful.

U+2020

```
https://github.com/JakeWharton/u2020
```

Jake Wharton is a prodigious contributor to the Android open source community. Among his many projects is the U+2020 app, which showcases a number of open source libraries including Dagger, Retrofit, Picasso, OkHttp, RxJava, Staggered Grid, and many others.

Lollipop Easter Egg

```
https://github.com/android/platform_frameworks_base/blob/
         master/packages/SystemUI/src/com/android/
         systemui/egg/LLand.java
```

Were you alive in 2014? Then you've probably heard of Flappy Bird. Perhaps even you or someone you love were unlucky enough to succumb to that terrible affliction. Well, now you can unleash it upon everyone you know who has Android 5.0 by tapping a bunch of times on "Android version" in Settings, and then long-pressing on the resulting lollipop. And if that's not enough, take a tour of the source code on Android Open Source Project (AOSP) using the link above.

Android Bootstrap

`http://www.androidbootstrap.com`

Building an app from scratch takes time. Android Bootstrap can be a great way to shortcut that process. It includes a full working implementation of Fragments, Fragment Pager, ActionBar via AppCompat, Navigation Drawer, ViewPagerIndicator, Retrofit, GSON, Robotium for integration testing, API Consumption with an API on Parse.com, and much more. It's no substitute for understanding how to build Android apps, but it can be a helpful tool to bootstrap your next Android project with a few commonly used tools.

The AOSP

`https://source.android.com`

Nearly everything about Android is open source. This means that the source code of the operating system itself, including many of the apps it ships with, is available online for you to browse at the Android Open Source Project (AOSP). The source is massive and you may find it a little difficult to navigate, so you may want to check out the GitHub mirror at `http://android.github.io`, which makes it easier to contribute to the source if you're a github user.

Chapter 22

Ten Tools to Simplify Your Development Life

. . . .

As a developer, you inherently build tools to become more productive — for example, to assist in asynchronous communication, XML and JSON parsing, date and time utilities, and much more. Before you write a ton of helper classes or frameworks to handle items for you, seek out tools that already exist. This chapter lists ten tools and utilities that can simplify your development life by increasing your productivity and ensuring that your app is up to snuff.

Android Lint

`http://developer.android.com/tools/help/lint.html`

If you've done other non-Android development, you may be familiar with the concept of lint tools, which helps you find the "lint" that collects around your code. Lint helps you flag code that may technically run, but it may not be doing exactly what you think it may be doing. Android lint is a sort of warning system on steroids for Android code. To run it, go to Android Studio and choose Analyze⇨Inspect Code. To run it from the command line, use the gradle target `check`; for example, `./gradlew check`.

Android Systrace

`http://developer.android.com/tools/debugging/systrace.html`

Are you interested in finding out why your app is so slow? Chances are that you are, or at least you should be. Android's Systrace tool can be instrumental to rooting out the causes of poor performance. Using it, you can get very detailed information about what your app is doing at any given time, an example of which is in Figure 22-1:

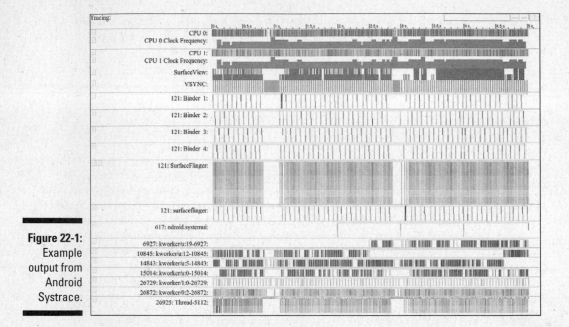

Figure 22-1: Example output from Android Systrace.

RoboGuice and Dagger

http://roboguice.org
https://github.com/google/dagger

No, RoboGuice isn't the latest and greatest energy drink marketed to developers — it's a framework that uses the Google Guice library to streamline dependency injection. *Dependency injection* handles the initializing of variables at the right time so that you don't have to. This concept cuts down the amount of code you have to write overall, and it makes maintaining your application a breeze. Where RoboGuice focuses on ease of use, Dagger is another popular dependency injection library focused primarily on speed.

Translator Toolkit

http://translate.google.com/toolkit

If you want to increase the number of people who can use your app, there's almost no better way to do it than to translate your app into other languages.

The answer is to use Google to find helpers to translate your app for you. The translations aren't as clean as if you found a native speaker to translate for you, but they're a great place to start on the cheap. You might consider getting the initial translations done by Google, then reaching out to your user community to find volunteers to edit the translations for you, or using an outsourcing website such as ODesk to find translators. Even craigslist can be a great resource!

Hierarchy Viewer

```
http://developer.android.com/tools/help/monitor.html
```

Working with various views inside the layout file to create a user interface isn't always a straightforward process. Hierarchy Viewer, located in the Android Device Monitor, lets you see exactly how your widgets are laid out onscreen graphically. This format lets you clearly see a widget's boundaries so that you can determine what's going on inside the layout. Hierarchy Viewer, the ultimate tool to make a pixel-perfect user interface, also lets you magnify the display in the pixel-perfect view to ensure that images and UIs display flawlessly on all screen sizes and at all densities.

UI/Application Exerciser Monkey

```
http://developer.android.com/tools/help/monkey.html
```

Don't worry: The UI/Application Exerciser Monkey doesn't need to be fed bananas to remain happy! You use Exerciser Monkey to stress-test your application. It simulates random touches, clicks, and other user events to ensure that abnormal usage doesn't make the app explode. Exerciser Monkey can be used to test apps on either your emulator or your own device.

Git and GitHub

```
http://git-scm.com
http://github.com
```

Git — a superfast, free, and open-source-distributed version control system — manages repositories quickly and efficiently, making it painless to back up work. Don't let a system crash ruin your day by not having a version control system for your next spectacular app. Git makes working with branching simple and effective, and it integrates into your workflow easily. Although Git is distributed, you'll likely want a remote location where the Git repository is stored. You can obtain a free, private Git repository from `http://bitbucket.org`. If your code is open source, you can create free repositories on `Github.com`, where there is a huge community of open source developers contributing to each other's open sourced projects. Also, the Github Android app is open source (see Chapter 21) and worth a good browse.

Picasso and OkHttp

```
http://square.github.io/picasso/
http://square.github.io/okhttp/
```

Images add much-needed context and visual flair to Android applications. Picasso allows for hassle-free image loading in your application — often in one line of code! You've already seen Picasso in use in the Tasks app in Chapter 9, but there's much more it can do for you in your other apps.

Picasso is built on OkHttp, which makes uploading and downloading information over `http` significantly easier than the built-in libraries included with Android.

Memory Analyzer Tool

```
https://developer.android.com/tools/debugging/debugging-
                memory.html
```

Java does a lot of memory management for you, but that doesn't mean that you can't leak memory on Java. In fact, memory leaks on Android are one of the most common ways that long-running apps can become unstable. The Eclipse Memory Analyzer Tool (MAT) can help you track down the cause of your memory leaks on Android. Visit the link above to get more information about how to use MAT and other tools to investigate your app's memory usage.

Travis-ci

```
http://travis-ci.org
```

Once you have a source code control system such as Git set up, the next step is to set up a Continuous Integration (CI) server such as Travis-CI. A CI system such as Travis-CI automatically builds your app every time you push a new change to GitHub. It also runs your test cases, checks Android lint, and can also build a release version of your app that's ready to be uploaded to the Google Play Store. Travis-CI is free for open source projects, but you can also buy a subscription if you want to build your closed source projects.

Index

About the Author

Michael Burton is the Director of Mobile Engineering at Groupon. He wrote the Digg, TripIt, OpenTable, and award-winning Groupon Android apps, among others. He's flown a project on the space shuttle. He's spoken on Android application development at conferences in London, Boston, Silicon Valley, Rio de Janeiro, and elsewhere. He's also the author of RoboGuice, the open-source dependency injection framework used by thousands of apps, including Microsoft, Nike, and others. Follow Michael on Twitter (@roboguice) or check out RoboGuice at `http://roboguice.org`.

Dedication

To a never-ending list of new desserts.

Author's Acknowledgments

A big thank you to the extended Android open-source community, including Carlos Sessa, Stéphane Nicolas, Manfred Moser, Michael Bailey, and Donn Felker among others, who contributed their code, expertise, and reviews of this book.

Thank you to my boss Greg and to the great Android team at Groupon — Carlos, Alan, Aliya, David, Eric, Hemant, Michael, Richard, Stéphane, Snow, Valampuri, Wentao, Cristian, Andrei, Bogdan, Marius, Alin, and Trevor, who have pushed me to deeply understand the Android platform.

I'd also like to thank my friends at Google, Roman, Boris, and Sarah, without whom the Lollipop sections of this book would have been that much more difficult to write.

Thank you to my team at Wiley for their tireless efforts, especially Maureen, Michael, Kyle, and Andy.

And finally, thank you to Carrie, my friends, and my family who have supported me through the many evenings and weekends I have spent working on this project over the years.

Publisher's Acknowledgments

Acquisitions Editor: Kyle Looper

Publisher: Andy Cummings

Project and Copy Editors: T-Squared Services

Technical Editor: Michael Bailey

Editorial Assistant: Claire Brock

Sr. Editorial Assistant: Cherie Case

Project Coordinator: Sheree Montgomery

Cover Image: © iStockphoto.com / Cary Westfall